Jung's Theory of Personality

This book provides a reappraisal of Carl Jung's work as a personality theorist. It offers a detailed consideration of Jung's work and theory in order to demystify some of the ideas that psychologists have found most difficult, including those in Jung's religious and alchemical writings. The book shows why these two elements of his theory are integral to his psychology of personality and goes on to propose a framework on which to base a collaborative research programme that could provide much-needed and, at present, unavailable validation data for some of Jung's key theoretical concepts.

Dividing the book into two parts, theory and practice, the author begins by emphasising the importance of religion and alchemy for understanding Jung's key concepts of individuation and the self, as well as the link between Jung's concept of the archetype and its function in the development and transformation of personality. The book considers the whole of Jung's work as a comprehensive theory of personality to which all strands, including his writings on religion and on alchemy, contribute. The second part of the book is both empirical and theoretical. Crellin reviews the history of the presentation of Jung's work in personality literature and discusses how inaccurate representation, the limitations of existing evaluation criteria, and consequent negative perceptions of Jung's theory in textbooks of personality psychology have contributed to the creation of a mythical Jung.

This book will appeal to both psychological practitioners who are unfamiliar with or only have a vague understanding of Jung's ideas, as well as Jungian psychoanalysts who are knowledgeable about Jung's writings but whose training may not have addressed the problem of theory evaluation in relation to Jung's theory.

Clare Crellin is a retired consultant clinical psychologist, psychoanalyst, and current external examiner based in the United Kingdom, with experience of mentoring and supervising counsellors, psychotherapists, and psychologists in adult mental health services in the National Health Service and private practice.

'Grounded in a thorough study of practically the whole of Jung's published oeuvre as well as an innovative survey of psychology textbooks, Clare Crellin's book makes a compelling case for the present-day relevance of Jung's personality theory. Crellin not only develops a helpful set of general criteria for evaluating personality theories, but also, when applying these criteria to Jung's distinctive model, maintains an assured balance in stressing the scientific character of his thought while not shying away from the integral importance of its religious and alchemical aspects. Scholarly, sensitive, and insightful, this is an important contribution to both Jungian studies and personality psychology'.

– **Professor Roderick Main**, Faculty of Social Sciences, University of Essex, UK

'The distinctive comparative and multi-disciplinary approach of this book makes it invaluable, both to encourage understanding of the relevance of personality theory for contemporary clinical practice, and to restimulate critical interest in Jung's work. The book goes beyond Jung's theory alone to offer a comprehensive framework for evaluating personality theories in general'.

– **Professor John Hall**, Centre for Health, Medicine and Society, Oxford Brookes University, UK

Research in Analytical Psychology and Jungian Studies Series

Series Advisor: Andrew Samuels

Professor of Analytical Psychology, Essex University, UK

The *Research in Analytical Psychology and Jungian Studies* series features scholarly works that are, broadly speaking, of an empirical nature. The series comprises research-focused volumes involving qualitative and quantitative research, historical/archival research, theoretical developments, heuristic research, grounded theory, narrative approaches, collaborative research, practitioner-led research, and self-study. The series also includes focused works by clinical practitioners and provides new research informed explorations of the work of C. G. Jung that will appeal to researchers, academics, and scholars alike.

Books in this series:

Time and Timelessness
Temporality in the theory of Carl Jung
Angeliki Yiassemides

Apophatic Elements in the Theory and Practice of Psychoanalysis
Pseudo-Dionysius and C.G. Jung
David Henderson

C.G. Jung and Hans Urs von Balthasar
God and evil – a critical comparison
Les Oglesby

Bridges to Consciousness
Complexes and complexity
Nancy M. Krieger

The Alchemical Mercurius
Esoteric symbol of Jung's life and works
Mathew Mather

Archetypal Psychotherapy
The clinical legacy of James Hillman
Jason A. Butler

Jung's Theory of Personality
A modern reappraisal
Clare Crellin

Jung's Theory of Personality

A modern reappraisal

Clare Crellin

Routledge
Taylor & Francis Group
LONDON AND NEW YORK

First published 2014
by Routledge
2 Park Square, Milton Park, Abingdon, Oxfordshire OX14 4RN

and by Routledge
711 Third Avenue, New York, NY 10017

First issued in paperback 2016

Routledge is an imprint of the Taylor & Francis Group, an informa business

British Library Cataloguing in Publication Data
A catalogue record for this book is available from the British Library.

Library of Congress Cataloging-in-Publication Data

Crellin, Clare.
Jung's theory of personality : a modern reappraisal / Clare Crellin.
pages cm
Includes bibliographical references.
1. Jung, C. G. (Carl Gustav), 1875–1961. 2. Personality.
3. Jungian psychology. I. Title.
BF109.J8C74 2015
155.2'644—dc23
2014000976

ISBN 13: 978-0-415-79167-0 (pbk)
ISBN 13: 978-0-415-87060-3 (hbk)

Typeset in Bembo
by Apex CoVantage, LLC

To my clients

Contents

Acknowledgements

I could not have written this book without the help and encouragement of many people. I am especially grateful to the late H.L. Dor for many long and fruitful discussions over the years, and to Michael Devitt for his enabling gift. My thanks go to Andrew Samuels, Karl Figlio, Renos Papadopoulos, Max Wheeler, Sandy Lovie, Elizabeth Valentine, Graham Richards, Sonu Shamdasani, Paul Stenner, John Nicholls, Christine Walker, John Evans, Paul Ford, Margaret Spelman, Sarah Boyd, Sally Stapleton, Vanessa Bryant, Hilary Smith, Tony Munn, Enrico Marcangelo, Robert Wycherley, my former colleagues at Sussex Partnership NHS Trust, my Jungian analysts, members of the History and Philosophy of Psychology Section of the British Psychological Society, Marilyn Ward, Gill Watt, Alison Evans, Paulene Ford, Debra Hall, Deborah Stewart, Fiona Gilles, and the staff and students of the Centre for Psychoanalytical Studies, University of Essex.

Introduction

A theory of personality attempts to account for human individuality, its characteristics and its functional and developmental processes, as expressed in the life of an individual, whilst setting this in the context of shared human characteristics. Theorists can legitimately view the human person from different perspectives, and there are wide differences of approach and method. Throughout the history of personality theory, there have been debates about what a 'good' theory of personality should include and what questions it should address.

A reappraisal of Jung's reputation as a personality theorist is long overdue, for three reasons. Firstly, his theory has been neglected by psychologists, particularly in the United Kingdom, as a consequence, I believe, of the way it has been introduced to them. Its continued marginalisation from academic psychology deprives us of potential research benefits, including application in the public provision of psychotherapy. Secondly, the number of attempts before now to systematically evaluate Jung as a personality theorist is limited, and few researchers have focused on Jung alone. Evaluations of Jung's personality theory have given rise to myths, misrepresentations, and misunderstandings about Jung's work. Thirdly, I reexamine the potential value of Jung's personality theory in the context of a broader investigation of what criteria and standards are appropriate for evaluating a personality theory.

This book sets out the elements of Jung's theory in an accessible way and shows that with the use of appropriate evaluation criteria, Jung's theory emerges as original and structurally coherent, its main constructs being capable of validation. It is a complex theory with unprecedentedly wide scope, having demonstrable and potential heuristic, moral, ethical, and therapeutic value. I hope that this approach to understanding and evaluating Jung as a personality theorist will bring to the attention of the psychological professions aspects of Jung's ideas of which they might otherwise be unaware. Reconsidering the value of Jung's work from the perspective of a psychological theory of personality should also be of interest and value to Jungian scholars whose knowledge of Jung comes from a different trajectory and who may not be aware of the ways in which the social history of psychology has done his work a disservice.

Personality theories seek to encapsulate, in concepts and hypothetical constructs, dimensions along which each individual person is recognisable and distinct. Personality has been defined by Pervin (1996: 414) as a complex organisation of cognitions, affects, and behaviours that give direction and pattern (coherence) to a person's life. I show how, throughout his career, Jung focused on those questions that personality theorists believe to be fundamental for elucidating the nature of human personality, such as the nature of and constraints on individuality, the degree to which personality or character is inherited or culturally determined, how complexity and individuality can be accounted for, and how to define the relationship between instincts and personality.

It is mainly in textbooks of the psychology of personality, in which Jung's work is featured alongside that of other theorists, that he has been evaluated as a personality theorist. The task for a textbook author of deciding what to include in a brief account of Jung's ideas is a difficult one. Jung's published work in English extends to more than twenty-five volumes, and there are besides many untranslated or unpublished manuscripts.[1] A particular challenge for the textbook author is that Jung's theory of personality is embedded within the entirety of his published work. Despite these difficulties, some textbook authors (Maddi, 1972, 1996; Maduro & Wheelwright, 1977; Massey, 1981) stand out for their in-depth appreciation of Jung's ideas and for having done justice to Jung's prolific writing in the confined space available to them.

Explanatory and evaluative accounts of Jung's ideas can also be found in the many introductory books about Jung.[2] These authors articulate and explain Jung's ideas from the perspective of psychoanalysis or psychology for the general reader. They do not compare Jung's work with that of other personality theorists or against criteria and standards specific to psychological theories of personality. In the 1950s, Ira Progoff (1953, 1956) expounded Jung's ideas for a public beyond the world of psychoanalysis and evaluated his contribution to general, social, and personality psychology. I have drawn on Progoff's work in devising my own evaluation criteria and in drawing my conclusions. I have approached this topic by considering whether it *is* possible to evaluate psychological theories objectively, since there is always the problem of reflexivity. One who evaluates psychology is also psychology's subject. My solution is to include a mixture of subjective and objective standards.

A question that interests me is whether carefully chosen criteria can provide a rational framework that supports and enables balanced judgment. My interest derives from my concern that Jungianism, the choice to live one's life in a Jungian way, involves both rationality and feeling. For Jung, feeling *is* a judgement and feelings are rational in a pragmatic way (*CW*6 1921 §725). However, the commitment to live a life guided by Jung's ideas becomes self-reinforcing. Over time, it is likely to become deeply ingrained and less questioned. I am aware that my commitment has the potential to override rationality. I have tried to balance my personal commitment with a rational analytic approach.

I adopt a hermeneutical rather than an adversarial approach. A theory needs to be understood before it is judged. I have sought to understand Jung's ideas through immersing myself in reading as much as possible of his writing. I read secondary sources and commentaries only after I had grappled with and responded to his work at first hand.

Although two volumes of the Collected Works, *Psychological Types* (*CW*6) and *The Development of Personality* (*CW*17), are explicitly concerned with personality, it would be misleading to assume that Jung's entire personality theory is to be found there. The theory's many themes and constructs emerged over Jung's lifetime and are distributed throughout his work. Although I have consulted the Index volume to the *Collected Works*, I could not rely solely on this. My understanding of Jung's personality theory has led me to appreciate that textual references indexed under apparently unrelated topics such as *Christ*, *Adam*, or *symbolism* are likely to have close links with personality concepts such as the *self* and *individuation*. I indexed all the statements in the *Collected Works* that I thought could have a bearing on how Jung conceptualised a *person* and on what personal development meant to him. As a result of doing so, I have come to appreciate that Jung's ideas on personality are distributed throughout his entire published work and embedded in every aspect of his writing. I thus regard the totality of Jung's currently published work as constituting the exposition of his theory of personality, even where he seems to be going down avenues and by-ways that do not immediately strike readers as being connected with personality. I observe that Jung's investigations in alchemy, for example, are crucial for understanding his concepts of the self and individuation. His theory of personality is grounded in his attempts to deal with religious questions, and this is nowhere more evident than in the background to his typology. Consequently, I have been as inclusive as possible in assembling the elements of his theory of personality.

In seeking to account for the fact that Jung's personality theory is often ignored or misunderstood by academic and practitioner psychologists, I have followed another line of enquiry. Recent scholarship suggests that some criticisms levelled at Jung are directed at 'Jung the myth' rather than arising from a studied overview of Jung's writings and other sources. Jung scholars such as Haule, Papadopoulos, Rowland, Samuels, Shamdasani, and Taylor[3] have sought to unearth the 'real' Jung which had been concealed under a tapestry of historical inaccuracy. Reviewing the treatment of Jung in a large sample of twentieth-century textbooks on personality, I have identified many flaws in the representation of his life and theoretical ideas. On the other hand, some of the most accurate and comprehensive presentations of Jung's work are also found in textbooks, especially the kind in which experts in each theory are invited to contribute chapters.

I subsequently reviewed the criteria that, explicitly or implicitly, had been used by textbook authors for evaluating theories of personality. Since there is no consensus as to what constitutes a good theory of personality, I have developed a set of criteria that have arguable advantages for reevaluating Jung's extensive work on personality. Finally, I give examples of how the criteria can be applied in relation to key aspects of Jung's personality theory, and I suggest possible directions for further evaluation and research.

The book is in two parts. Part I describes Jung's theory and discusses its religious and alchemical aspects. The importance of Jung's concept of the archetypes is explored as well as the themes of transformation and creative imagination within his theory of personality. Part II focuses on evaluation: it examines the treatment of Jung in textbooks of personality psychology, discusses Jung's views on the nature of theories, and sets out a framework for reappraisal.

Part I comprises Chapters 1 through 5. In Chapter 1, I explain what I understand *Jung's personality theory* to be. In the second section of the chapter, I discuss my reasons for agreeing with psychology's categorisation of Jung as a personality theorist. In the four chapters which follow, I highlight what I consider to be the most important themes in Jung's personality theory. These are the themes of religion, alchemy, and the archetypes, and the transformative function of creative imagination. I have chosen these specific themes because they are centred on individuation and the development of the self, and because these elements in Jung's theory are the ones that some people have found difficult.

Chapter 2 explores the religious and philosophical roots of Jung's interest in personality, his interest in gnosis and in the historical emergence of Christianity. I draw attention to Jung's interest in mystic writers such as Jakob Böhme and Meister Eckhart and his emphasis on religious experience rather than belief. I explore Jung's close association of the idea of God with the psychological idea of the self and the very close links between Jung's idea of 'the God within' and his concept of individuation. I argue that Jung's idea of an encounter with the God-within is central to his theory of personality.

Chapter 3 deals with Jung's ideas on psychological types and highlights the importance of creativity. I stress the significance of Jung's practice of 'active imagination' for the development of his theory. This significance has become much more evident since the publication of Jung's *Red Book/Liber Novus* in 2009 (Jung, 2009). The typology is regarded by many psychologists as the most approachable and conventional aspect of Jung's work. I argue that Jung's *Psychological Types* is in fact a cryptic work hiding some of Jung's most radical ideas under a veil of scientific orthodoxy.

In Chapter 4, I give a thematic and chronological exposition of Jung's fifty-year engagement with the subject of alchemy. I show that, far from being a regrettable deviation from empirical personality psychology, Jung's exploration of alchemical concepts is, in fact, fundamental to his development of the concept of *individuation* and therefore of central relevance to his personality theory.

Chapter 5 concerns Jung's concept of *archetype* in relation to his theory of personality. I argue that theoretical constructs such as the archetype function as higher-order abstract concepts that structure thinking. They do not have to be independently verifiable empirically. For Jung, archetypes have direct influence on character. They do so by superimposing a set of preferred orientations which are expressed behaviourally as personality types. Jung held that individual personality is in part derived from the personalities of our internal archetypes. Thus, in Jung's way of thinking, archetypal structures underlie differences of personality. I emphasise that Jung's is an abstract and radical antibehavioural approach to the psychology of personality inasmuch as Jung proposed that inborn, inherited 'empty' ideas searching for form and shape drive the intrapsychic processes of personality development. I compare his concept of a dynamic archetype capable of driving the process of personal development with the ancient idea of the Divine imagination believed to be the creator of form in a formless cosmos.

Part II comprises Chapters 6 through 8 and the concluding reflections. In Chapter 6, I examine how Jung's work has been construed within the field of personality psychology by reviewing the treatment of Jung's work in more than fifty textbooks on personality theory published in the United States and the United Kingdom from the 1930s to the early years of the twenty-first century. I show that Jung's work has been treated dismissively by some authors, that a significant number of authors base their accounts on a very limited selection of sources, quote uncritically from secondary sources, and fail to question myths that have grown up around Jung's life and work. As a consequence, misunderstandings of Jung as a personality theorist and criticisms based on myths have run on unchallenged, handed down through generations of students. I argue that, in some cases, evaluation criteria have been applied to Jung's theory without a full understanding of its nature.

In Chapter 7, I identify criteria used by personality theorists and textbook authors either implicitly or explicitly to inform their views of what a good theory of personality should be. I use these as a basis for developing my own criteria, adding some which were absent in earlier lists. I suggest that different criteria are appropriate for different types of personality theories. Some 'hard science' criteria are appropriate for theories that emphasise single aspects of personality, such as behaviour or cognition, or for typologies. I propose additional 'soft science' criteria which include morality; the theory's potential for abuse, distortion, and harm; and the way in which the notion of 'person' is being constituted. I present and argue for the utility of a set of standards that includes ethical, aesthetic, logical, social, cultural, and empirical perspectives, and I show how these can form an evaluative framework.

In Chapter 8 I focus on the criterion of structural coherence and show that a clearly discernible and coherent structure of the kind that corresponds to models of scientific theories of personality underpins Jung's theory. I take two of Jung's significant theoretical constructs, the conscious and unconscious psyche, and the archetype, as contrasting examples and consider them in relation to validity. Using these two examples as detailed models and reviewing the theory in the light of other criteria, I offer a different view of Jung's value as a personality theorist and suggest directions for a comprehensive reappraisal based on a synthesis of existing and new research.

Notes

1 See Martin (2005) on the number of manuscripts and the amount of other unpublished material that exists such that 'we anticipate that our work will take upwards of thirty years to complete and will likely reach thirty additional volumes beyond the *Collected Works*'. See also Shamdasani (2005b) on the 'mountain' of unpublished manuscripts, correspondence and seminars of Jung; and Taylor (2009: 143) on the many seminars Jung gave of which there are transcriptions in the libraries of Jungian Institutes, such as *Visions seminars* (1930–1934) and *Kundalini Yoga Seminars* (1932). *Children's Dreams Seminars 1936–1940* (Jung, 2008) and the correspondence *The Jung-White Letters* (Lammers & Cunningham, 2007) have recently been published.

2 Examples are those by Cox (1964), Dry (1961), Fordham (1953), Hyde and McGuinness (1992), Jacobi (1962), Mattoon (1981), Meier (1977), Singer (1973), Storr (1973), and Tacey (2006).

3 See, for example, Haule (2011), Papadopoulos (2006a), Rowland (2002, 2010), Samuels (1985, 1989), Shamdasani (2003, 2005a), and Taylor (2009).

Part I

The theory itself

Chapter 1

Jung's theory of personality

> *Personality is the supreme realization of the innate idiosyncrasy of a living being . . . the most successful adaptation to the universal conditions of existence coupled with the greatest possible freedom for self determination.*
>
> (C.G. Jung, *CW*17 1934a §289)

Psychoanalysts have tended to see Jung, Freud, Adler, and others primarily as psychoanalytical thinkers, whereas it is university departments of psychology that have included them in the study of the psychology of personality. Chapter 1 is in two sections. First is a brief summary of Jung's personality theory to introduce the theory for readers not already familiar with Jung's concepts and to establish what I am including. Section 2 introduces the question of how to evaluate Jung's theory and defends the categorisation of Jung's theory as a theory of personality by clarifying the degree to which Jung is concerned with the questions that a personality theory addresses. I argue that, in addition to being viewed (uncontroversially) as a psychoanalytical theorist, Jung should indeed also be considered a personality theorist inasmuch as his work has many themes in common with those of personality theorists contemporary with him. Hence his work can be evaluated systematically using a framework of criteria for evaluating personality theories.

1 The theory

Introduction

I begin with some general observations. In defining Jung's theory of personality broadly I am proposing that what in his work may be thought of as metaphysics (alchemy), thought processes (archetypes), and ethos (religion) are best understood as integral elements of his personality theory and that it is these very elements that make Jung's a challenging, innovative, and useful theory today.

Jung's is an unconventional developmental theory and a total theory of human nature. The developmental aspect of his theory predominates. Jung pioneered an account of the intrapsychic organisation at each stage of life, covering both moral and spiritual development. Life is described in terms of positions and outlooks rather than functions. One of Jung's assumptions is that there are tasks and moral aspects to being a person, in the sense of the need to attend to one's duties to oneself as well as those of profession, family, and society (*CW*4 1913 §419, §423–424). The assumption that there are inner duties of life that must be fulfilled touches on religion (see *CW*18 1916b §1095; *CW*13 1929d §80–81; *CW*18 1945 §1378; and *CW*10 1958c §722, where Jung compares individuation with Bunyan's *Pilgrim's Progress*). This assumption underlies Jung's interest in Eastern approaches such as Taoism, Buddhism, Zen, and yoga, which emphasise a way of living supported by the practice of inwardly directed tasks.

Inherent in Jung's theory is a deep challenge to psychoanalytical theories which forefront parental influences and, indeed, to postmodernist ideas that people are predominantly culturally determined. Unlike object-relations theories which emphasise the formative influence of parents, Jung's theory emphasises constitutional elements. Although the predetermined elements are modified by experience, the process is guided by inherited archetypes within the personality itself (see Chapter 5). Jung also posed questions for the field of personality theory by thinking differently about it. For example, his well-known typology is more about being than doing. The introvert–extravert difference is as much about a fundamental and possibly constitutional difference of attitude and epistemological approach to the world as it is about behaviour. Jung's answer to the question 'What causes personality as it is subjectively experienced?' brings an element of mystery, of something ineluctable that is inherent in human nature and also purposive.

Whereas all theories of personality have implicit notions of a healthy, well-adapted, or well-adjusted way to live, in Jung's theory this perspective is prominent and overt. However, whilst it is the case that Jung's theory has much in common with religion in its emphasis on transformative and transpersonal aspects, it is not itself a religion – rather, it is a psychological theory of personality that suggests how religious ideas about the self can be understood in a modern secular world (see Chapter 2).

Jung used metaphysical and philosophical terms, such as *psyche*, *soul*, and *archetype*. To put this into a historical context, in the early decades of the twentieth century, university chairs in psychology were situated in departments of philosophy, there being no departments of psychology as such. Philosophical issues such as the nature of free will were debated, while laboratory studies of memory were based on philosophical concepts (association of ideas). Meanwhile, a behavioural approach within pedagogical and comparative psychology (the comparative study of animals and plants) was developing. Between 1897 and 1930, entries in the *Psychological Index*, one of the earliest bibliographies of psychology, reveal that the categories of *attention*, *emotion*, *conation* (will), and *aesthetics* were major areas of psychological research (Crellin, 1987). The emerging discipline of psychology at this time took its information from a wide range of other disciplines including anthropology, philosophy, medicine, and natural history. In his early years, Jung had followed Wundt's laboratory approach in his development of the word-association experiments. By 1913, he had come to find this unsatisfactory and focused increasingly on the images found in dreams and visions as a source of data for his developing ideas.

General characteristics of Jung's theory

Jung's concept of a person encompasses a basic inherited human ground plan which is at once physical and psychological; an organic substrate embodied and governed by instinct; the *psyche*, which consists of both unconscious and conscious processes; the *persona* (the outer social role); the *ego* (a self-conscious, self-reflecting autonomous complex); and the *self* (the potentially realisable expression of individuality). Jung was aware of the evolutionary history of the brain, which he conceptualised more in terms of processes than of structures.

Jung's thoughts on the relationship of the conscious to the unconscious mind were influenced by early experimental psychology, such as the work on attention. In 1927, he stated that the unconscious should not be seen as 'below' but 'around' the conscious. Following William James, he proposed that consciousness emerges when a segment of the neural field is illuminated temporarily by conscious focused attention, the remainder of the field simply not having reached a sufficient threshold of activation to become visible (*CW*8 1927/1931b §382fn). For Jung, consciousness is the phenomenological aspect of a continuous dynamic unconscious process of which it is a part.

Jung's *unconscious* included inherited (collective) aspects such as the instincts, as well as personal aspects such as memories, knowledge, and experience. It is an organised and highly dynamic network of changing relationships between properties, such as temporary states and configurations, permanent innate capacities, learned skills, acquired memories, and immediate sense experiences and feelings.

Jung maintained that personality development involved exchanges of contents (information) between functions of the psyche. He proposed that these exchanges could bring about reconciliation between environmental demands and desired inner states which would otherwise be in conflict. An *inversion*, a movement of attention inwards, can lead to the discovery of a new attitude or position which balances compliance with social demands and the desire to follow instinctive urges. The notion of an optimal adaptation to both inner and outer environments combined individuality with social responsibility. Jung maintained that developed individuals have dual duties – to themselves and to others, as social beings. However, Jung states unequivocally that 'duty to self is incomparably more important' than the demands of social convention (*CW*4 1913 §189), from which the individual needs to redeem his or her self by means of an introspective attitude. These ideas are contained in the concept of *individuation* (see what follows).

Inherited characteristics

Jung followed what are now largely regarded as uncontroversial Darwinian ideas[1] about inherited characteristics, which is to say that he supported the idea of a nature/nurture interaction, the inherited component of which is a universally human basic ground plan. The ground plan included temperament, which contributes to the person's type, orientation, and dominant mode of functioning. He believed that inborn qualities, such as the child's degree of sensitivity, create 'a special way of experiencing infantile events so that such events are experienced more powerfully, are therefore remembered, and continue to exert an influence on the person's development' (*CW*4 1913 §399).

Jung noted that children may scarcely resemble their parents, as the ancestral inheritance from earlier generations may dominate (*CW*17 1927/1931a §93). He held that psychic inheritance derives from the child's ancestral stock as much as, if not more than, from parents: 'The mind . . . consists of the sum of ancestral minds, the "unseen fathers" whose authority is born anew with the child' (*CW*8 1928c §101). In genetic terms, this is a conventional notion, in keeping with the principles of Darwinian (Darwin, 1859: 210) and of Mendelian genetic inheritance, but its psychological implications required an expansion of the notion of the unconscious to include a *collective unconscious.*

Parental and other cultural influences

Jung did not deny a role for social factors, experience, and learning in the development of personality. He stated, for example, that the will 'is a psychological phenomenon that owes its existence to culture and moral education' (*CW*6 1921 §844). However, he emphasised unconscious forms of social transmission. His professional interest in similarities between children and their parents in their reaction-type data dates from his 1904 word-association tests. Jung explained these similarities as the result of a form of 'identification' with the mother in which the child enters into what he came to call a '*participation mystique*' (a term he borrowed from the philosopher and anthropologist Lévy-Bruhl,1857–1939). This resulted in the 'daughter having the mother's attitude . . . she simply took it over from the environmental influences' (*CW*17 1910/1946 §55). While he acknowledged this as a form of environmental influence, he stressed that the means of its transmission was neither conscious learning nor imitation (copying behaviours modelled by others such as parents). Instead, he proposed an unconscious process of identification (*CW*6 1921 §742) in which unconscious projections founded on perceived similarity with the external objects and driven by the power of an innate 'parent' instinct become fused with memories of actual experiences. The resulting emotionally charged dynamic image is individually expressed in the form of the parental *imago* in the child's psyche.

The child inherits the potential to create parental imagos as part of the human ground plan. The imago itself is formed from the inherited parent instinct and the influence of the actual parent/child experience together with the libido (life energy) invested in that experience, which provides a dynamic field of energic activity. The result is that 'the children are infected indirectly through the attitude they instinctively adopt towards their parents' state of mind' and as a function of their level of sensitivity to their parents' attitude (*CW*17 1926/1946 §154).

One important element of the parents' attitude was the degree of completeness of their own psychic development. Children, Jung said, may 'get wind of' and 'live out' aspects of the parents' incomplete selves, their 'unlived life', and unwittingly become enslaved to their parents' goals and desires rather than pursuing their own (*CW*17 1928a §107). In this way, Jung's developmental theory made a place for both nature and nurture. In the case of the child's psychological development, it was the propensity to identify with the parents that Jung regarded as an inherited instinct. The 'nurture' element was the particular aspect of the parents' mental life that the individual child identified with and adopted. Jung was exploring ideas about the nature of family relations and their unconscious influence very early in the twentieth century, before the development of family therapy and systemic approaches such as those of Bateson (1904–1980), Minuchin (1921–), or Palazzoli (1916–1999).

Jung held that, in addition to parents and family members, teachers influence children to the degree that they have fulfilled their own personality development. Consequently, Jung advised teachers to fulfil as far as possible the external and internal demands of their own lives. If successful, teachers could help to free children from their unconscious identification (*participation mystique*) with the parental environment. By developing a temporary relationship with a teacher as a substitute for the parent, 'the child can let go of the infantile parental environment, from unconscious identity with his family' and become 'properly conscious of himself' (*CW*17 1928a §107–108).

Jung's teleology

In a letter to Loÿ in 1914, Jung said 'in the past nothing can be altered, and, in the present, little, but the future is ours and capable of raising life's intensity to the highest pitch' (*CW*4 1914b §668); he also asserted, 'the task is to be oriented towards the future through a deeper knowledge of the present' (*CW*5 1911–12/1952 §78 n. 18). Jung's particular understanding of teleology underpins his idea of *how* a life should be lived. He held that the blueprint for the future is in the present and the past. It can be reached and made conscious by developing awareness. But its detail is not yet worked out and so cannot be known except in the outcome of all the individual choices that have been and are being made. Jung saw the task of individuation as teleological. However, although Jung assumes an inner movement in each individual to seek individuation, so that each individual has the goal of her or his own life, this does not result in overall progress for humanity. For Jung, 'whilst we are the culmination of the whole history of mankind', 'we are also the disappointment of the hopes and expectations of the ages' (*CW*10 1928/1931 §154). The apparent civilisation of society only drives the more savage tendencies temporarily underground.

Significant theoretical constructs

The main concepts or hypothetical constructs of Jung's personality theory are the unconscious, the ego, the self, the psyche, instincts, archetype, the soul, spirit, individuation, the religious instinct, the attitude, the transcendent function, the will, psychological tasks, psychological types, neurosis, and psychosis. The remainder of this chapter summarises these concepts and their function within Jung's theory. For convenience, I have arranged these concepts in three groups: characteristics of the psyche, developmental processes, and types and psychopathology.

Characteristics of the psyche

Jung's *unconscious* is a process rather than a place. It is dynamic and interactive, having the possibility of influencing and being influenced by consciousness. Jung hypothesises the unconscious as the source of individual self-development with archetypes as innate drivers of this process. It is the ground and source of inherited patterns of behaviour and the source of the formative capacity itself. In addition, the unconscious is the totality of the personal experiences which have not reached a sufficient threshold level of energy to be the focus of conscious attention.

In 1921 Jung described the ***ego*** as 'the centre of my field of consciousness' (*CW*6 1921 §706). The conscious ego brings the capacity to deviate from the instincts by voluntary choice. Jung viewed the ego as capable of experiencing itself, a self-reflecting executive function controlling and directing conscious behaviour, an autonomous part of consciousness but not the whole: 'the *ego* is only the subject of my consciousness' (*CW*6 1921 §706).

Jung held this position from the start of his career. This can be seen from his very early statement of 1904: 'The conscious self is merely the marionette dancing upon the stage to a hidden automatic impulse' (*CW*2 1904–7/1910 §246 and note 2). However, shortly before his death he said that he had not wished to depreciate the importance of consciousness by giving the unconscious a supreme role. Rather, he sought to reestablish a balance by devoting his chief efforts to the elucidation of the nature of the unconscious psyche (*CW*18 1956/1957 §1585). For Jung, the unconscious had the capacity to 'take the ego into its service' and enrich consciousness, which meant that 'the extent of the personality . . . cannot be limited' (*CW*11 1942/1954 §390).

Jung discerned various sense consciousnesses within the ego. However, although 'sense perceptions tell us that something is, they do not tell us what it is.' 'This,' he said, 'is told to us . . . by the process of apperception', a kind of recognition that derives from a thinking process (*CW*8 1927/1931b §288).

Ego consciousness is the means by which unconscious contents, archetypal and individual, can be discerned, or, in Jung's language, apprehended ('made aware', 'recognised'). The process of recognition is unconscious, or at least automatic, but the result of this process (recognition itself) is conscious, apprehension of the situation and the impulse to act being aspects of the same vital activity (*CW*8 1919 §282). An important function of ego consciousness is to expand consciousness through enabling conscious awareness of thoughts, feelings, and instincts that exist 'in potentia' in the form of archetypal images and thoughts that are not yet fully formed. Hence, for Jung, conscious and unconscious processes are interdependent.

For Jung it is the *self* that develops in the process of individuation. The centre of the self was not the ego but a point of unity between consciousness and the unconscious, psyche and soma, of oneness which corresponded with Christ's function as the unifier of divine with human nature. For Jung, the self is the product of a dialogue between ego and the instincts, formed at the meeting point of the instincts and the outside world (*CW*7 1928b §297–298). Through integration, the centre of the personality is displaced from the limited ego into the more comprehensive self, 'the mid-point about which true personality turns' (*CW*18 1943 §1817). The self is the centre of the psyche, whereas the psyche is 'the totality of all psychic processes' (*CW*6 1921 §797) which can be brought under the influence of a will. In a more symbolic sense, the self is also the 'God-within'. I will return to this point in Chapters 2 and 3.

Jung understood the *psyche* to mean the collective and the personal unconscious, plus consciousness. It included dreams and fantasies inasmuch as they function as image forms driving the process of psychological development. In Jungian analysis, 'free associations are considered with respect to their aim and not with respect to their derivation' (*CW*6 1921 §702), and dreams and fantasies may be seen as 'symbolic expression[s] which anticipate a coming phase of psychological development' (*CW*6 1921 §701). The psyche is the source of the drive towards individuation. In referring to the psyche as the totality of both conscious and unconscious, Jung understands the conscious mind to be an ephemeral phenomenon occurring within the psyche. Although psyche is both conscious and unconscious, as when both the personal and the collective unconscious act together, Jung's *collective unconscious* is not conscious since it is impersonal. That aspect of 'the human psyche is as little personalistic as the body. It is far rather something inherited and universal' (*CW*3 1939a §527). However, since psyche as a whole is conscious of itself, it is capable of 'knowing' a goal different from the goal of the unconscious. This distinguishes psyche from 'blind instincts' (*CW*8 1947/1954 §380).

Jung saw *instincts* as 'typical modes of action' (*CW*8 1919 §273). Jung's instincts are both drives and inherent capabilities, somewhat akin to Chomsky's notion of inherited language tendencies (Piattelli-Palmarini, 1980). They are potentialities which lay down a path of possible development but which need environmental experiences to set the development in motion. Jung's perspective on instincts anticipated later developments in psychology and ethology, such as the experiments in the 1960s investigating the development of visual recognition in kittens (Hubel & Wiesel, 1959, 1962), and Thorpe's (1961) studies of birdsong, which revealed that such abilities consist of an innate blueprint that is shaped by individual experience.[2] In Jung's theory, instincts and archetypes account for uniformity and regularity. However, within the limits of human variation, each individual has a set of choices. Jung asserted that the range of choice for each individual is influenced by a combination of inheritance (implied in the psychological type which is part of the ground plan of a person's own nature and disposition; *CW*6 1921 §560), individual experience and education (*CW*17 1928a §103–104), and socialisation (*CW*17 1934a §289).

Jung thought that civilisation was attained at the cost of a loss of contact with the instincts and that the huge increase in cultural and social pressures that followed civilisation has left individuals needing to rebalance external and internal demands. He had found that refocusing on the inner world gave a vital role to dreams and symbols, which he thought were the image forms of instincts and therefore future oriented. They could be the means by which information about what is not yet fully conscious is conveyed to consciousness. He made use of *active imagination* (a conscious, deliberate exploration of fantasies and symbols) and painting, drawing, and writing as ways of turning conscious attention towards these images.

Archetypes are Jung's postulates of dynamic form-shaping influences which set the directions or the paths along which the instincts can flow.[3] The archetypes drive specific aspects of the process of psychological development and give direction to the shaping of this in each individual. Scholastic philosophers described them as 'natural images engraved in the human mind, helping it to form judgements' (*CW*8 1919 §275). In Jung's theory, archetypes function as explanatory hypothetical constructs that helped him to articulate the process by which individual personal growth is driven, energised, and expressed. Jung conceptualised archetypes as ***instincts*** clothed in images and given imaginative form. He said they are 'intuitive concepts for physical phenomena' – the effects of man's experiences – 'but equally they appear as the factors which cause such experiences' (*CW*7 1917/1926/1943 §151 and fn). This paradoxical statement introduces Jung's hypothesis of a dynamic aspect of the archetype which shapes individual development intuitively from within (see Chapter 5 for a more detailed account of Jung's theory of archetypes). Archetypes have both an empirical reality in their imaginal forms *and* a theoretical function as an explanatory linking principle providing internal consistency in Jung's overall theory.

Jung was also interested in the long past of the human psyche. In his view, the basic questions psychology seeks to address, such as what a person is and what this means for how life should be lived, were taken up first by the world's religions and subsequently by secular philosophy. Hence he viewed the history of religions as a history of humankind's struggle with these issues, long before they became the concern of psychology. To Jung, the use of religious terms such as *soul* for transcendental aspects of the psychology of personality was not problematic.

Jung saw the *soul* as autonomous enough to become a personality in itself (*CW*6 1921 §797). He described the soul as the sense of the inner self which becomes individuality through conscious effort, by bridging inner and outer with a conscious attitude. The inner attitude, he said, is the sense of the inner self known to the individual alone. I acknowledge that there are a number of problems with Jung's failure to distinguish *soul* from self, and whilst it may seem desirable to clarify this distinction, I am cautious about doing so because of the danger (of which Levinas, 1930, warns) of 'grasping' knowledge rather than perceiving and experiencing it and consequently reducing the wide connotations of meaning that this word had for Jung and that it gathered over centuries of use. In contrast to the *soul*, which reflects the whole self, Jung saw ***spirit*** as the life of the body seen from within and the body as the outward manifestation of *spirit*, though he also uses the conventional meaning of *spiritual* (*CW*10 1928/1931 §195).

Developmental processes

As I mentioned, for Jung, civilisation was gained at the cost of a loss of contact with the instincts. The cultural and social pressures following from civilisation mean that individuals need to rebalance external with internal demands through *individuation*, which Jung saw as 'the complete actualization of the whole human being' (*CW*16 1934d §352). Refocusing on the inner world gives an active and vital role to dreams and symbols as the means by which that which is not yet fully conscious is conveyed to consciousness. This inwardness is seen as an essential precursor to and preparation for self-development.

Because of the danger of psychosis, Jung felt that the task of individuation was something of a heroic quest. Jung referred to the initial phase of separation from maternal origins as *differentiation*, a state which he contrasted with *symbiosis*. He thought that 'hero' mythology *reflects and encapsulates* the preexisting instinctive blueprint for this internal quest in timeless thought-forms and images. He understood the goal of the heroic quest to be the self: 'The hero seeks the treasure from the dark cavern: the treasure is *life*: it is himself' (*CW*5 1911–12/1952 §580). Jung pointed to the extreme antiquity of this idea, citing an image from the Rig Veda of 'the self-begotten egg from which he (man) hatches himself' (*CW*5 1911–12/1952 §589).

Jung understood individuation as a task and the resulting fullness of personality as an achievement. For Jung, personality (self) development is the result of the self shaping its own person and is expressed through the actions and experiences of the lived life. He compared individuation in its social and collective sense with the historical process of civilisation. Jung held that man's struggle is with the collective (in this case understood as social, familial, and cultural influences), from which people must free themselves through a lifetime developmental process of separation, differentiation, and individuation, to achieve a new synthesis between inner and outer conflicts. Implicit in Jung's notion of individuation is the strong idea that individual balance and harmony lead to raised levels of *social* consciousness.

Whilst Jung understood the urge to self-development to be instinctual, he maintained that the response to the urge is not. Rather, it should be understood as a consciously fostered process aided by developmental practices, an idea more usually associated with religious activity. Thus Jung conceptualises personal development in spiritual, moral, and religious ways (see Chapter 2 for the links between individuation and Jung's religious ideas and Chapter 4 for the link with alchemy) whilst staying within an evolutionary model of optimal adaptation. The notion of adaptation to both inner and outer environments bridges what otherwise might be conflicting elements.

Jung was unapologetic about the similarity between his concept of individuation and a *religious* attitude to life, saying, 'it was of profound psychological significance when Christianity first proclaimed that the orientation to the future was the redeeming principle for mankind' (*CW*4 1914b §668). Jung postulated a 'religious/spiritual instinct', while acknowledging that this was not equally strong in every individual. The role of the *religious instinct* or attitude is examined in more detail in Chapter 2.

According to Jung, individuation is brought about when a *new* conscious ***attitude*** is formed as a result of previously unconscious material being brought into conscious awareness. Jung used the term *attitude* in a philosophical way to mean 'a point of reference, a position, an orientation' and in a psychological way to mean 'a predisposition, expectation, readiness to act in a certain way, or habit born of experience or training'. Jung states that he derived this latter meaning from Ebbinghaus – 'To have an attitude means to be ready for something definite . . . an *a priori* orientation to a definite thing' (Ebbinghaus, 1905–1913) – and from Wundt's concept of *apperception*, which recognises the relatedness of newly perceived contents to the already existing contents of the psyche and promotes 'the perception . . . of everything similar to itself' (*CW*6 1921 §688). He felt that this function of apperception resulted in one-sidedness of the conscious orientation and of the personality *type*. 'Were it not for the absolutely fundamental importance of attitude, the existence of an individual psychology would be out of the question' (*CW*6 1921 §690).

In addition to giving rise to psychological type through a preferred orientation, an attitude may be a maxim or guiding spirit. This may be via another personality revered and emulated or, more abstractly, a living of life 'in a certain spirit' that makes life worth living (*CW*8 1926 §645). The attitude or guiding spirit, he said, is 'an intention of the unconscious, superior to, or at least on a par with, the ego' (*CW*8 1926 §643). This makes the unconscious into a kind of higher consciousness guiding the ego, not a subconscious. Thus the guiding superego, for Jung, is an unconscious as well as a conscious influence.

Conscious ideals and unconscious attitudes also expressed by Jung as an aspect of the meaning of 'spirit' 'give meaning to life and the possibility of its greatest development' (*CW*8 1926 §648).

The new position is achieved through the *transcendent function*, a hypothesised functional element in the developmental process that, like archetypes, has or is a form of goal-directed energy.

> The transcendent function . . . leads to the revelation of the essential man. . . . The meaning and purpose of the process is the realization, in all its aspects, of the personality originally hidden away in the embryonic germ-plasm; the production and unfolding of the original, potential wholeness.
>
> (*CW*7 1917/1926/1943 §188)

In calling this finding of a new attitude the transcendent function, Jung adapted a term from mathematics to mean the union of conscious and unconscious contents (*CW*7 1917/1926/1943 §79 fn1), the transition from one attitude to another (*CW*6 1921 §828).

Fundamental to Jung's assertion that individuation is both a task and a goal is the concept of ***will***. Development as a person is not limited to a biological growth sequence, though this is included in the notion of the stages of life. Jung conceptualised personal development in a *spiritual*, *moral*, and *religious* way whilst also framing it in terms of an evolutionary model of optimal adaptation. The question arises of exactly how Jung understood the concept of *will* and whether the new direction could be brought about by conscious effort alone. He offered a paradoxical answer. The new direction or transcendent function is not determined by the will, which is not available to the whole psyche. Jung saw self-development as an tendency inherent in human nature (just as nest building is in birds) but in which there are elements of conscious choice.

The tendency towards individuation is expressed in the form of *tasks*. Jung described these tasks as being predetermined by inherited 'collective blueprints' which 'produce culture in man with the same logic as in the bird they produce the artfully woven nest, and the antlers in the stag' (*CW*4 1914b §665). He described these determinants or tendencies as due to the peculiar attributes of living matter itself. But:

> The psyche does not merely *react*, it gives its own specific answer to the influences at work upon it, and at least half the resulting formation is entirely due to the psyche and the determinants inherent within it.
>
> (*CW*4 1914b §665)

This gives a powerful role to individual creativity. However, Jung implies that creativity is not under conscious control. It is an aspect of nature that can be neither inhibited nor voluntarily produced. But Jung's notion of will *is* conscious. To make sense of this, one needs to remember that Jung linked the central task of individuation with introversion. It is the degree of introversion, or inner focus, that Jung saw as the individual's 'specific answer to the influences at work on it'. An individual's 'answer' to the demands of life also involves personal values, moral and spiritual ideals, and choices based on these. This is the Jungian *task,* to make choices and decisions at pivotal points in life, guided by an increasingly conscious knowledge of one's own nature, to be oriented towards the future via a deeper awareness of the present, *and* to find a new form of expression. Again and again Jung emphasised a complex interplay between biological determinism and choice. Development for humans was not a biological flowering in preordained stages but the satisfying and fulfilling expression of inherent possibilities through making conscious choices.

Types and psychopathology

The *typology* is often thought of as 'Jung's theory of personality', but, although important, it is not the core of his personality theory. The core is individuation, a position of balance and unity. Jung put forward an eightfold *typological matrix* consisting of two main *orientations, introversion* and *extraversion*, and four *functions: thinking, feeling, intuition*, and *sensation*. Each of the four functions may be introverted or extraverted. The functions have an organising role as they represent different ways of approaching and understanding the world. In Jung's typological matrix, the four functions are in a different arrangement and balance within each person. One of the functions will be a person's dominant mode and one will be the least preferred or nondominant function. The *thinking* function is characterised by rational thinking, perception, and judgement. The *feeling* function is concerned with value. *Intuition* is concerned with possibility, meaning, and potentiality, and *sensation* is the empirical function giving awareness of events in the field of experience. The combinations of types give rise to subtle differences in behaviour and approach to life as well as complex interpersonal dynamics among the types.[4] A well-known psychological test, the Myers-Briggs Type Indicator (Myers, 1962), is based on Jung's typology.

Jung held that a one-sided attitude developed as a result of an overreliance on the dominant features of the person's type can lead to neurosis, which itself may become the stimulus for setting out on a path of individuation. Integration of the less dominant attitude and functions and a rebalancing of the typological aspects of the personality are conscious tasks of the individuation process. As I have suggested, other aspects of individuation are less conscious and driven by archetypes (see Chapter 3).

Jung had observed that *neurotic* conflicts seemed to produce a kind of crisis through which a person is forced to look inward and is compelled to seek a new attitude. In Jung's view, it is not the outside world that causes *neurosis* but rather, it occurs 'because [a person] does not know how to use his external adaptedness for the good of his most personal and intimate life and how to bring it to the right pitch of development' (*CW*17 1926/1946 §172). This is consistent with

Jung's idea that emotional disturbances might have a purpose. If there was no conflict with oneself, there would be no drive to turn inward.

While neurosis could motivate beneficial change, Jung understood ***psychosis*** to be a pathological adaptation. Psychosis is also a state of introversion. In this state, feeling-toned complexes become dominant and intrude into consciousness accompanied by intensive affect as a consequence of their possessing 'a value that sometimes exceeds that of our conscious intentions' (*CW*8 1934e §200). Not being disposable by will, they tend to remain unchecked by conscious meaning and may be difficult or impossible to integrate. Jung's observations of his own experiences and those of his patients led him to conclude that these intrusive images and feelings can have an abnormally strong influence on the psyche, creating such disturbance that they are likely to be projected and reexperienced as bizarre thoughts, hallucinations, and delusions. Even when projection was not a feature, one could become fascinated by the images themselves, in which case nothing would be gained as there was no integration of them. Psychosis could therefore be distinguished from creative processes and 'Divine madness' inasmuch as the latter are characterised by reflection, analysis, and integration.

Concluding comments

Any attempt to encapsulate Jung's theory by enumerating his main concepts leaves half of the story untold. Its unique aspect is the fusion of Jung's psychological concepts with his knowledge of religious and cultural history. In the chapters that follow, I will expand on both the religious aspects of Jung's theory of personality and the contribution of Jung's alchemical studies to the development of his concept of individuation and his concept of self. But first I wish to return to the question of why it is justified to treat Jung's theory as a personality theory.

2 Setting the context for treating Jung as a personality theorist

By psychologists, Jung is classified as a personality theorist along with most of the other early psychoanalytical writers. However, psychoanalysts think of Jung as primarily a psychoanalytical theorist. The early psychoanalysts neither published their work as 'personality theories' nor described themselves as 'personality theorists' – it is a retrospective categorization. Consequently, insofar as I am addressing psychoanalysts, it may be useful to review the reasons for accepting the classification of Jung's work as a theory of personality. In the following section, I summarise the focus and overall approach to personality theory taken by personality theorists contemporary with Jung, namely, Gordon Allport (1897–1967), Gardner Murphy (1895–1979), Henry Murray (1893–1998), and Abraham Maslow (1908–1970), and also by more recent expert commentators and theorists, namely, Maddi (1972), Mischel (1999), Schultz (2001), and Magnavita (2002). I suggest that there is common ground between the questions that Jung's theory addresses and those of other significant personality theorists and commentators sufficient to justify inclusion of his work within personality psychology.

Jung compared with contemporary personality theorists

Jung and Gordon Allport

Like Jung, Gordon Allport deemed an exclusively scientific approach to personality unsatisfactory. He contrasted science's 'generalised human mind' with the 'living individual human models from which it is drawn' and maintained that personality theories should represent change and variation. For Allport, individuality was about uniqueness and distinctiveness ordered within a single individual (Allport, 1937: 3, 14).

Jung's theory accounts for both the uniqueness of people and their shared characteristics by proposing a species-specific (collective) inheritance and an individual personal inheritance from the ancestral line (see above: 4–6). Allport's theory also combined *nomothetic* (emphasising general laws) and *idiographic* (emphasising individual differences) approaches (Allport, 1937: 22–23). Like Jung, Allport was interested in genetic principles and attempted to understand the laws of 'mind in general' while also seeking to understand the 'lawful tendencies of minds-in-particular' (1937: 23).

Allport's seminal book, first published in 1937, set out a programme for psychologists to follow. His challenge for psychologists was to account for personality *as a whole* (the macrocosm), but he accepted that there was value in studies of any one of the elements of personality separately (the microcosm; Allport, 1937: 17, 21, 22). Allport emphasised that personality theory should give an account of the processes of maturation and development and of adaptation achieved through the experience of managing conflicting desires and needs. He maintained that growth over the life span must be the result of integrating experience with the person's own characteristics in a 'self' (1937: 138–147). Jung also saw individual development as a sequence having several stages, similar to the stages of an alchemical transformative process: an initial separation stage followed by a differentiation stage and then a stage of individual flowering of the fully developed and unified self, tempered by contact with the outer environment and all its influences.

Allport's programme included the element of aspiration and transcendent capability that Jung expressed as his concept of the transcendent function (see above: 13). Like Jung, Allport acknowledged that such concepts are theoretical, that is to say hypothetical (1937: 365). He concluded that there are many ways to study the human person, but the best way would be to study the person fully as an individual who transcends descriptions, strives for his or her own integrity, and struggles, hopes, and plans even in adversity (1937: 566).

In *Becoming*, published in 1955, Allport argued for the need to include a concept of a 'religious sentiment' that develops as a result of seeking a theory of Being. This requires a balance between intellect and feeling and brings to the person a feeling of being meaningfully linked to the whole of Being (Allport, 1955: 94–95). Jung also postulated the existence of a religious/spiritual instinct (*CW*17 1926/1946 §157). For Allport, the development of a religious orientation was comparable with the development of other 'high level schemata that influence the course of becoming', such as ideologies, philosophies, notions, and hunches about life that guide the person. For Jung, it was an instinctual and inherent aspect of human nature.

Although sympathetic to a holistic approach to human psychology, Allport held that some areas could not be addressed scientifically and consequently was not as inclusive as Jung. What Jung included as amenable to scientific study was philosophically and spiritually almost limitless, and this is perhaps his particular hallmark (see Chapter 8: 171).

Jung and Gardner Murphy

Gardner Murphy (1895–1979) proposed that each of the different ways of approaching the study of personality had its own 'membership character' in a system and that the system should itself be viewed as an organised, unified conception (Murphy, 1947: 12). Jung saw himself as defining the field for a general psychology of human personality whose scope was not to be limited to being a branch or subfield of psychology.

Murphy's conception for theorising personality featured a series of levels in a biosocial system arranged in order from the simplest to the most complex (1947: 18–21). Jung did not outline a tiered system for theorising personality and was cautious of reducing the complexity of human nature to simple components. Jung's view was that human nature might be almost impossibly complex, but it was the proper subject for a psychology that was a synthesis of knowledge from many fields. By contrast, Murphy's view was that psychological theorising on personality must acknowledge what is not yet known *and* what is ultimately unknowable:

> Man is a sample of the stuff of which the cosmos is made . . . we do not know to what extent the principles operating within man are identical with general principles which operate elsewhere in the universe . . . it seems to be nothing but arrogance to insist that man's place has been discovered with finality. We know neither man, nor the cosmos, nor his relation to the cosmos.
>
> (Murphy, 1947: 916–917)

Whilst there were differences in their approaches, there were similarities in their philosophical positions. Both Jung and Murphy leaned towards Vitalism.

Murphy remarked that what emerges from a study of human personality is 'the impulsive nature of the life process, the continuous effort at satisfaction and fulfilment of which Bergson never tired of writing' (Murphy, 1947: 917). Jung too was strongly influenced by Vitalist ideas, especially Bergson's as expressed in his 1907/1923 book *Creative Evolution* (Shamdasani, 2003: 208–209).

Jung and Henry Murray

In 1949, Jung's former analysand,[5] Henry Murray (1893–1998), wrote that, since personality is motivated by an intricate pattern of forces, an organismic conception of personality as a whole was required. This should represent unity across single events and unity across the successive developments that constitute a life, together with its long-range goals. For Murray, unity of personality came from resolution of conflicts and was formed as a result of repeated choices being made between alternative or opposing 'percepts, concepts, needs, goals, loyalties, philosophies, tactics or modes of expression'. Hence he felt that it was sometimes necessary to wait for years until a structure had been completed to comprehend the events leading up to it. Interestingly, in relation to the cross-fertilisation of ideas between these two figures, the example Murray gave to illustrate this point is one Jung repeatedly said was the most central and abiding influence on his development and on his life's work, namely Goethe's *Faust* (Murray & Kluckhohn, 1949: 4).

Jung also regarded personality as unfolding over the course of the lived life. As we have seen in the previous section, his theoretical constructs conceptualised both constituents of the human psyche and developmental processes. In addition, Jung anticipates future development, though he stops short of claiming to predict individual behaviour. For Murray, however, a representation of personality was a hypothetical and selective formulation, a sufficient formulation for a specific purpose which should 'explain past and present events; predict future events; and serve as a basis for control' (Murray & Kluckhohn, 1949: 7).

Murray defined personality as the organisation of all the integrative processes in the brain (Murray & Kluckhohn, 1949: 9). Like Jung, Murray asserted that need systems generate images of difficult and distant goals (Murray & Kluckhohn, 1949: 16). For Murray, formal analysis of personality requires observation of the relative dominance and differentiation of psychological processes. No conception of personality could be complete without reference to development, most of which could be described in terms of differentiation and integration (Murray & Kluckhohn, 1949: 29–30). So for Murray, understanding and theorising personality required following its development through time, studying the processes of differentiation and integration, and developing knowledge of the personality's endowments (Murray & Kluckhohn, 1949: 32).

Jung anticipated Murray in maintaining that personality can only be seen in the stages of an entire lived life rather than observing moment-to-moment occurrences of particular behaviours. After his analysis with Jung, Murray went on to establish a branch of personality theory known as 'personology' which, following Stern (1871–1938) and Allport in the 1930s, emphasised the importance of a continuous narrative of the self.

Whilst Murray may have distanced himself from Jung's later work which focused on alchemy, there was considerable influence of Jung's ideas on Murray's. Both emphasised the importance of the lived life as the expression of a unique combination of genetic inheritance and cultural influences and the importance of instincts. Both were concerned with the nature and development of individuality. However, Jung emphasised the importance of collective or species-inherited aspects of human nature more than Murray did.

Jung and Abraham Maslow

Jung construed the human individual as moving forward towards the future and as seeking to fulfil needs and pursue goals in relation to his or her process of 'becoming'. Abraham Maslow (1908–1970), a contemporary of Jung's later life, suggested that a theory of personality must include a theory of human motivation, and, like Allport, Murphy, and Murray, asserted that it must be conceived as dynamic not static (Maslow, 1954: 23).

Most of Jung's major works in which he made similar points in relation to individuation were available and well known by the 1950s; hence there is the possibility of cross-fertilisation. Maslow makes several references to Jung in *Motivation and Personality* (1954) in connection with self-actualisation and instinctual needs, including a need or drive for growth (Maslow, 1954: 35, 68, 78, 93). From the middle of the twentieth century onwards, it is increasingly difficult to ignore the possibility that personality theorists may have been influenced by Jung, whether or not this influence was consciously acknowledged, since Jung's work was widely available.

I will briefly mention some of the personality theorists who followed Jung and brought the psychology of personality into the late twentieth and early twenty-first centuries to illustrate the point that, although later personality theory tended to be increasingly founded on experimental research, there are evident correspondences between Jung's concerns and those of later personality psychologists.

Later personality theorists and Jung

Salvatore Maddi, Walter Mischel, Duane Schultz, and Jeffrey J. Magnavita have been major contributors in the field of personality in the later years of the twentieth century, Maddi and Schultz as commentators and authors of textbooks whose many editions have spanned several decades and Mischel and Magnavita as theorists and innovators. These authors take a holistic perspective as well as acknowledging the contribution of experimental studies of specific traits, behaviours, attitudes, and motivating factors. Furthermore, Maddi advocates that personologists should integrate the information from all areas of psychology into 'an overall account of the functioning of persons' (Maddi, 1972: 9). Similarly, Duane Schultz listed the questions about human nature that a theory of personality should address as: free will/determinism, nature/nurture, past/present, uniqueness/universality, equilibrium/growth, and optimism/pessimism (Schultz, 2001: 35), issues that Jung actively engaged with throughout his life (see above and Chapters 2–4).

Jung and Salvatore Maddi

Both Jung and Maddi valued different modes of knowing as ways of theorising the complexity of human life. In Maddi's view, theories in any field are

> virtually never restricted to statements based on empirical knowledge alone, and personality theories are not based solely on empirical knowledge. Intuitive knowledge, operated upon by reason could become rational knowledge and may merge with empirical knowledge, but, at any point, a theory of personality, which is a product of a person, may be 'a conglomerate of intuitive, rational and empirical knowledge.'
>
> (Maddi 1972: 11; 1996: 9–10)

The three types of knowledge Maddi mentions correspond with the epistemological preferences described by Jung for his intuitive, thinking, and sensing types (*CW*6 1921 §556–671). Maddi's respect for intuitive knowledge and non-empirical statements is in harmony with Jung's overall purpose and approach.

For Maddi, personality characteristics are 'stable or structural entities or tendencies that are used to explain not only the movement towards goals but the fact and content of the goals themselves' (Maddi, 1972: 10; 1996: 8). That is to say, personality theory should encompass hopes, aspirations, ideals, and philosophies, as recommended by Allport. Jung, who stressed the importance of final causes and the creative aspects of the psyche, would have agreed.

Jung and Walter Mischel

At the time that Jung was developing his theory, the field of psychology drew from many other disciplines, as the boundaries between disciplines were not yet established. By the 1970s, when disciplinary separation had been achieved, personality theorists like Mischel were once again ready to recognise that, whilst psychology had produced useful experimental data, field boundaries should not be too tightly drawn. Walter Mischel emphasised complexity and advocated the need for a holistic approach (Mischel, 1999: 3).

By the late 1990s it was becoming clear that data from many types of research, taken together, were beginning to produce a synthesis of information on how human tendencies, including motivation and biogenetic processes, interact to influence an individual's distinctive patterns of adaptation through the life span. Like Jung, whose work encompasses philosophy, religion, and anthropology, Mischel acknowledges the degree to which the study of personality overlaps with other fields of study and is at the crossroads of most areas of psychology. The study of personality, he said, is the meeting point of the study of human development and change, abnormality and deviance, competence and fulfilment, emotions and thought, learning, social relations, and the biological foundations that underlie human qualities (Mischel, 1999: 5).

Maddi and Mischel recognise that theories of personality do not lend themselves to precise scientific testing and suggest that they may function either as general guidelines or orientations or for interpreting results from a certain perspective or framework (Mischel, 1999: 9). For Mischel, the value of a personality theory is as much in its function for stimulating research and its real-life applications such as therapy as in its capacity to find clear support or disconfirmation (1999: 9). His view was that, although the main ideas within psychoanalytic approaches have been difficult to test, recent developments of sophisticated methods could make it possible to reconceptualise some of the insights of psychoanalytic personality theory in such a way as to allow them to be incorporated into current personality theory (1999: 12).

Jung and Jeffrey J. Magnavita

Finally, when speaking of the need for a synthesis of approaches in *Theories of Personality: Contemporary Approaches to the Science of Personality*, Magnavita (2002) cites Rychlak (1973). Rychlak, a philosopher, not a personality theorist, attempted to provide a philosophy of personality theories, and, in particular, theories developed by psychotherapists. He distinguished between a 'discriminal' style for theories (attempting to tie together behavioural sequences) and a 'vehicular' style (analysing the laws that tie the sequences together; Rychlak, 1973). Rychlak regarded psychotherapy as an experimental forum within which to diagnose, measure, and treat personality, saying that the resulting marriage between psychotherapy and personology produced seminal personality theorists, most of whom (like Jung) were both psychiatrists and psychoanalysts (Rychlak, 1973: 18)

Rychlak regarded psychotherapy as a legitimate test of the applicability of a theory, albeit that it lacks rigorous experimental controls, and advanced the notion that good theoretical systems offer alternative understandings of the nature of humankind and of the possibility of behaviour and personality change (Rychlak, 1973, cited by Magnavita, 2002: 15). Apart from his self-observation and self-experimentation recorded in *The Red Book* (see Chapter 4), Jung both discovered and 'tested' his ideas through his work with patients and analysands. His entire work, from *Psychological Types* (1921) to his work on alchemy in the 1940s and 1950s, circled around transformative processes in personality.

Magnavita acknowledges that abstraction in theories ranges from lower to higher levels, and there are gains and losses in each of the possible positions. On the one hand, psychoanalytic theorising is highly abstract and consequently stays less close to empirical data than does a theory like behaviour theory. On the other hand, although behaviour theory stays close to empirical data, it describes the complexity of the personality system less well. In his earlier years, Jung researched personality experimentally using word-association tests but found that his results revealed further questions that, in his view, required a more abstract approach if they were to be pursued satisfactorily.

Concluding comment

This overview of past and contemporary positions on theorising personality shows many correspondences between Jung's approach and areas of interest and those of other influential personality theorists. In particular, there was agreement that personality must ultimately be understood as a unified whole, that personality is constituted from a complex nexus of conscious and unconscious drives, desires, and aspirations, and that the person's position in relation to their goals and aspirations and religious outlook could be included as legitimate aspects of the psychological study of personality. These different theorists and commentators and Jung agree that theories of personality contain subjective elements as well as objective data and that personality theories are perspectives for assembling, arranging, and viewing a potentially unlimited mass of data.

This chapter has described the significant constructs of Jung's theory as I have defined it and shows that, though there are differences of position, Jung and other significant personality theorists and analysts of personality theories address similar questions. This suggests that it is reasonable to continue to classify Jung as a personality theorist and to reappraise his work on the basis of its status as a theory of personality. I return to this issue in Chapter 8, where I compare the structural coherence of Jung's theory with structure of scientific personality theories.

The next three chapters examine in detail the role and functions of four important themes in Jung's personality theory: religion, alchemy, the archetypes, and the transformative functions of creative imagination.

Notes

1 Some of Jung's statements about inherited images have given rise to the view that he supported Lamarckian ideas on the inheritance of acquired characteristics. Jung strenuously denied this, though it is not clear what alternative mechanism he proposed for the inheritance of universal psychological experiences, such as mating or parenting, in the form of *archetypes*, if not through the inheritance of that which has been experienced. However, Haule (2011) suggests a possible mechanism whereby experience can modify brain structures in such a way as to alter the capacities of future generations (11–16).

2 Hubel and Wiesel reared kittens in conditions of sensory deprivation and found that kittens have a basic neural blueprint for sight but need exposure to lines and curves in the visual field to stimulate the development of specific visual abilities. Thorpe made detailed analyses of recordings of the songs of birds reared separately and showed that although young birds can sing even if they are reared in isolation, their song only becomes recognisable to other birds when it is shaped by hearing the pattern of song sung by their own family group.

3 See Progoff (1956, chapter VI, especially p. 176).

4 See Cox (1964) and Storr (1973) for descriptions of the Jungian typology which I have drawn on for summary.

5 Byrne (1966: 286).

Chapter 2

The place of religion in Jung's personality theory

Analytical psychologists are familiar with Jung's blending of psychology and religion, but other psychologists have found it problematic. Jung has been criticised on the grounds that his writing is arcane and difficult to follow (Schultz, 1976; 2001). This perception may be a consequence of the way he interweaves religion, mythology, and alchemy with psychology. Some empirical psychologists, for example Eysenck (1953: 226–235), disliked Jung's attempt to reinsert religion into psychology, seeing his ideas as subjective, mystical, and unscientific. Others, such as Allport (1937), Murphy (1947), and Ryckman (1993), have been inspired by the breadth of scope in Jung's theory. Some have considered Jung's scope unparalleled (for example, Hall & Lindzey, 1978: 149). This chapter explains why Jung's radical religious ideas are inseparable from his general theory of personality and why understanding this aspect of his work is the key to understanding his personality theory. I focus particularly on the religious meaning of Jung's key concept of *individuation*.

Personality as vocation

Jung was primarily interested in the transformative phenomena of mature self-development: in how individuality might be shaped from within. A single quotation will illustrate the importance Jung gave to the task of self development: 'To the degree that a man is untrue to the law of his being and does not rise to personality, he has failed to realize his life's meaning' (*CW*17 1934a §314). Jung held that experiences that remain unconscious may be detrimental to the wholeness of the personality, since experiences that do not come into conscious awareness fail to be integrated. In addition, adopting society's rules uncritically takes the individual away from his or her self. Jung quotes Rousseau: 'You must choose between making a man or a citizen, you cannot be both at once' (*CW*6 1921 §134); hence the cost of true individuality is a degree of social isolation. Jung knew from his own self-searching period recorded in *The Red Book* that its consequences led him away from his earlier public successes on to a more solitary path. He described the driving force of personality development as a task and a vocation whose challenging nature was such as to need Divine assistance:

'It is what is commonly called a *vocation:* an irrational factor that destines a man to emancipate himself from the herd and from its well-worn paths. True personality is always a vocation and puts its trust in God' (*CW*17 1934a §300).

Religion and individuation

As I have indicated in Chapter 1, Jung's emphasis on individuation as the goal of personality development is unique to his theory, as is his proposition that the process of individuation is driven by symbols, forms of archetypes, which he defines as nonrational guiding images, not yet fully formed and arising from the instincts (see Chapter 5). It is helpful to recall that Jung proposed an innate instinct for self-realisation. Postulating innate instincts and drives was by no means peculiar to Jung – Freud proposed life and death instincts, and McDougall (1923: 121–177) lists thirteen basic instincts. Jung conceptualised the instincts as having the capacity to form images which may appear in dreams and fantasies (*CW*3 1908/1914 §565), become manifest to consciousness through active imagination, or find expression in forms of art, myths, and religious symbols. He held that images and symbolic forms produced by the instincts had the power to influence, and indeed drive, psychological and cultural development (*CW*16 1946 §471).

Jung understood the cross to be a psychological symbol for the union of opposites in consciousness and thus of individuation. He postulated that contemplation of the symbols of the cross and the Trinity could bring about a conscious realisation of the complementary relationship of the dichotomous and separate aspects of the symbol. A bridge or connection between the conscious and unconscious parts of the psyche is created. He saw parallels here with his proposed mechanism for the psychological process of individuation, in which diverse or scattered parts of the personality are brought together in symbolic form, in a dream, or in other creative expressions. Contemplation of a dream image or a potent symbol could establish links between unconscious and conscious material, creating the potential for dialogue between different parts of the personality.

However, to come face to face with the inner core of oneself in a dialogue between one's conscious and unconscious self is to encounter something that is both familiar and wholly other. Jung's experience in psychiatry made him aware that confronting this duality within oneself could be awesome and unnerving. In his later years, Jung concluded that 'fear of God' could be understood as a projection of the psychological experience of coming face to face with one's whole self, both conscious and unconscious. On the other hand, Jung saw religions as 'great psychic systems of healing' (*CW*13 1945/1954 §478). Some religions, he felt, offered symbolic ways of containing the tension between unity and duality in the self as well as in the God-image. Jung pointed to the Christian concept of the Trinity, which holds in one symbol the idea of three persons. Another example was the idea of duality in the transformation symbolism of the Roman Catholic mass. Although the Roman Catholic mass has changed in style and language since Jung wrote his *Transformation Symbols of the Mass*, the underlying symbolism in the central rite of the mass, the consecration, in which Christ is both sacrificer and sacrificed, is essentially the same as that described by Jung. In Jung's interpretation, the symbolic meaning of the mass is that, through the self-sacrifice of the crucifixion reenacted in the mass, God returns to his divine unity, but the symbol retains the opposites of good and evil which Jung held are contained in the dual nature of the God image (*CW*11 1952b §659–664).

Jung speculated that the sense of mystery shared by the great religions was perhaps the result of humanity's fascination with this ineluctable internal teleological process. It seemed to him that the sense of mystery did not come from looking outwards towards an external God but from an intuition of an internal psychological process that was no less mysterious. He held that this went some way towards explaining why strong religious feeling has been expressed by so many people in the past, though apparently lost to 'modern man' (Jung, 1933: 235–237). Jung researched numerous comparative examples of archetypal images such as those found in religious rites, myths, stories, art, and dreams in search of evidence for his assumption that the action of archetypes through images and symbols was a universal phenomenon. In explaining this phenomenon as spontaneous generation, he neglected to explore the possibility of alternative explanations such as cultural transmission between cultures and consequently overemphasised the spontaneous generation of similar symbols across time and cultures. Further research is needed to clarify the status of Jung's explanatory hypothesis that cultures spontaneously produce similar symbols, but his documentation of the widespread occurrence of similar of symbols is systematic and scholarly, and the facts of his observations are less questioned than his conclusion that they were incontrovertible evidence for a collective unconscious.

From 1912 onwards, Jung explored the idea that religious experience could be interpreted as a manifestation of the psychological experience of individuation. In addition to alchemical texts, Jung explored a classical Chinese Taoist text, *The Secret of the Golden Flower* (*CW*13); *The Tibetan Book of the Great Liberation* (*CW*11); *The Tibetan Book of the Dead* (eighth century, *CW*11); and the *I Ching* (fourth–third century BC, *CW*11). Approaching ancient Christian and Eastern religious texts from a psychological angle, he believed he had discovered a layer of psychological meaning in their symbolic images and metaphysical language.

He concluded that the texts described universal patterns of the human mind and, in particular, the experience of individuation. For example, he proposed that the ubiquitous motif of the hero's quest found in heroic literature, religious texts, and secular mythology could be interpreted as a representation of the psychological journey towards individuation (*CW*5 1911–12/1952 §580). In addition, Jung spent many years researching the hypothesis that the various anthropomorphic and heroic images of God were projections of the self with all the divine aspects that Jung associated with a transcendent, self-creating, unified self. He found that initially the images were of a sun-God, then of a man-like God, and eventually the fully embodied Christ-made-man (*CW*12 1944a §455, §469–470; *CW*9.1 1940/1950 §229).

The issue of duality

The importance for Jung of the dual nature of God and, by implication, of the self is crucial for understanding Jung's view of the psyche. Jung noted that the image of God in the early history of Judeo-Christianity was two sided, as in early pagan conceptualisations of divinity: as, on the one hand, the embodiment of light, wisdom, and benevolence and on the other, arbitrary, malevolent, disastrous (*CW*18 1954 §1538). He understood the Old Testament God and the later Christian God as society's attempts to deal with the darker aspects of life. However, he regarded the Christian Church's doctrine that God was all good (the *Summum bonum*) and that evil was the absence of good (*privatio boni*) as weak.[1] He interpreted the doctrine of *Summum bonum* psychologically, as an unsuccessful attempt to deal with the problem of evil by relocating it 'outside' the person and outside the image of God. For Jung, this conception meant that darkness and destructiveness were no longer aspects of God's own power and instead seemed to threaten God's goodness. A God or self conceived in this way would no longer have control over evil. The eruption of violence in Europe in World War I and the shock of the revelations of the death camps at the end of World War II led Jung to wonder if conscious striving for goodness and a failure to acknowledge unconscious evil had caused evil to be pushed to the margins of the collective psyche, where it could flourish unchecked.

Jung's understanding of this doctrine has been questioned by White, Philp, Hostie, and Segal on theological and philosophical grounds. Segal (1992) suggests that Jung's view, if taken as ontological rather than a psychological statement about the status of evil, would be heresy. My understanding is that, however much Jung argues that he is speaking as a psychologist and not as a theologian, his personal standpoint was indeed heretical from a traditional Christian point of view. However, this does not mean that he was making a theological argument. Jung took pains to avoid taking a public doctrinal position.

Jung wanted Christianity to renew itself by dispensing with the one-sided notion of God as wholly good and to rediscover something of the Old Testament idea of the ambivalence of God that he felt corresponded more accurately with the reality of the human psyche, of which the God-image was a reflection. Evil that could be consciously acknowledged could be assimilated and controlled. Through viewing itself from a psychological perspective, Christianity might acknowledge the dynamism of the tension of its own opposites and, as a result, contain its negatives and revitalise itself.

The brief description I have given in the preceding two paragraphs may give the impression that Jung wrote about religion *as* religion, that is to say, theologically. But it was never separated from his psychology of personality. Although in 'Answer to Job' (*CW*11 1952b) Jung directly explores the problem of Evil and the historical change of the image of God from the dualistic Yahweh of the Old Testament to the reformed God of the New Testament, he offers a *psychological* explanation of the transformation of the God-image. The suggestion that the God-image or archetype was in need of alteration is a startlingly radical idea and may be difficult to understand without some familiarity with the many ways in which Jung uses the term *archetype* (see Chapter 5). However, if I can attempt to summarise the theme of this complex book in a few brief phrases, Jung's thesis is that salvation meant saving man from God's cruelty as portrayed in the book of *Job*. This could only be achieved, Jung asserts, by making the image of the God archetype into one that embodied a capacity for reflection. Phrased in psychological terms, the God image is produced by humanity by means of projection and is transformed from a relatively unthinking image of extreme righteousness and power into the image of a God made self-conscious through becoming man-like. Ultimately the God-image is recognised as a projection of the divine in the human self.

In contrast to 'Answer to Job', which deals with the image of God and its transformation through God's relationship with humanity, Jung's several volumes on alchemy (*CW*12, 13, and 14), the essays on Chinese and Indian philosophy (*CW*11), the preface to 'Commentary on *The Secret of the Golden Flower*' (*CW*13 1929d), 'Yoga and the West' (*CW*11 1936a), and the 'Psychological Commentary to The Tibetan Book of the Dead' (*CW*11 1939/1954) are more directly concerned with individual self-transformation. These are psycho-hermeneutical works in which Jung presents religions *as* systems of personality development, as systems for bringing about a metaphysical process of transcendence, which he believed corresponded with his psychological concept of individuation.

Summary

The preceding section introduces the religious aspects of Jung's concept of individuation. We have seen that Jung found complex links between religious symbols and fundamental psychological processes, so much so that he articulated these processes through the language of religion and, even more, through the language and imagery of alchemy (see Chapter 4). Very near the end of his life, in a letter not intended for publication, Jung took his analogy between psychological and Christian spiritual development a step further than he had in his published work. In his reply to a letter from the Rev. David Cox (September 1957), Jung stated that key psychological and religious terms could be interchangeable:

> [I]nstead of using the term God, you say "unconscious", instead of Christ "Self", instead of incarnation "integration of the unconscious", instead of

> salvation or redemption "individuation", instead of crucifixion or sacrifice on the cross . . . "wholeness". I think it is no disadvantage to religious tradition if we can see how far it coincides with psychological experience.
>
> (*CW*18 1956/1957 §1664)

The continuation of this chapter takes Jung's juxtapositions of these terms as a framework.

The unconscious and God

Jung thought that the vast potential of the unconscious, its unknowability compared with consciousness, and its timelessness, together with its accompanying emotions of awe, longing for completeness, and sense of mystery, could substitute for the notion of 'God' and perhaps was God, in the alchemical sense of nature reflecting the Divine. Like the unconscious, God is seen as timeless, ceaseless, and constantly creating life out of its own matrix. In 'Answer to Job', Jung stated categorically, 'we cannot tell whether God and the unconscious are two different entities' (*CW*11 1952b §757). He speculated that pre–Christian people and both Christian and non–Christian alchemists projected the unconscious and thought of it as a God-entity. However, Jung's unorthodox idea was that man's God-likeness was not confined to the higher conscious and civilising aspects of personality but included the 'base elements'. It was the total, complete human. Its higher potential *and* its darker instinctual aspects were projected onto 'God' and became the God-within or the image of God in the human psyche.

Jung has been criticised by Glover (1950), Hostie (1957), Philp (1958), Heisig (1979), and Palmer (1997)[2] for irreligiously reducing religion to a psychological phenomenon and for stepping beyond his area of competence into philosophy and theology. Heisig and Palmer have criticised Jung's theory on the ground of poor methodological thinking and inadequate and erroneous logic, seen from a philosopher's perspective. On the other hand, Schaer (1950) and Nagy (1991) view the religious and philosophical ideas within his psychology favourably and with an appreciation of his subjectivist epistemological stance. Under heavy pressure to defend his position, Jung always insisted that he made a distinction between a God entity and the God images that he saw as originating in the human mind. He repeatedly said that he was not discussing the existence or otherwise of a superordinate God entity. Taking this position was necessary as it addressed the concerns of those who wished to defend disciplinary boundaries. However, I believe that a better argument can be made that Jung could not have been reducing religion to psychology since his view of the unconscious as infinite in time and space, autonomously creative, and reaching to the edges of biological matter and beyond has so much in common with a God entity as to be indistinguishable from it. For Jung, the unconscious is part of the cosmos and the cosmos is part of God. It is precisely because Jung sees the unconscious in a religious way that his psychologising of religion is not reductive. This transcendent aspect of his psychology is nowhere more manifest than in his picture of the unconscious and of the self.

Christ and the self

As he worked on unpicking the links and similarities between the symbols of earlier religions and those that were wrapped around the theological as opposed to the historical Christ, Jung argued that some New Testament authors were concerned to elevate Christ and, in effect, to treat him as an archetype. In a surprising departure from his usual style of writing, which tends towards amplification, Jung summarised in condensed form the manner in which New Testament authors had inserted the Christ figure into a preexisting historical niche which 'required' God to become man. The long preparation for 'restyling' the God image, he said, went through a continuous series of psychological transformations through which man came to acquire divinity:

1 Gods
2 A Supreme deity ruling the gods and demons
3 The deity shares a human fate, is betrayed, dies, is resurrected, and becomes just through acquiring wisdom in the form of the Holy Ghost.
4 God becomes man in the flesh and thus historical.

(*CW*18 1956/1957 §1658)

The chain of transformations suggests that the religious attitude implies an attitude to the self. Its history was both the history of religious traditions and of the changing status of the self. In an earlier essay, Jung made this point:

> All creation *ex nihilo* consists of nothing but God, with the result that man, like the rest of creation is simply God become concrete. . . . It was only quite late that we realized (or are beginning to realize) that God is reality itself and therefore – last but not least – man.
>
> (*CW*11 1952b §631)

My understanding of this statement is that Jung is saying that, although in the Christian world, we are on the verge of realising that we are 'God', the Christian world cannot accept this. The East seemed to Jung to be much more comfortable with the idea that God is inside humanity, not outside. In 1955 he commented, 'it is the rooted conviction of the West that God and the ego are worlds apart. In India . . . their identity was taken as self-evident' (*CW*14 1955–56 §131). Christians contemplating Christ will only say, like Paul, 'Christ liveth in me' (Gal. 2.20), whereas, in contrast, the Buddhist Sutra says, 'thou wilt know thou art the Buddha' (*CW*11 1943b §949). For Jung, the notion of Christ-within symbolises the self as unifier of the psyche and amounted to being a God-within; the problem was that Christianity found this difficult to accept.

Incarnation and integration of the unconscious

Jung expressed the integrated self or self complex, which develops at the interface between consciousness and unconsciousness, in religious terms:

> The dissolution of the mana-personality through conscious assimilation of its contents leads us back to ourselves as an actual living something poised between two world pictures . . . I have called this centre the Self. . . . It might equally well be called the 'God within us.'
>
> (*CW*7 1928b §397–399)

We have noted that, for Jung, the self comprised both the conscious ego and a limitless unconscious on which it is presumed to rest. Adult personality development proceeds by the expansion of the conscious self as a consequence of the withdrawal of external projections, as well as through the influence of education and experience. Jung suggested that what is projected outwards is lost to the self. Consequently the self is diminished. For self-realisation to be achieved, the ego must assimilate that which emerges from the older historical part of the psyche, the unconscious:

> Through its integration the centre of the personality is displaced from the limited ego into the more comprehensive self, into that centre which embraces both realms . . . and unites them with each other. This self is the mid-point about which true personality turns.
>
> (*CW*18 1943/1969 §1817)

We need to consider the unconscious contents that Jung believed must be assimilated for the self to develop to understand why taking in unconscious contents leads to awareness of the 'God within us'.

In 1939 Jung described the contents of the unconscious as 'a total vision *in potentia* from which consciousness singles out tiny fragments from time to time' (*CW*11 1939c §897) and in 1947 as 'everything which involuntarily and without paying attention to it, I feel, think, remember, want and do; *all the future things that are taking shape in me and will sometime come to consciousness*' (*CW*8 1947/1954 §382, italics mine). It can be seen that Jung was increasingly articulating the idea that the unconscious was the dynamic source of the creation of the future self. This included its darker possibilities which required assimilation and integration. Admitting the validity of the 'other voice', the conflicting 'shadow side' of the self, he said, gives equal weight to both the position and the complementary counterposition in the psyche. Even if only tiny fragments of unconscious contents become conscious, consciousness is widened or can be widened provided the fragments are integrated (*CW*8 1916/1957 §184–193). The unconscious did not become less unconscious; however, some contents could cross over into (or reach the threshold for) consciousness more easily than before the process was started. The previously unconscious contents could therefore be examined and 'illuminated by consciousness' (*CW*14 1955–56 §211). In this way, what started by merely happening to consciousness (through contact with symbols) later became integrated in it as the result of its own activity, and 'any accumulation of unconscious acts of this sort will have the effect of strengthening and widening consciousness' (*CW*11 1942/1948 §238).

The moral significance of the widening of consciousness has to be understood in relation to the importance of opposites in Jung's interpretation of the dual nature of the Gnostic God and his view that the Christian God-image had lost this duality with consequent loss of power. Consciousness widened by assimilation of its darker side more closely resembled the dual aspect of the Gnostic God-image than the Christian God-image, which Jung found one-sided. Segal (1992: 25–33) questions Jung's interpretation of the Gnostic position on good and evil on the grounds that Gnosticism did not unify them as Jung suggests. However, much Jung's interpretation of Gnosticism may be open to criticism on historical grounds; the important point in relation to his ideas on personality is that he emphasises the *psychological* need to unify these two opposites within the personality and in the God-image. He amplifies this point with his interpretation of the Gnostic God-image. Projection or not, this is the essence of the God-like aspect of Jung's concept of self.

Jung's comparison of the self with the Christian God-image involved several convolutions. Introjection of projections unifies, transforms, and expands the knowable Self. Similarly, incarnation united God with the human self and resulted in a more self-conscious, self-reflective aspect of the God-image being manifest in Christ. In tracing the history of ancient symbols of the self, Jung's concern was to show how, in a similar process, the mature individual's 'confrontation of conscious (rational) data with those that are unconscious (irrational) results in a beneficial modification of standpoint' (*CW*14 1955–56 §257). Thus the concept of God's incarnation could be understood as a human *psychological* development process. Indeed, the confrontation of consciousness with the unconscious was, for Jung, *the* central psychological process leading to a sense of unity and completeness.

'Individuation' and salvation or redemption

In 'Answer to Job', Jung argued that incarnation transformed God on a theological level. Through becoming human, God was modified and, consequently, could take a new standpoint. The salvation of the cross could be understood as God's own salvation through an increase in Divine self-consciousness and God's increased capacity for reflection through participating in human consciousness, itself an aspect of Divine creation.

We have seen that Jung's concept of self is both human *and* divine, just as God is both divine *and* human. This idea is also linked with alchemists' philosophical notion that creation reflects the Divine creator and is expressed in the formula 'as above, so below'. Religious contemplation aims to put individuals more deeply in touch with God. The ultimate goal of most religious systems is expansion and transformation of the self through recognition of one's centre, the God-within, the Divine light of the soul. Jungian psychotherapy aims to help people to become more fully themselves, to individuate (see Chapter 1, pp. 11–12), and psychotherapy in general aims to put individuals in touch with themselves and the world of which they are a part. Since Jung argued that God could be conceptualised as a projection of the universal total self and redemption as the retrieval of that projection, we can conclude that in Jung's view, humans may become more consciously divine through the realisation that divinity is an aspect of their projected self.

Moreover, Christian redemption was achieved when the son of God was made human and then taken back into the father. In the Son-of-God-made-man, humanity could recognise that which is God-like in itself. Similarly, in psychological integration, Jung asserts that consciousness, the offspring of the unconscious, takes in its 'father', its own unconscious parental matrix, with the result that it recognises and comes to know that which was unconscious within itself. For Jung, individuation and redemption are achieved though integration. The result for God and for the human psyche alike is an expansion and deepening of conscious experience through incorporating its own unconscious aspect.

There is another sense in which Jung understood Salvation to be the same process as psychological individuation. In 1952, Jung remarked that the Old Testament God had a threatening aspect as well as a benign aspect as man's helper. Jung gives the example of Yahweh, who he says in 'the old rabbinical view . . . hide(s) the righteous from his wrath under his throne, where, of course, he cannot see them' (*CW*11 1952b §664). This was the side of God Jung thought was experienced by Job. This aspect of the God-image was not self-aware, just, or merciful but was formed of unreflecting power. Jung named this threatening aspect 'divine unconsciousness' (*CW*11 1952b §383n). In this form, the God-image (thought righteous) was implacable, lacking a capacity for moral reflection and so, ironically, needed to 'empty himself of his godhead' and 'become man' in order to acquire a human reflective capacity (*CW*18 1956/1957 §1622). Thus, Jung says, God, in the shape of his own son, 'rescue[d] mankind from himself' (*CW*11 1952b §664). According to Jung, the work of salvation, portrayed in the death of God's son on the cross, was that it modified God so that men need not fear God's unthinking power. Before this, God, as Yahweh, was the totality of opposites, and that was the source of his immense power (*CW*11 1952b §567).

The consequence for humans, as Jung saw it, was that humankind reincorporated and transformed its image of God. However, Jung observes that there were some challenging and painful consequences in terms of human psychology since humanity now had to contain these opposites:

> [Man] finds that God in his 'oppositeness' has taken possession of him, incarnated himself in him. He becomes a vessel filled with divine conflict . . .

> we hesitate to describe such a painful experience as being 'redeemed'. . . . It is on the one hand a deliverance from the distressing state of dull and helpless unconsciousness and, on the other hand, a growing awareness of God's oppositeness, in which man can participate. . . . Only through the most extreme and most menacing conflict does the Christian experience deliverance into divinity.
>
> (*CW*11 1952b §659)

As Jung expressed it, an important consequence of psychological individuation is that the divine duality of implacable evil and infinite good is internalised and understood as part of our own human nature. All that the individual is 'saved' from is having to fear it coming from outside. People could now deal with evil as part of themselves, no longer having to 'drive it over some frontier or other . . . like the Old Testament scapegoat which was supposed to carry the evil into the wilderness' (*CW*10 1957b §572). The consequence and purpose of salvation and of individuation was that we would be at odds with ourselves rather than with others.

With salvation came a sense of internal opposition and a greater potential for moral and psychological conflict. Since humans learned that good and evil are categories of our own moral judgment, therefore relative to man, the way was opened for a new model of the self (*CW*18 1956/1957 §1657). For Jung, this position is closely linked with social morality.[3] From mid-life onwards, it became Jung's mission to urge people to recognise the moral dangers and destructive potential of one-sided ego development.

In taking this view of salvation, Jung was pitting himself against traditional Christianity. Putting aside the question of the historical accuracy of his account, his criticism that a sense of the inherent ambivalence of human nature had been lost to twentieth-century Protestantism may hold true. In Jung's view, the (Protestant) Church and to some degree the Catholic Church resolved the problem of evil by means of denial. This is important for understanding his concept of individuation as a transformation of consciousness by means of the incorporation and integration of unconscious aspects of the personality. From a psychological perspective, a state of awareness of God's (and hence also humans') dualism was, in Jung's view, a developmental and moral advance since 'consciousness . . . cannot exist without discrimination (differentiation, separation, opposition, contradiction, discussion)' (*CW*18 1956/1957 §1630), and 'without dualism there is no cognition at all, because discrimination is impossible' (*CW*18 1956/1957 §1639).

Crucifixion and wholeness; sacrifice and the self as unifier

Since Jung's conception of salvation led to a recognition of duality in God and the self, one might be misled into thinking that there was no place for unity in Jung's concept of the self. But Jung held that internal opposites could be united without losing their separateness. This crucial psychological point has far-reaching consequences for Jung's conceptualisation of individuation and for the development of Jungian psychotherapy. Jung described the process thus:

> One should listen to the inner voice attentively, intelligently and critically . . . because the voice one hears consists of the 'right' and 'left' streams, i.e. of opposites. They have to be separated so that their positive and negative aspects become visible. Only thus can we take up a middle position and discover a middle way.
>
> (*CW*18 1956/1957 §1622)

To understand how individuation could be compared with an experience of many-in-one, we need to turn to Jung's exploration of the symbolism of the mass. In the sacrifice of the mass, as interpreted by Jung (*CW*11 1942/1954), the human participant undergoes a symbolic death and renounces human functions for the sake of a spiritual, unworldly goal. Jung felt that the attempts over the centuries to renounce human functions in favour of spiritual goals alienated humanity from its own nature and from nature in general. He argued that this had resulted in an overdevelopment of consciousness that needed rebalancing. His solution involved a psychological view of the crucifixion that radically changed its meaning to signify a new balance between the conscious spiritual aspect of the self and its unconscious, instinctual aspect. In its new meaning, the cross could be seen as a symbol of the uniting of opposites in the psyche. Jung explained that the two pieces of wood that make up the symbol of Christ's cross are joined, 'crossed' in the form of four opposing points that are linked, rather in the manner that the four functions of thinking, feeling, sensing, and intuition are linked in the personality, by complementarity, but are also opposed as dimensional poles or opposites in Jung's typology. If psychotherapy could succeed in linking the four functions in individuals' awareness, each function could inform and serve the others in a balanced way, within the personality. This he felt could lead to a sense of wholeness. The cross could therefore be understood psychologically as a symbol of opposites *and* as a symbol of the self as the unifier of opposites within the psyche (*CW*11 1942/1954 §434–5; *CW*18 1956/1957 §1661).

The point Jung makes here is crucial to his personality theory. It is that through the reinterpretation of the symbol of the cross as the self, a conscious individual can be seen as a unity of opposing tendencies. His or her centre is singular whilst also made up of opposites. Achieving psychological unification of the hypothesised dual self would entail withdrawing the following projections:

1 that evil resides in the 'other',
2 that God is outside, and
3 that God and humankind must be all good.

Jung denies that integrating a united God–self schema must lead to inflation, arguing, on the contrary, that it involves accepting that the rational ego which otherwise *could* become inflated is subordinate to the self. One significant consequence is that, because it remains largely unconscious, the total self in Jungian personality theory is ultimately unknowable, as unknowable as God.[4]

Conclusion

The religious vector of Jung's psychology brings interesting and challenging implications to the practice of psychotherapy. Being consciously dualistic, that is to say, becoming fully aware of the inherent potential for evil as well as for good in oneself, is not the explicit goal of standard psychological therapies, such as cognitive therapy, for example.

As far as the consequences for psychotherapy are concerned, since individuation can only be achieved insofar as dualities can be acknowledged and reflectively analysed, whether the idea of the Self as God is beneficial or a dangerous delusion depends on acceptance of the duality of the God-image. If both God and the Self are understood to be dual natured, this belief is as humbling as it is aggrandizing, since neither God nor human individuals can be 'all good'. The specific behavioural consequence of awareness of an internalised dual-natured God-Self is self-examination and the operation of what might be called a psychological form of conscience. His position also has implications for Christian practice, since he eschews all notions of neutralising the dualism of good and evil in the self by striving for goodness. Jung makes it clear that both good and evil must retain their potency in the psyche and be consciously recognised.

In 1948, Gerhard Adler, a Jungian who knew Jung personally, was careful to say that Jung was not talking about God as such and that the existence or not of an Absolute God is not a matter for psychology (or, by implication, for personality; Adler, 1948). I think that we must now conclude that, rightly or wrongly, Jung was at times talking about his personal *idea* of God and that he *was* saying that religion is and always was a psychological matter, because God and the Self in its widest sense are one and the same. Jung believed that reflection, consciousness, and introversion are essential for cultural development, that instinct is resistant to cultural change but its expression can be modified by culture, and that, ultimately, self-consciousness civilises, provided that it can maintain consciousness of its own 'oppositeness'. As the unavoidable complexity of the subject matter of this chapter may indicate, when Jung says that God is a psychological experience, his intention was clearly not reductionist. He felt that religion, and Christianity in particular, might be given a new meaning through being conceptualised as the centre of a psychological cosmology.

This chapter shows why Jung cannot simply be described as a psychological theorist who was also interested in religion. Rather, he should be acknowledged as the originator of a theory of personality that fuses religion with psychology. I have used Jung's juxtaposition of the terms *God*, *incarnation*, *salvation*, and the *cross* with *unconscious*, *integration*, and *wholeness* as a framework for explaining why the central concepts of Jung's personality theory need to be understood in the light of his religious position. I have shown that Jung's provocative suggestion that the key terms of his personality theory can be substitutes for the central concepts of Christian doctrine is in fact reasonable. The terms share many connotations of meaning. Through making these links, Jung was able to show to a secular world that psychology and religion are concerned with similar questions about the relation between mind and matter. Happold (1964: 113) refers to these concerns as the 'coinherence' of God and man and of spirit and matter. Happold sees this coinherence as a central assertion of the Church but one which is difficult to demonstrate logically. This is also Jung's position. Like every other personality theorist, Jung takes up a position on fundamental debates such as the nature/nurture question. Jung's position on the spirit/matter question is that they are together, each participating in the other, as one. I return to this point in Chapter 4.

Through his concept of the self and his view of personality as having both timeless and limitless aspects, Jung engaged with a debate that underlies the formation of Christian creeds. His view of the self as unifier concurs with the early Christian blending of Sufism ('I am God' achieved through loss of the self), Hinduism (there is nothing that is not God), Taoism (God is opposites in balance), and Buddhism (the self is transformed, not lost, in enlightenment).[5] This is the mystic vision expressed in terms of Jung's concept of self and transformed into a psychology of personality.

Notes

1 The catholic doctrine of the *privatio boni* was first propounded by Origen (A.D. 185–254), whose definition of God as the *Summum bonum* (1936: III.6.1) was the effective source for his characterisation of evil as the diminution of good. The doctrine became established during the early centuries of the Church and was fully developed by St Augustine of Hippo (Bennet, 1985: 119n.) See also Lammers and Cunningham (2007: 142 n 36) on its roots in Platonism and systematisation by Aquinas.

2 There is a tendency for Jung's theory to be judged as if it were a philosophical edifice or a psychology of religion and to find it inadequate, but Jung was not building a philosophical argument or a psychology of religion. As Heisig puts it (1979: 144–145), to judge Jung's theory either as a natural science theory or as a philosophical theory is to misconceive a theory that is best judged by criteria more applicable to theories in the humanities (see Chapters 7 and 8).

3 See *CW*10 'A Psychological View of Conscience' especially §855, 1958a, and 'God and the Devil' (Jung, 1957a).

4 This is possibly an instance of Jung speaking of his personal 'God' rather than the God-image in the person. One can understand that such statements may be the source of the criticisms made by Palmer and others that Jung was inconsistent in distinguishing God from the God-image. This can be understood without accepting the conclusion that Jung was advancing theological claims. To have a private theological position and to have a personal 'God' is not the same as making a public argument for or against the existence of a superordinate God with specific characteristics.

5 See Happold (1964: 18, 97, 110–113).

Chapter 3

Psychological Types, creativity, and the active imagination

Introduction

Chapter 1 gives a brief description of Jung's typology. Chapter 2 shows how closely religious themes are fused with the most important theoretical constructs of Jung's personality theory. I now turn to Jung's seminal book *Psychological Types* (*CW*6 1921). This chapter explores the relationship between the book *Psychological Types* and the religious themes and ideas of transformation expressed during the same period in *Liber Novus, The Red Book*, Jung's illustrated journal of active imagination. The second part of the chapter focuses on two examples taken from *Liber Novus* to illustrate the similarities of themes being worked out in Jung's personal experience and in his presentation of his theory of personality in *Psychological Types*. My purpose is to show why *Psychological Types* is only fully comprehensible when it is understood as a dual text which conceals within a landscape drawn from world literature a theory of personality that was in fact derived from personal experience.

This volume of the *Collected Works*, especially the sections which describe the types, is the one most widely read by psychologists interested in personality. They expect to hear Jung in his scientific persona, and they do. But alongside the voice of the scientific Jung, the voice of a less direct and more covert Jung can be heard throughout *Psychological Types*. This second voice articulates the transformation of personality brought about by the emergence of a uniting symbol in the unconscious. The unresolved tension between the overt and covert agendas may account for the commonly held perception among psychologists that his work is 'arcane' and 'difficult to understand'. Nevertheless, *Psychological Types* is the work that most clearly reveals Jung as a personality theorist precisely *because* this is where he introduced his understanding of the process of personality transformation.

Background

In the years between 1913 and 1919, while Jung was working on *Psychological Types*, he was also engaged in the 'psychological experiment' in active imagination that he recorded in *The Red Book, Liber Novus* (Jung, 2009). There are a number of interlacing themes in *Liber Novus*: the theme of the loss and refinding of his soul, the connections between his personal visions and world events such as the outbreak of war and aspects of the general Zeitgeist, and the problem of 'the opposites'. For Jung, the problem of opposites was closely linked with the theme of duality in humanity's image of God. In *Psychological Types*, Jung's elaboration of parallels from the history of Christianity and from other cultures takes up more than half of the total text.

The typology

In Chapter 1, I outlined the structure of Jung's typology, the two fundamental orienting attitudes of introversion and extraversion, the four modalities – thinking, feeling, sensation, and intuition – and the principle of dominance and inferiority of the preferred and least preferred functions. In chapter X of *Psychological Types*, Jung gave conventional descriptions of the prototypical character types that his typology suggests, thereby conforming to a long-standing tradition of characterology. For example, he describes the extraverted and introverted sensation types and the extraverted rational and the introverted intuitive types and explains the interpersonal interactions between them. This well-organised and parsimonious typological framework attracted the interest of psychologists like Hans Eysenck (1916–1977), who went on to develop his own definitions of introversion and extraversion.

Jung also spoke of introverted and extraverted attitudes as being differential conscious and unconscious attributes of individuals (*CW*6 1921 §568–576). He proposed a theory of neurosis as the result of intrapsychic conflict which might be the result of an imbalance of the attitude and functions within the personality (*CW*10 1934b §362–364). He elaborated historical and cross-cultural parallels in which the matrix of orientations and functions is seen from an intrapsychic ('within-person') rather than from an interpsychic ('between-person') perspective (*CW*6 1921 chapters I–V). The importance of this was Jung's realisation that intrapsychic conflict often led to the emergence of a resolving and redeeming new attitude, capable of bringing about profound personality change with a consequent release of vital energy (*CW*8 1916/1957 §189). This, he asserted, was brought about by nonrational processes emerging spontaneously in the unconscious (*CW*7 1928b & 1945 §368), the personal experience of which he had privately documented and illustrated in *Liber Novus*.

Psychological types

Jung was at the forefront of the trend in psychology that was taken up a few years later by Watson and the behaviourists in providing scientific definitions for his theoretical terms. However, the chapter headings of *Psychological Types* reveal the book's dual purpose. The history of the early church, transubstantiation, the problem of opposites, the uniting symbol, and the relativity of the

God-concept are all listed in the book's contents. Where you might expect to see a conventional history of characterology, you see early Christian and medieval Church history. Instead of literary examples of character types, Jung focuses on metaphysical themes in literature, such as the theme of redemption and transformation in Faust; symbols of God's renewal in Spitteler's *Prometheus*; the concept of *rta* – order, destiny, and direction in the Indian Vedas; and on Eckhart's conceptualisation of the relativity of the God-concept in Man. Most of the section 'The Type Problem in Poetry' is not about the types but about individuation. A reader may have difficulty in making sense of this focus without the perspective of Jung's personal preoccupations. What, for example, do *rta* and Tao have to do with personality types? It is that, for Jung, they are expressions of the directions of flow of energy, the vital feeling within the personality that is renewed at moments of transformation and redemption, when the typological attitude is in balance.

Psychological Types reviews the problem of types in the history of classical and medieval thought, initially correlating Gnostic philosophy's three types (*pneumatikoi*, *psychikoi*, and the *hylikoi*) with Jung's thinking, feeling, and sensation types (*CW*6 1921 §14). The lives of two figures from the early Christian church, Tertullian (lascivious to his thirty-fifth year and a passionate thinker thereafter), and Origen (who castrated himself in his early thirties and then became an erudite scholar), are explained in terms of introversion and extraversion and the sacrifice of a one-sided attitude. Jung follows this comparison with a discussion of disputes within the early Christian Church (Scholasticism, transubstantiation) seen from the perspective of different types of thinking arising from differences in psychological types (*CW*6 1921 chapter I). He ends with the philosophical 'solutions' offered by Abelard and Kant and compares these solutions with his idea of the new solution or new attitude that he subsequently called the 'transcendent function'.

Jung also examined other typologies, Schiller's aesthetic types (*CW*6 1921 chapter II), Greek typological traditions, the Apollonian and the Dionysian (*CW*6 1921 chapter III), Jordan's introverted and extraverted types (*CW*6 1921 chapter IV), the Brahmanic conception of opposites, the Brahmanic, Taoist, and Christian ideas of the uniting symbol (*CW*6 1921 chapter V), and the philosophical conception of opposites in William James's typology (*CW*6 1921 chapter VIII). Finally (*CW*6 1921 chapter X), he gives a detailed description of his own typological matrix. So, for nine chapters, Jung appears to be setting the scene, putting his own ideas into a long lineage, wrapping his ideas in the lives and words of others, and taking the opportunity to explore themes such as the nature of the uniting symbol and its relation to the Godhead, themes that are not normally found within a psychological typology. The impression is of a long process of thinking from which the theory was rationally and logically derived. However, the material Jung uses to demonstrate the types pulls the text towards religion and philosophy, enabling Jung to explore his long-standing personal preoccupations. It becomes clear, as Shamdasani suggests, that this is an encrypted Jung, concealing the personal and experiential origins of his psychology in a wealth of comparative literature (Jung, 2009: 219).

In most of his published work, Jung concealed the personal source of his ideas, believing that his own experience of a transformative process would not be acceptable to the scientific community as valid empirical evidence. He used parallels from Indian and Chinese sources in *Psychological Types* as an indirect way to introduce ideas that he arrived at through the creative exploration of his own psyche as the basis of a theory of individuation. His strategy was to comment on analogous developments in esoteric practices (Jung, 2009: 219).[1]

This was Jung's first attempt to weave religion and personality, as opposed to psychiatry, together in his published work. It is here that Jung first presents the idea that dynamic images could be involved in the putative process of individuation (see the discussion of the problem of opposites and function of the uniting symbol in *CW*6 1921 chapter V). It is also here that Jung introduces the idea of Tao as a dynamic symbol of the balance of opposites, the idea of sacrifice as part of a psychological transformational process, and the theme of the renewal of God through a transformation of attitude (*CW*6 1921 §324–326, §348–370).

As well as religious ideas, there is also a strong epistemological theme in *Psychological Types*. Introversion and extraversion are presented as differences in ways of thinking. Chapter VII 'The type problem in aesthetics' focuses on *empathy* and *abstraction* understood as aspects of introversion and extraversion. The meaning of this focus becomes clear when it is understood in relation to Jung's epistemological ideas, his Kantian notion that the object is not seen directly but through either a projection or an abstraction, which Jung relates to extraversion (projection) and introversion (abstraction). We begin to see that Jung gives greater importance to differences between ways of thinking in his theory of types than to behavioural differences. This is one of the themes that he also explores in *The Red Book*.

Liber Novus/The Red Book

Earlier I said that difficulties in making sense of *Psychological Types* may have contributed to psychologists' negative reception of Jung's work. Because we now have the 'other side' in *The Red Book*, the companion work written in a symbolic style that grew alongside *Psychological Types*, we are in a position today to make sense of Jung's purpose in writing *Psychological Types* (Jung, 2009: 223 translators' note). One reason this is important is that it illuminates the process by which personal experience can be transformed into a theory with general application and value.

Jung himself was well aware of the importance of the question of how personal experience could be translated into theory. His 'gnostic' view that knowledge *is* experience meant that he prioritised psychological experience as data for a scientific psychology. In his discussion of Spitteler's Prometheus, Jung explored the function of poets and artists who are tuned in to the events and atmosphere of their time and give voice to its unconscious aspects. He concludes that artistic expression is not enough (*CW*6 1921 §434). Instead, Jung's language was to be the language of science, notwithstanding his reservations about the limitations of science. In 'Scrutinies' (Jung, 2009: 336), Jung's soul says to him, 'Science is too superficial, mere language, mere tools. But you must set to work'. In *Black Book 5*, where Jung made direct notes of his fantasies, Jung's soul continues by saying, 'You are not supposed to dissociate yourself, but consider that science is merely your language' (Jung, 2009: 336f).

His life's work thenceforth would be to theorise scientifically the psychology of personal transformation that he had discovered through close self-observation and the analysis of his own experience.

The process of theorising

In *Liber Novus* Jung is already working out the theoretical implications of his self-observations. Jung, as a psychologist, observes and investigates his own imagination. *Liber Novus* is a study of the function of imagination in his self-transformation through dialogues and interactions with imaginary figures. In addition to the record of the fantasies, there is a layer of personal reflection which relates the events in the fantasies to Jung's immediate situation, his search for his neglected soul and his confrontations with opposing tendencies in his own psyche. A second layer of commentary elaborates the 'collective' meaning, such as Jung's premonition of war, and his psychological interpretation of the struggle between opposing tendencies in the world. The layer 2 commentaries were added at various times, sometimes a year or more after his immediate notes recorded in the *Black Books*. These reflections, interleaved into the text of *Liber Novus*, contain Jung's thoughts on the wider collective significance of his visions and his ideas about their potential psychological meaning. The three layers constitute a record of the flow of thinking between his original experience and the formation of his theory.

Jung was unique in having documented the flow of his thinking from personal analysis to theory in an introspective tradition. Thus *Liber Novus* has important implications for the psychology of creative theorising as well as for the psychology of personal transformation. It challenges the belief that theories are arrived at through a process of deduction or rational thinking and suggests instead that theoretical ideas are derived from intuition or inspiration and are subsequently reformulated in academic or scientific language. In Jung's later published work, the connecting thinking process is missing. As he worked out his theory, he increasingly gave his ideas 'in translation'. As Shamdasani notes:

> Jung's work after 1930 could be considered as an extended amplification of the contents of *Liber Novus*, and an attempt to translate its contents into a form acceptable to the contemporary outlook. Some of the statements

> made in *Liber Novus* closely correspond to positions that Jung would later articulate in his published works, and represent their first formulations. . . . The *Collected Works* can in part be considered an indirect commentary on *Liber Novus*. Each mutually explicates the other.
>
> (Jung, 2009: 219)

With *Liber Novus* in one hand and *Psychological Types* in the other, psychologists can now follow the genesis of Jung's thinking process and judge for themselves the quality of the reflective and analytical thinking that turned inspired vision into a psychology of personal transformative processes.

In *Liber Novus*, Jung's thinking takes various forms, including dialogues with imaginary/projected symbolic figures such as Philemon, dialogues with himself as the mirrored 'I', and analytic reflections which include conclusions and decisions. In these dialogues, it is often the symbolic figures who speak the thoughts, with Jung as the listener or recipient. At other times, he addresses questions to the figures or considers what they have said. In 'Scrutinies', the third and final part of *Liber Novus*, these forms of reflection merge, becoming less differentiated.

To follow Jung's entire process requires a detailed comparison of both texts which is outside the scope of the current work, but I will try to give a flavour of Jung's self-debate in *Liber Novus* on themes that are central to his typology and his concept of individuation in the following examples summarised from *Liber Novus*. This illustrates the subjective origins of his theorising, which is of historical interest, and it allows one to see more clearly what Jung had in mind when he developed these ideas. This makes for greater accuracy in reading his subsequent texts and understanding his significant concepts.

Example 1 – The balance of the types within the personality

The vision – summary

I lay in a dark depth. I see an old man like one of the old prophets with a black serpent at his feet. A house with columns some distance away. A beautiful maiden steps out of the door. She is blind. The old man waves me to follow, and I follow to the house at the foot of a sheer wall of rock. The serpent creeps behind us. It is dark in the house. We are in a high hall with glittering walls, and a bright stone the colour of water. I see in it the reflection of Eve, tree and serpent. A door opens into bright sunshine. We step out. The old man asks if I know where I am. The old man says he is Elijah and this is Salome, his daughter. I am shocked – the bloodthirsty woman. Elijah says she is blind. I am shocked. How are these two together? Salome asks me 'Do you love me?' I. 'How can I love you?' S. 'You will love me. I love you.' I. 'Leave me be. I dread you.' Salome tempts me with a look to the future. Elijah says Salome loved a holy man. She loved the prophet who announced the new God to the world. Elijah says: 'Consider this: I and my daughter have been one since eternity'.

In his layer 2 commentary, as he ponders on the symbolism of Elijah and Salome, Jung notes their associations, Elijah with forethinking (Elijah is a prophet) and Salome with sensual pleasure. He then links forethinking with the mythical figure of Prometheus, about whom he wrote extensively, in *Psychological Types* (*CW*6 1921 chapter V §275–326) as an example of introversion. In *Liber Novus* he writes:

> The powers of my depths are predetermination and pleasure. Predetermination or forethinking is Prometheus who without determined thoughts brings the chaotic to form and definition. Forethinking needs pleasure to be able to come to form. Pleasure needs forethinking to be able to come to form. . . . Only in man does the separate existence of both principles become apparent. . . . One cannot live with forethinking alone. You need both. . . . But men prefer one or the other. Some love thinking and establish the art of life on it . . . so they lose their pleasure. . . . The others love pleasure, they practice their feeling and living. Thus they forget thinking. Therefore they are young and blind. . . . You find truth and error in both. . . . The way of life writhes like the serpent from right to left and from left to right, from thinking to pleasure and from pleasure to thinking. . . . He who prefers to feel than to think leaves his thinking in darkness where it spins its nets in gloomy darkness. . . . The thinker feels the disgust of feeling, since the feeling in him is mainly disgusting. So the serpent lies between the thinker and the one who feels. They are each other's poison and healing.
>
> (Jung, 2009: 247–248 *Liber Primus*)

Jung reflects on the figures he encounters in this vision in relation to his personal association, that, in him, thinking and sensory aspects are not separate but interdependent. At the same time he considers their more general psychological meaning, as representing one-sided developments of aspects of the psyche which should be in balance. We see how the problem of opposites, their interdependence, and the need for balance underpins his personal and his psychological thoughts. It is the foundation for his approach to typology. We also see that his approach to the psychology of thinking is very much bound up with his theory of types and with his concept of the archetype, the image, as a thought-in-formation. We see how Jung's thoughts flow through personal, collective, and abstract theoretical levels, eventually to be expressed at an abstract theoretical level in the text he was writing in the day. In *Psychological Types* Jung writes:

> [Spitteler's] Prometheus, the 'forethinker', stands for the introvert and Epimetheus, the man of action and 'afterthinker', for the extravert. The conflict between these two figures is essentially a struggle between the introverted and extraverted lines of development in one and the same individual . . . .
>
> (*CW*6 1921/1977 §276)

> If we fuse Prometheus and Epimetheus into one personality we should have a man outwardly Epimethean and inwardly Promethean – an individual constantly torn by both tendencies . . . .
>
> (*CW*6 1921/1977 §287)

> For the man who always stands in the middle the soul has a human and not a dubious, daemonic character, neither does his neighbour appear to him in the least problematical.
>
> (*CW*6 1921/1977 §281)

On the nature of thinking, he says in *Liber Novus*:

> My thoughts are not myself, but exactly like the things of the world, alive and dead. . . . Thoughts are natural events that you do not possess, and whose meaning you only imperfectly recognize . . . thoughts grow in me like a forest, populated by many different animals.
>
> (Jung, 2009: 250)

From this we can see that, for Jung, a person does not 'think' thoughts. Rather, they happen to the person. They are the primary data that emerge from the conscious/unconscious mind and are the subject of psychology in their original form. Images and fantasies are as valid 'ideas' as their later formulations.

Jung is clearly stating the kind of empiricism that he espouses, and we see how he can logically bring philosophy and metaphysics into his psychology of personal transformation while simultaneously maintaining that he is first and foremost an empiricist. He observes himself, engages in an empirical self-experiment, in which he observes the irrational. But the subsequent analysis of his observations is rational and philosophical, calling on knowledge of many kinds and making philosophical distinctions. For example, Jung ponders on the relation between thinking and feeling in anticipation of the theme of balance of the four functions and the danger of one-sided development generally, within the personality and in himself:

> If I endorse the pure principle, I step to one side and become onesided. . . . If you go to thinking, take your heart with you. If you go to love, take your head with you. Love is empty without thinking, thinking hollow without love. The serpent lurks behind the pure principle. Therefore I lost courage, until I found that the serpent led me across to the other principle.
>
> (Jung, 2009: 253)

The image of the 'way of life' that writhes like a serpent between pleasure and thinking *is* the thought in formation, 'seen' before it could be expressed verbally in the form of reciprocal dependency between matter and mind, consciousness and the unconscious, that was to become the ground of Jung's concept of individuation. Here the movement of thinking flows from a general principle back to the visionary image (the serpent) and back again to 'general advice', then returns to the immediacy of the experience, where the transformation is enacted by the serpent who leads the one-sided Jung across to the other side, where the balance that he now sees as a necessity can be realised. In *Psychological Types* he expressed the struggle between thinking and feeling as the struggle between science and feeling (life):

> The goal of totality can be reached neither by science, which is an end in itself, nor by feeling, which lacks the visionary power of thought. The one must lend itself as an auxiliary to the other, yet the opposition between them is so great that a bridge is needed . . . the bridge is already given us in creative fantasy . . . if psychology remains for us only a science, we do not penetrate into life.
>
> (*CW*6 1921/1977 §85–86)

Example 2 – The heavy personal cost of individuation

The vision – summary

After many angry words with myself, I noticed that I began to bear being alone with myself. Then I heard a voice one night from afar. It was the voice of my soul. She came from above me, from a world apart, and could hardly see me in the smoke of the earth. I spoke to her about the suffering in the world (1914), and I heard her voice happy and bright, rising higher, as her wings grew, because of the suffering, the blood of human hearts. She rejected my compassion and advised me to stay on my way and not run away from myself. I did not know what I suffered from (since this happened two months before the outbreak of war). I wanted to understand. Belief and knowledge must strike a balance but it is dangerous to believe too much because today everyone has to find his own way and encounters in himself a beyond full of strange and mighty things. We need differentiating knowledge to clear up the confusion which the discovery of the soul has brought in. I spoke to my soul and asked 'Is that all to be accepted?' She replies 'I understand you – but it has to be accepted'.

In this second example which is taken from 'Scrutinies', the third part of *Liber Novus*, Jung becomes painfully aware that differentiation (individuation) brings solitude. It cuts one off from other men. He expressed his concerns to his soul:

> Jung: The solitude of this acceptance terrifies me. I dread the madness that befalls the solitary.
>
> Soul: I have long predicted solitude for you. You need not be afraid of madness. . . . You must go your way, unconcerned about others, no matter whether they are good or bad.
>
> (Jung, 2009: 336)

Jung reflects:

> I . . . did not want to accept this way that forces me into dialogue with my soul. I preferred to speak with men. But I felt compelled toward solitude and I feared at the same time the solitude of my thinking which departed from accustomed paths.
>
> (Jung, 2009: 336)

In *Psychological Types*, he says: 'The path is *rta,* the right way. This path is also fate. . . . It is the path of our destiny and of the law of our being' (*CW* 6 1921/1977 §355). The layers of vision and analysis are not so clearly separated in 'Scrutinies'. Jung's thinking is taking place within the visions. Nevertheless, we can see how he is beginning to develop his concept of individuation as separation and differentiation achieved through solitude and at the cost of 'being one's own task'. In his definition of differentiation in *Psychological Types*, Jung says:

> So long as a function is still so fused with one or more other functions . . . that it is unable to operate on its own, it is in an *archaic* condition, i.e. not differentiated. . . . Undifferentiated thinking is incapable of thinking apart from other functions. . . . Without differentiation direction is impossible . . . only a differentiated function is *capable* of being directed.
>
> (*CW* 6 1921/1977 §705)

This theme of the necessity for differentiation is taken up in *Liber Novus*, when Philemon speaks. In the first sermon to the dead (Jung, 2009: 347), the symbolic figure of Philemon contrasts a differentiated state with the oneness of nondifferentiation:

> Philemon: Our very nature is differentiation. If we are not true to this nature we do not differentiate ourselves enough . . . You ask 'What harm is there in not differentiating oneself?' If we do not differentiate, we move beyond our essence, beyond creation, and we fall into nondifferentiation . . . we fall into the Pleroma[2] itself and cease to be created beings. We lapse into dissolution, into nothingness. This is the death of the creature. Therefore we die to the same extent that we do not differentiate. Hence the creature's essence strives towards differentiation and struggles against primeval perilous sameness. This is called the *principium individuationis.* This principle is the essence of the creature.
>
> (Jung, 2009: 347)

Shamdasani's footnote at this point indicates that the *principium individuationis* is a reference to Schopenhauer's 1819 notion of the possibility of multiplicity and that this was taken up by von Hartmann, who thought it originated in the unconscious. Von Hartmann saw it as a psychological concept meaning the uniqueness of the individual set against the 'all one unconscious'. From 1916, Jung was to define individuation as 'the process of the formation and particularization of individual beings, especially the development of the psychological individual, as a being distinct from generality, from collective psychology . . . having for its goal the development of individual personality' (*Psychological Types* §758 cited by Shamdasani in Jung, 2009: 347 fn 85).

Philemon continues: 'Not your thinking but your essence is differentiation. Therefore you must not strive for what you conceive as distinctiveness, but for *your own essence*' (Jung, 2009: 348). Earlier in his layer 2 commentary in *Liber Primus*, Jung spoke of the pain of individuation: 'To live oneself means to be one's own task. Never say that it is a pleasure to live oneself. It will be no joy since you must become your own creator' (Jung, 2009: 249). At the close of *Liber Primus*, Jung uses religious language as he reflects on the powerful influence the experience of his visionary journey had on him:

> I saw it. I know that this is the way. I saw the death of Christ and I saw his lament. . . . I saw a new God, a child. . . . The God holds the separate principles in his power, he unites them. The God develops through the union of the principles in me. He is their union. . . . The mystery showed me in images what I should afterward live.
>
> (Jung, 2009: 254)

This image of a God who unites the opposites within the personality was to become Jung's concept of the Self that is formed at the midpoint where opposites are held in balance.

Finally, at the close of *Liber Secundus*, we see that Jung had begun to sense the work to come, that is to say, the project of transforming the images and his analysis of them into a theory of the self:

> An opus is needed, that one can squander decades on, and do it out of necessity. I must catch up with a piece of the Middle Ages – within myself. We have only finished the Middle Ages of – others. I must begin early, in that period when the hermits died out.
>
> (Jung, 2009: 330)

In a corresponding footnote, Shamdasani mentions that in 1930 Jung explained that by 'regression to the Middle Ages', he did not mean a personal regression but a historical regression into the past of the collective unconscious, adding that this occurs 'when the way ahead is not free, when there is an obstacle from which you recoil, or when you need to get something out of the past in order to climb over the wall ahead' (Jung, 2009: 330 fn. 334). This need to step back to find what is needed for going forward may have been the motivation for Jung's subsequent explorations of the ancient and medieval art of alchemy. He used this as a means of disclosing to himself the detailed working out of the nature and process of individuation, to which I turn in Chapter 4.

Summary and conclusions

This chapter explains that *Psychological Types* is to be understood as a text with a dual purpose. On the one hand, Jung presented his typological matrix in the scientific style of objective descriptions or prototypes based on observations of individual differences in behaviour and styles of being. On the other, he was concerned with finding a language for his concept of individuation and with validating its universality by demonstrating its cross-cultural and historical parallels. This resulted in some unconventional choices of examples that are adequately explained when *Psychological Types* is seen as a dual text in which Jung first offered to the world the fusion of religious and psychological ideas that was to become his theory of individuation.

The second part of the chapter demonstrates how insights from Jung's *Liber Novus* can clarify and enrich a reading of *Psychological Types*, and, indeed of Jung's subsequent work. *Liber Novus* is where we see Jung's developing ideas in the very process of formation through the images of his creative imagination and where we can discern the flow of his thinking from self-analysis to generalisation, from personal experience to the formation of the general principles and concepts of his psychology. I conclude that *Psychological Types* is the work that most clearly reveals Jung as a personality theorist, not primarily because he presented a typology of personality differences but because it is here that he articulates his concept of individuation as a transformative process within the personality.

This chapter should enable the remaining chapters in Part I, on the function of alchemy and archetypes in relation to personality, to be better understood. My project parallels Jung's in a small way. I am trying to find a language to communicate Jung's ideas for a modern audience of the psychological professions. Now that we have access to this key to Jung's thinking, his writing can be approached in a different way, as I hope I have demonstrated, with the result that his ideas make more sense and less is 'lost in translation'.

Notes

1 Shamdasani mentions that, in his 1925 seminars to the Psychological Club, Jung discussed some of the fantasies from *Liber Novus*, indicating how they formed the basis of the ideas in *Psychological Types* (Jung 2009: 210–211).

2 Shamdasani explains *Pleroma* as a term from Gnosticism which Jung understood to mean a state of fullness in which the pairs of opposites are together; thus it reflects the unity underlying the multiplicity of the empirical world, a state of preexistence and potentiality (Jung 2009: 347 fn 82).

Chapter 4

Alchemy and individuation

Introduction

Jung's work on alchemy is often regarded as a deviation from his psychological purpose. In fact, Jung's fifty-year fascination[1] with alchemy lies at the heart of his thinking. A full understanding of the subtleties of meaning of the main concepts and theoretical constructs in his theory of personality is not possible without understanding the alchemical ideas that helped to shape these concepts.

This chapter offers a thematic account of four periods in Jung's life, his early, middle, mature, and later years, showing the emergence and fleshing out of Jung's concepts of self, individuation, and the transcendent function as a result of his alchemical investigations. Jung's discovery of alchemy offered him an analogue for the practice of 'active imagination' as a means for self-development. Throughout his life, Jung simultaneously lived out and developed his ideas, systematically reflecting on his own experience and subsequently amplifying his reflections with cultural examples. The ensuing chapter introduces alchemy and cosmology and shows the specific ways in which alchemical ideas and images shaped Jung's approach to therapy and his concept of the collective unconscious with its intimations of immortality.

Alchemy

Alchemy has been described variously as an art and a science (Holmyard, 1957), as a sacred science (Eliade, 1978), as a science of the cosmos, and as a royal art (*ars regia*; Burckhardt, 1997). Its practice was concerned with blending and transforming metals and distilling elixirs for medical purposes. However, Holmyard distinguishes between alchemy's exoteric practice and its hidden esoteric and symbolic aspect. Its outward (exoteric) practice was primarily concerned with the making of gold. This was to be achieved through attempts to prepare a substance, the Philosopher's Stone or Lapis, which would have power to transform base metals into precious metals (Holmyard, 1957: 16). Even this practical goal carried symbolic significance. Holmyard reminds us that gold had been regarded as a sacred metal since long before it was used as a measure of commercial transactions. Burckhardt

(1997: 11) notes that gold and silver were regarded as earthly reflections of sun and moon and of spirit and soul and that preparation of ores was the prerogative of priests in ancient Egypt. Alchemy's hidden (esoteric) nature had arisen from the belief that the Stone could only be obtained through divine grace. This led to the development of a devotional system in which the transmutation of metals became the symbol for the transformation of a human into a perfect being through prayer and submission to the will of God (Holmyard, 1957: 15–16).

In addition, alchemy had a well-developed medicinal aspect. Distillations of minerals combined with organic substances were used in classical times and throughout the Middle Ages to produce elixirs and salves to treat wounds and infections (Ball, 2006: 171–172; Porter, 1997: 79–80, 190–194). Whereas illustrated medieval herbaria and books of plant lore, such as Pseudo-Apuleius's Latin herbal, the fourteenth-century Italian *Tractatus de Herbis*, and *Liber de Simplici Medicina*, a fourteenth-century dictionary of drugs from Salerno (see Telesko, 2001: Introduction), transmitted knowledge of their medicinal properties in a transparent way, available to everyone, the esoteric and highly symbolic language of alchemy guarded and concealed a spiritual purpose that transcended its more mundane applications.

The several strands of alchemy are linked with different geographical cultures. These are: Egyptian alchemy (though metallurgy and embalming practices to ensure the immortality of the soul), pre–Islamic alchemy (emphasising the soul's development in its quest to become closer to God), Chinese alchemy (linking the idea of immortality with the untarnishability of gold), and Indian alchemy (linked with the practice of yoga). Historians of alchemy have had difficulty in tracing exactly which texts came into Europe, when, and from where. Some Hermetic ideas were incorporated into Islam and reached Europe via Moorish Spain. A flood of texts, in Latin translations, came to Western Europe in the Renaissance of the fifteenth and sixteenth centuries. The alchemical texts known to Jung were from the late Middle Ages (Arnaldus of Villanova, Ramon Llull), the Renaissance and late-Renaissance periods (Paracelsus, Pico della Mirandola, Marsilio Ficino, Michael Maier), and the seventeenth and eighteenth centuries (Nicholas Flamel and Isaac Newton). In addition to European alchemy, Jewish, Arabic, Chinese, and Indian traditions are represented in the collections to which Jung had access. In addition to Middle Eastern influences, alchemy incorporated ideas from cosmology, speculations on the nature of the universe which reach as far back in time as the earliest origins of thought itself. It is these cosmological ideas that are in the background of Jung's thinking, with ideas about the immortality of the soul being most relevant in relation to his conception of the soul.

Cosmology

Cosmologies were attempts to describe topographically and theologically the entire Divine Grand Design of Creation. Cosmologists were concerned with questions like: What is God? How did God create the universe? What might have been the process? What has God as Divine Intelligence to do with creation? Preclassical and medieval cosmology answered these in the following way: The world is the result of God's imagination. Matter reflects and embodies God's imagination, although it is not wholly contained in matter. The sun's energy and light enliven matter, changing and transforming it. This transformation is the direct result of God's energy, which is an aspect of God's intelligence and imagination. The spark or scintilla, the tiny bit of light in every creature, is the result of the sun's (therefore God's) action on matter. Matter is not inert but receives light and then actively participates in the transformation. This active principle of matter relates to deeply held ideas about the male/female principle. The female (earth/mother) is acted upon but participates equally in the transformative process, bringing her own nature to the field of change.

Cosmological manuscripts are richly illustrated with complex diagrams cross-referenced with symbols and allusions.[2] Ideas are expressed through the language of signs embedded in a 'puzzle picture'. These elaborately symbolic diagrammatic works of art incorporated all that was known from physics, mathematics, philosophy, theology, astrology, mythology, and chemistry (Roob, 2006: 8). A cosmological world view would encompass the entire known universe, which included Heaven and the celestial spheres as well as dimensions of time and space. Often, a process of creation reminiscent of *Genesis* 1–10 is depicted as bursts of light and fire, coming out of darkness, from which orderly divisions are gradually formed through the action of Sun (Divine fire and light) on unformed Chaotic Matter (the *materia prima*).

All cosmologies start with the principle of undivided unity (oneness) and move through many levels of division from binary (such as the polarities of male/female) through further subdivision to multiplicity and the entire diversity of Creation. The levels of spheres representing different states of being in relation to The One are conceptualised variously as concentric circles, triads (superimposed or overlapping), tree diagrams (such as the Sephiroth or Tree of Life), and ladder diagrams which represent the movement of the soul through the spheres towards participation with Oneness and God.

Creation is understood as 'Emanation', that is to say the manifestation of Divine Imagination and of Divine Nous (knowledge). Theories of Emanation are believed to derive from Zoroastrianism. Ball (2006: 149–150), Cheetham (2003: 26), and Nagy (1991: 82) note the importance of the fifteenth-century philosopher and translator of classical and alchemical works, Marsilio Ficino, who traced a line of succession from Zoroaster through the Egyptian Hermes Trismegistus and the Orphic mysteries to Pythagoras and Plato. Ficino's genealogy suggested a cosmological basis for later Greek ideas. This link between cosmology and Greek philosophy was the basis of alchemy but also underpins Christianity through Platonic and neo-Platonic philosophy.

Ficino's genealogy hinted at a mystical and religious context that links Pythagorean numbers with celestial harmonies. What lies beneath Pythagorean mathematics is the goal of Gnosis. God is seen as Unity, Creation as the many. At the same time, God is *in* the many since the Divine Mind is present in creation and in the harmony of numerical relations. Thus the microcosm is a reflection of the cosmos. This came to be expressed within the Hermetic alchemical tradition as 'as above, so below'. Ficino's genealogy of great teachers of theology traced Christian mysticism back to neo-Platonism. Both Gnostic and neo-Platonist influences have been identified in Jung's work (see Chapter 4 in Nagy, 1991, for examples).

Jung's alchemical sources

The Index of the *Collected Works* reveals that Jung consulted a number of Renaissance collections of alchemical tracts, mainly in Latin versions.[3] Through these collections, Jung had access to most classical alchemical authors in translation (from original Arabic and Greek mainly into Latin). For example, he had access to the visions of Zosimos of Panopolis, Maria Prophetissa, the Egyptian Magus, Hermes Trismegistus, and many famous illustrated texts such as the *Rosarium philosophorum* and the *Chymical Wedding*. The most striking features of alchemical texts are their coded[4] illustrations and their rich visual and literary symbolism. Alchemists describe their theories, operations, and materials in 'language efflorescent with allegory, metaphor, allusion and analogy' (Holmyard, 1957: 16). Modern textual exegesis relies on the comparative study of different texts. The meaning contexts in which terms occur are compared for illumination and amplification. According to Marie-Louise von Franz, the Jungian writer and researcher into alchemy, this was also Jung's method (von Franz, 1977: 21). Common themes in alchemical texts are transformation, healing, spiritual openness, individual life in relation to the cosmos, the oneness or unity of the self, and the male and female principle.

Jung's psychological interpretation of alchemy

In 1942, Jung gave lectures to the Swiss Society for the History of Medicine on Paracelsus, the sixteenth-century Swiss healer-alchemist. Paracelsus believed that healing assists God because it assists nature. Because it is God's work: 'You must be of an honest, sincere, strong, true faith in God, with all your soul, heart, mind and thought, in all love and trust' (Paracelsus, *Paragranum*, cited in *CW*13 1942 §146). Distillations of minerals and organic matter were used to restore balance and assist nature's healing powers in the body, thus helping God's purpose by accelerating nature's task. To heal a body was to heal nature itself, but more than healing was involved. Jung tells us that, for Paracelsus, the alchemist's task was 'bringing to perfection the divine will implanted in nature' (*CW*13 1942 §236).

Jung's psychological interpretation was to suggest that alchemists' activities could be understood as a projection which 'results in the activation and development of a psychic centre, a concept that coincides psychologically with that of the self' (*CW*13 1942 §189). The unconscious psychological process consisted firstly of a confrontation with inner darkness, then dissolution, and finally a transformative resolution. For this reason, Jung claimed that alchemy was the forerunner of the psychotherapy of the unconscious (*CW*13 1942 §237). At the same time, the alchemist was concerned with transforming and perfecting the self so as to achieve sufficient closeness to God for 'the work' to succeed. The alchemical adept sought connection with the Divine in attempting to create Nature's perfect metal (gold). The intensity of spiritual openness required a guide if the adept was to avoid what might now be termed depression and psychosis.[5] There is similarity with Jung's idea of the dangers of the psychic journey towards individuation and the protective function of the psychic guide (psychotherapist).

Jung used alchemy as a veil to draw attention away from the highly subjective origins of his ideas. He could say through alchemy what he could not say directly: 'Alchemy . . . has performed for me the great and invaluable service of providing material in which my experience could find sufficient room, and has thereby made it possible for me to describe the individuation process' (*CW*14 1955–56 §792). This is why it is essential to look closely at his work on alchemy to understand the meaning connotations for his key theoretical terms.

The very early years: 1896 to 1918

The idea that the Divine order was reflected in creation was expressed by alchemists as the macrocosm in the microcosm, or 'as above, so below'. We find a similar theme in Jung's earliest writing in the Zofingia lecture of 1896 'The Border Zones of an Exact Science': 'We behold the infinity of the world in the microcosm, we behold it in the macrocosm' (Jung, 1983 §63). In these early years, Jung was preoccupied with the problem of opposites and the existence of inherent 'primordial ideas' in the unconscious, which he later called the archetypes. He was interested in Gnostic ideas, especially the duality or ambivalence of God.

Symbols of Transformation (*CW*5 1911–12/1952) was Jung's first attempt to demonstrate his method of dream interpretation based on a systematic amplification of dream images by comparison with myths. The book contains a wealth of mythological and symbolic material, some of which is alchemical. However, at that time Jung used alchemical texts primarily as sources of literary allusions, whose purpose was to support his concept of the 'collective unconscious' and its hypothesised autonomous contents, the primordial images. Most of the alchemical references were in fact afterthoughts for the revised edition, but a few are embedded in the text itself. For example, a reference to the alchemical *athenor* or 'melting pot' (*CW*5 1911–12/1952 §245) is part of a long list of fire and 'fiery furnace' symbols in a chapter devoted to enumerating mythological examples of the transformation and canalization of libido.

Jung had not yet fully worked out an alchemical theory of individuation or the elaborate alchemical metaphor for psychotherapy. However, during this early period, other evidence suggests that he is developing a cosmological view of humankind that is very much in resonance with the alchemical model. His first published mandala picture, the *systema munditotius* (*Jung History* 1.2. 2006 Front Cover), which dates from about 1916, expresses his cosmological world view, showing opposites in relation to unity and a dual-natured God-image (Jeromson, 2006). Thus, although there is evidence before 1918 that Jung was aware of alchemical ideas which were perhaps working in him, he was not yet drawing on them in the formation of his main theoretical concepts.

The midlife years: 1918 to 1935

Jung's serious study of alchemy began in the late 1920s. Jung is reported (in Jung & Jaffé, 1963) to have said that he took a more active interest in studying alchemy after 1928 when he read a translation of the Chinese text *The Secret of the Golden Flower*[6] and that he recalled commissioning a Munich bookseller to notify him of any alchemical texts that came into his hands. Subsequently, over a period of ten years from around 1930, he made a lexicon of key phrases 'as if I were trying to solve the riddle of an unknown language' (Jung & Jaffé, 1963: 231).

In the period 1918 to 1935, Jung began to express psychological processes in alchemical terms. By 1928, he was moving away from using dreams to support his concept of the collective unconscious and towards seeing dreams as bringing about the transformations that he observed in himself and his patients. Alchemy was helping him to understand psychotherapy in terms of moving through stages, like the steps of the alchemical process. In his subsequent discussions of the stages of psychotherapy and its techniques, Jung used alchemical imagery as a direct means of expression of the stages and processes involved. In 'The technique of differentiation between the ego and the figures of the unconscious' (*CW7* 1928b Pt 2 chapter III), Jung compares differentiation as a change of personality that involves a transformation of general attitude (*CW7* 1928b §360) with the concept of Tao, the 'middle way' of Lao-Tzu (*CW7* 1928b §365), in which the creative centre and equilibrium of all things is achieved by a transformation brought about by a transcendent function. Jung gives a twentieth-century case example in which transformation of personality is brought about by the patient's active participation, merging herself in the unconscious processes and gaining possession of them 'by allowing them to possess her' and consequently opening her consciousness to unconscious contents. Jung expressed this psychological process as 'transmutation in the alchemical heat, the genesis of the "subtle spirit" that is the transcendent function born of the opposites' (*CW7* 1928b §368).

Later in the same essay, Jung warns that bringing unconscious material into consciousness can lead to a temporary 'God-like' state. His use of the term 'godlikeness' has echoes of the alchemists' search for the Anthropos or the divine man. The Gnostic Anthropos referred to Adam, the first human being, who was the origin of both genders, the primal man, the fundamental being before its division into individuals. The idea has many different connotations in different religions and cultures. These include 'King of light' in Manichaeism, primeval 'mind' in Gnosticism, the spiritual Second Adam, the Word made man or Christ the Redeemer of St Paul (see *CW*11 1942/1954 §400–401; *CW*13 (1938/1954a) §116 fn 112; §173 & §210).

Part IV of 'The technique of differentiation between the ego and the figures of the unconscious' (*CW*7 1928b) has two long quotations from Goethe's *Faust*, reminding the reader of Jung's early fascination with Faust's description of personal transformation.[7] In Part V, Jung expresses the idea that imagination is the creative source of all that has made progress possible to human life (*CW*7 1916a §492). The route to individuation is 'hermeneutic treatment of imaginative ideas' (*CW*7 1916a §497). Development of individuality is a divine pathway, a duty, a moral task, just as the alchemical adept had a divine duty to prepare spiritually for the sacred task. Individuation of the personality is presented here as a moral aim whose outcome is to take both oneself *and* the outside world equally seriously 'with a sound sense of the general good' (*CW*7 1916a §502).

Alchemy and psychotherapy

Jung first presented his idea that psychotherapy fosters individuation in 'Problems of Modern Psychology' (1929a), translated by Baynes and Dell for publication in *Modern Man in Search of a Soul* (Jung, 1933/1981). In 'The practical use of dream analysis' (1934d), he moved away from using dreams to support his hypothesis of the collective unconscious and instead emphasised their role in psychotherapy in which conscious assimilation of dreams can be used to 'bring about a change in and through the unconscious' (*CW*16 1934d §326). He explains the process of Jungian psychotherapy in the 'Tavistock Lectures' (1935), introducing his concept of dynamic unconscious archetypes and the technique of amplification. In lecture IV, he says people feel less isolated if they see that the archetypes of their dream images are not merely particular and personal but are universally human (*CW*18 1935 §232–233). He may likewise have felt less isolated when he found parallels in alchemical writings for his own experience of a powerful transformative process.

Through alchemy, Jung arrived at an understanding of psychotherapy as a cycle of separation, regeneration, and transformation. He described the stages in detail. The first stage was to see the subjective value of the images that create difficulties for patients and to encourage the patient to try to 'find out why they are a part of himself' (*CW*18 1935 §367), then to assimilate the contents of the neurosis. The second stage, when this has been achieved, leaves projections that 'belong to the structural elements of the psyche' and are important protective features (*CW*18 1935 §368). These projections feel as if they are located outside one's ego and do not belong to one. Jung is differentiating here between the personal and the collective unconscious. He reminds us that archetypes, although irrational, have a tremendous fascination and are powerful enough to change history:

> The powerful factor, the factor which changes our whole life, which changes the surface of our known world, which makes history, is collective psychology, and collective psychology moves according to laws entirely different from those of our consciousness. The archetypes are the great decisive forces, they bring about real events, and not our personal reasoning and practical intellect. Before the Great War all intelligent people said "We shall not have any more war, we are too reasonable to let it happen" . . . and now look at reality! . . . Man's unconscious psychology decides, and not what we think and talk in the brain-chamber up in the attic. (*CW*18 1935 §371)

The patient had to have a full recognition of the importance of his or her archetypal images. Jung thought that alchemy, religion, and therapy seek the same treasure and that this treasure is the self. When describing the technique by which the patient objectifies collective (nonpersonal) images from the unconscious, he expresses the healing and transformative process through the language and imagery of alchemy, behind which is the language and imagery of religion. First, he said, the patient has to 'secure the treasure in the unconscious', since in the unconscious which is nature, 'there *is* gold, there *is* the treasure and the great value' (*CW*18 1935 §375). The person no longer places the guarantee of his happiness outside of himself but 'comes to realize that everything depends on whether he holds the treasure or not. If the possession of that gold is realized, then the centre of gravity is *in* the individual and no longer in an object on which he depends' (*CW*18 1935 §377). Healing, he tells us, has to do with detachment, acceptance and transformation, as in 'Eastern practices of detachment and . . . all the teachings of the Church' (*CW*18 1935 §377). If the individual could be helped to relate to the images that have taken on form and are living their own characteristic life in him, 'he is in touch with that vital function which from the dawn of time has been taken care of by religion' (*CW*18 1935 §378).

The mature years: 1936 to 1944

We have seen how in midlife, Jung's conviction that alchemy had psychological as well as a spiritual meaning led him to think about the healing process of psychotherapy in terms of stage-process. He developed his technique of 'hermeneutical treatment of imaginative ideas' through a series of steps that resembled the stages of the alchemical process. During this period, he began to differentiate between a personal and a suprapersonal collective unconscious, and he speaks of psychotherapy as enabling the patient to detach from outer objects so as to realise possession of the treasure within, which he later expressed as the God-self or the God-within.

During the years 1936 to 1944, alchemy became the main focus of Jung's writings. In his lectures of 1935 to 1936, alchemical symbols and dream symbols signified a parallel process (*CW*12 1944a p. x; *CW*14 1955–56 §705; §711). The step-by-step alchemical process worked in matter to release the world-creating spirit, and the same processes also work in the individual psyche to bring about the unified self (*CW*14 1955–56 §759–760).

Jung's most substantial published work on alchemy can be found in Volume 12 of the *Collected Works*, which is based on two lectures given at the Eranos conferences of 1935 and 1936. The lectures were 'Traumsymbole des Individuations-prozesses' *Eranos-Jahrbuch* 1935 and 'Die Erlösungsvorstellungen in der Alchemie' *Eranos-Jahrbuch* 1936 (see *CW*12 1944a p. vii). It is difficult to know where to place this text chronologically in Jung's work. Editors' notes indicate that Jung revised the text in 1940. It appears that he was working on it from some time before 1935 to at least 1943. He made revisions and additions in 1952 for the published version of the lectures. The substance is a comparative analysis of a series of dreams recorded by a colleague (unnamed in the text, but now known to have been the physicist Wolfgang Pauli; see Brown, 2011: 198–199). Here Jung states his view that alchemy's redemptive work releasing Christ in the individual is both spiritual and psychological (*CW*12 1944a §557). He saw this as an age-old, prerational process that uses an intuitive and pragmatic form of thinking (see next section) which senses what does and does not benefit the psyche. At a simple level, such pragmatic judgements are essential for survival; at a more developed level, they are essential for the human psyche to develop itself.

Pragmatic logic

In the third of his collection of three essays (1902–1932), 'Phénomènes occultes', which deal with the question of the soul's existence after death, Jung proposed the existence of an intuitive and feeling-based pragmatic logic that he believed must have existed before reason and before any kind of philosophical thinking. The significance of this for investigating Jung's use of alchemy to articulate his personality theory is his proposition that this kind of logical 'test' is what makes humans able to make use of symbols as an inner guide. In speaking about the usefulness of unverifiable ideas like immortality, Jung says:

> We know that salt is indispensable for our physiological health. We do not eat salt for this reason, however, but food with salt in it tastes better. We can easily imagine that long before there was any philosophy, human beings had instinctively found out what ideas were necessary for the normal functioning of the psyche.
>
> (*CW*18 1938 §743)

While there is no way of knowing whether there is a life after death, the psyche may benefit from assuming that there is. You can tell if ideas are useful by living reflectively and seeing if they are beneficial or toxic to your being. Here we see Jung restating the goal and purpose of psychotherapy, of dream analysis, and of active imagination. No longer presented as a matter of adaptation to inner and outer contingencies, personality development is now conceptualised as a universal process of self-regulation and self-development that is instinctual. In its most basic form, it is fundamental to the survival of all animal existence, and, in its more developed form, fundamental to all human psychic development.

We have touched on Jung's reasons for believing that psychotherapy and alchemy were similar, not only in terms of the stages of their process but also because they were achieving the same psychological goal. We have seen that Jung proposed the existence of a pre-rational form of logic that enables the psyche to make beneficial use of ideas and images and how Jung was able to explore this as a universal process in which development takes place through the action of symbols. I now turn to the images themselves, in particular the circular mandala images that have an important role in Jung's theory of individuation.

Mandala symbols

Chapter 3 of *Complete Works* Vol. 12 deals with the symbolism of the mandala[8]. From their symbolism in different cultures, he came to interpret mandalas as image forms of archetypes that brought the self into being (see Chapter 5, pp. 76–78). This crucial section of Jung's work is elaborated in great detail, indicating the importance Jung gave to the concept of individuation. The mature Jung was stating something that had been forming in his thinking for a very long time. Having been observing 'these processes and their products for close on thirty years on the basis of very extensive material drawn from my own experience', he concluded, 'they signify nothing less than a psychic centre of the personality not to be identified with the ego' (*CW*12 1944a §126). At the same time, Jung was developing his theory of archetypes. He argued that an individuation process must be universal, as

> in the last analysis, every life is the realization of a whole, that is, of a self, for which reason this realization can also be called "individuation". All life is bound to individual carriers who realize it, and it is simply inconceivable without them. But every carrier is charged with an individual destiny and destination, and the realization of these alone makes sense of life.
>
> (*CW*12 1944a §330)

The section on mandala symbols flows into the third and largest section in this volume (*CW*12), titled 'Religious ideas in alchemy'. Here Jung describes the alchemical process, its chemical elements, stages, vessels, the terminology, and the symbolic language used, stating that alchemy's project was to explore the nature of matter, which was a mystery. In exploring this 'unknown', the alchemist involuntarily projected 'yet another mystery – his own unknown psychic background – into what was to be explained' (*CW*12 1944a §345). Jung contended that the alchemist was, in psychological terms, experiencing the mystery of his own unconscious.

Since Jung believed that unconscious processes are universal, it was no disadvantage to his project that alchemy is an ancient or obsolete practice. On the contrary, the fact that these processes could be revealed in times other than our own supported his universality hypothesis and gave him an external vantage point from which to view the psyche. He notes that the terms for the first alchemical stages point to psychic processes, *cogitatio*, *meditatio*, and *imaginatio*, and that the term *meditatio* meant an inner dialogue and hence 'a living relationship to the answering voice of the "other" in ourselves' (*CW*12 1944a §390). The function of one of these stages, *imaginatio*, is important because, in early cosmology, God's imagination created the cosmos. Jung cites Ruland (1612, *Lexicon alchemiae*), who states that although what the soul 'imagines' happens in and to the mind, the soul has 'absolute and independent power to do other things than those the body can grasp' (*CW*12 1944a §396). The alchemist used imagination to bring about the release of the world-creating spirit that is imprisoned in matter. Jung used imagination to bring about the release of the world-creating spirit that is imprisoned in every individual psyche.

Turning to other texts, in 1936, Jung began to write about yoga. In 'Yoga and the West', he says that yoga offers a welcome system of development as well as a profound philosophy, and he recognised its parallels with his own ideas about the 'purposiveness of unconscious tendencies with respect to personality development' (*CW*11 1936a §875). In addition to the comparative material that Chinese Taoist yoga afforded to Jung for interpreting the collective unconscious, its added value for Jung's personality theory was its use of active imagination techniques to 'help the unconscious to reach the conscious mind', though he acknowledged that the West needed to produce its own method for this (*CW*11 1936a §875).

The new self

Jung expanded his concept of self in his 'Commentary on *The Secret of the Golden Flower*', an eighth-century AD Chinese Taoist text concerning meditation (*CW*13 1929d). The golden flower image resembles a mandala symbol. Jung held that the pictures that arise spontaneously from the unconscious and from life are 'an intuition of the self, of one's own individual being'. Through these symbols, he said, 'what is unconscious becomes conscious in the form of a living process of growth.' A reciprocal relationship is set up. 'When the self finds expression in such drawings, the unconscious reacts by enforcing an attitude of devotion to life . . . *the mandala reacts upon its maker*' (*CW*13 1929d §36, italics mine).

The Chinese text acknowledges the paradoxicality and polarity of all life. Further on in his commentary on *The Secret of the Golden Flower*, Jung looked back to his earliest work, the 1902 study of his cousin, the somnambulist fifteen-and-a-half-year-old girl who produced a circular diagram showing in its centre a spring of 'primary force' or life energy, whose emanations she portrayed as clashing with a contrary spatial principle (*CW*13 1929d §37). Now, with hindsight, Jung explained that the circular movement depicted in such mandala-like diagrams could be interpreted as a movement 'around oneself so that all sides of the personality became involved'. He adds, 'the poles of light and darkness are made to rotate. There is night and day' (*CW*13 1929d §38). Self-knowledge of the light and dark forces of human nature is brought about, as Jung puts it, 'by means of self-brooding', and through contemplation of the self-produced mandala. Jung believed that the function of the mandala's circle was to protect and depotentiate the unconscious from having a disintegrating effect on consciousness. Yoga instructs the conscious, which is struggling to disentangle itself from demonic forces within itself in order to enter into individual unity, described as a 'centre of emptiness [where] dwells the god of utmost emptiness and life'. The author of *The Secret of the Golden Flower* speaks of detachment as a move towards 'a conscious void of content, which nevertheless permits all contents to exist' (*CW*13 1929d §64) and acknowledges that, ultimately, its goal is an idea that can be realised only in death (*CW*13 1929d §56), which, in personality terms, can be seen as the ultimate point of realisation of one's becoming.

Jung subsequently elaborated his idea of the psychic structure of the self, saying that the new centre, the self, free from ego domination, is a personality 'that is detached and is a superior personality' (*CW*13 1929d §67–68). He compared this with the image of 'holy fruit' and 'the diamond body' mentioned in the Chinese text, and 'any other kind of incorruptible body', which could be understood as 'an attitude that is beyond the reach of emotional entanglement and violent shocks – a consciousness detached from the world' (*CW*13 1929d §68).

The author of *The Secret of the Golden Flower* regards the detached consciousness as timeless and in harmony with the religious spirit of all ages, as did Jung, who sees timelessness as a quality of the collective unconscious and, hence, of the self. Jung notes that Chinese yoga is based on an idea of the symbolic begetting and birth of a 'spirit-body' which ensures the continuity of detached consciousness beyond death. The goal of Chinese alchemy was immortality. Jung had discovered that he could articulate his theory of a psychological development through life and beyond death by emphasising the links with Taoist yoga. Jung's contemplation of the images of Yoga and alchemy functioned as 'midwives' to the formation and expression of his theory of the immortality of the collective unconscious in exactly the same way as meditating on images brought about the formation of the new self in the personality.

Continuing with the theme of the immortal aspect of the self, Jung published, in 1939, his 'Psychological Commentary on *The Tibetan Book of the Great Liberation*'. This text gave Jung a further opportunity to align his conceptualisation of innate intrapsychic drivers of transformative personality development with the insights of earlier authorities. He cited the Chinese philosopher-alchemist Lao-Tzu, who, in *Tao Te Ching*, stated that, in our character, 'high stands on low' (*CW*11 1939/1954 §791). Jung interpreted this statement to correspond with his own view that consciousness stands on the basis of unconscious instinct. Jung is not offering this as proof of the correctness of his ideas but rather as evidence of the existence of an ancient lineage with a continued tradition of ideas similar to his own and which inspired and enriched them.

Jung and Paracelsus

In June 1929, Jung gave an address (reprinted in 1934) in the house where Paracelsus was born. He was interested in Paracelsus, the 'spiritual man' (*CW*15 1929c §9). He had not at that stage fully incorporated Paracelsian ideas into his theory, but his lecture emphasised that Paracelsus saw healing as the work of God released by man through an alchemical process. In 1942, Jung returned to Paracelsus in 'Paracelsus as a spiritual phenomenon' (*CW*13 1942), in which he gives a detailed account of Paracelsus's unique alchemical philosophy. The main implications for Jung's personality theory are that Paracelsus held that a star or firmament existed in man's body which was a microcosm of the heavenly firmament. Paracelsus, Jung states, recognised two kinds of knowledge: temporal, which springs from the light of Nature, and eternal, from the light of the Holy Spirit. Knowledge in Nature came from the stars in the flesh and blood, not from the flesh and blood itself. Alchemy, astrology, and magic all come from this source.

Both diseases and their medicine came from the stars, as the *astra* (stars) are constellations which originate with the individual's birth horoscope. The Paracelsian physician, Jung said, practised the art of 'charming' an illness, as the ancient Egyptians did. The 'light of nature' gave the patient instructions which the physician must discern and follow intuitively. The physician is only the means by which nature is put to work, and healing is achieved through the physician's attunement with nature. Jung was to develop a form of psychotherapy in which the psychotherapist needs intuitive attunement to discern and reveal the inner God/Self in his patients.

Jung understood the stages of the alchemical operation Paracelsus was engaged in as follows: separating the *prima materia* into the active principle, soul, and the passive principle, body, then reuniting these after separation in personified form in the *coniunctio*, expressed as the ritual union of Sol and Luna from which the son, the *filius sapientiae* or *filius philosophorum*, was the symbolic product (*CW*13 1942 §157). These chemical procedures with their symbolic names correspond to Jung's stages of personal transformation in the following way:

Jung frequently described personality development as a process of separation (from the mother or the parental milieu), a dissolution of previous alignments of the parts of the personality (type, persona, ego), and a reunification into a transformed form. By means of separation and reunification, the 'eternal star' in the nature of the self is given new life as the product of the new union.

Paracelsus put forward a concept of a self-forming principle which he called the *Iliaster* (Paracelsus, *De Vita Longa*, 1562). He advanced the notion that, in every man, an *Iliaster* dynamically formed the individual's character and unique qualities. The *Iliaster*'s length of life of was determined by a natural 'balsam', by means of which the body is kept alive. The same balsam, in this case known as *mumia*, preserved the body after death. In the alchemical approach to healing, the body must be purified by separating its four elements. For Paracelsus, the purpose of this was to raise man to be equal with the *Enochiani* (those who attain long life like Enoch). Jung points out that this was achieved simultaneously in the alchemist's furnace and in the alchemist's mind by meditation (*imagination*).

Jung understood the *Iliaster* to be both a formative principle and a 'principle of individuation' (*CW*13 1942 §171). Paracelsus proposed two other concepts which, together with the *Iliaster*, form an individual person. These were the *Aquaster* and *Ares*. Jung compared Paracelsus's *Aquaster* with his own conception of the unconscious. He saw similarities between Paracelsus's *Ares* (a supra-celestial body whose function is as the assignor of the peculiar nature of each species and its individual form) and individuation in its biological sense (*CW*13 1942 §176). Paracelsus describes *Ares* as being capable of producing out of nothing a corporeal imagination to be thought of as a solid body. For example, Jung says, by thinking of a wolf, a wolf appears. These imagined creations (creatures) both are like the ones composed of four elements and are also not like them. For Jung, Paracelsus's *Ares* is creative imagination personified, and creative imagination (Divine imagination reflected in nature) gives rise to individuality in nature.

One can see how Jung could identify himself closely with Paracelsus's philosophy since there are so many echoes within it of Jung's personal discoveries of the transformative powers of his own and his patients' creative imagination.

The final section of 'Paracelsus as a spiritual phenomenon' illustrates Jung's method of analysis in a particularly vivid way. On vertically divided pages, Jung set out, on one side of the page, Paracelsus's *De Vita Longa* and, on the other side, Dorn's 'Commentary' on it (*CW*13 1942 §213–215). In a manner similar to biblical exegesis, Jung showed how comparison and amplification could be used to determine the meaning of the text. Jung then added his own commentary, expanding the text's meaning with reference to his own psychological concepts. This was Jung's method of amplification that he used for the analysis of dreams, the practice of psychotherapy, understanding myths, and exploring the 'collective' human mind through 'collective' human culture. Apart from his occasional use of questionnaires,[9] it was to become Jung's main scientific method after he abandoned the experimental method that he had used in the word-association tests.

The self as God

In two brief texts of 1943 and 1944, Jung compared Western and Eastern perspectives on consciousness, God, and the self. The culture of the West, he said, seeks to uplift towards consciousness, whereas the East turns back into the 'maternal depths of nature' (*CW*11 1943b §936). 'An ethical dilemma divides us in the West from our shadow', whereas 'the spirit of India grows out of nature: with us Sprit is opposed to nature' (*CW*11 1943b §941). For a Buddhist, the Buddha is oneness with the Deity. Speaking of 'the Holy Men of India', Jung comments that, while the equation of self with God may be shocking to the European, it is not to Indian culture, where the self as the originating ground of the psyche is not differentiated from God; not only is it contained in God, but it actually is God (*CW*11 1944b §957).

Jung concluded that the goal of Eastern religious practice is the same as that of Western mysticism, 'the shifting of the centre of gravity from the ego to the self, from man to God . . . the ego disappears in the self, and man in God' (*CW*11 1944b §958). This goal-like quality of the self was not dependent on consciousness, which was often in opposition to the developing self. The changing relations between ego and self constituted a field of experience which Eastern introspection had exploited to a far greater degree than the West had done. However, the wisdom and mysticism of the East could remind us that our culture can recover access to something similar which it has forgotten (*CW*11 1944b §963).

We have seen that in Jung's mature years, alchemy became the main focus of his published writing. He explored the psychological meanings of the stages of the alchemical process, using them as a parallel model for the transformational processes he placed in the centre of his theory. Through alchemical philosophy, he was able to bring the issue of the immortality of the soul into the arena of personality, at least to acknowledge its historical importance. Through alchemical parallels, Jung was able to hint at some of his deepest convictions, such as the creative power of imagination and the Self-God-likeness and to bring these into his theoretical framework.

The later years: 1945 to 1961

The preceding sections traced the roots of Jung's alchemical and cosmological thinking from his earliest writings through his midlife and mature years and outlined the development of his thought on individuation and the self through his interest in alchemy. The following section covers the points of significance in the alchemical publications of his later years, the sixteen years leading up to Jung's death. The main development in relation to his personality theory was his articulation of his concept of the archetype and the presentation of further alchemical research. It was a period in which Jung repeated, explained, and clarified the psychological vision that alchemy helped him to develop.

There were several publications during this period. The first major one was his *Psychology of the Transference: interpreted in conjunction with a set of alchemical illustrations* (*CW*16 1946). This complex work gives a detailed comparison of similarities Jung perceived between the alchemical processes depicted in the allegorical illustrations to the text *Rosarium philosophorum* (1550) and transference phenomena he observed in psychotherapy. In 1946, Jung also published a foreword to a Yale University Library catalogue of books and manuscripts from the collection of Paul and Mary Mellon in which he asserted his projection theory of alchemy. On this occasion, Jung reflected that alchemical language is perhaps intended to reveal rather than conceal: 'Alchemical language . . . does not disguise a known content but suggests an unknown one, or rather, this unknown content *suggests itself*' (*CW*18 1946/1948 §1691). I think that exactly this is true of Jung's own use of an alchemical language, to enable an 'unknown' content to suggest and reveal itself to him and to his readers.

Jung's essay 'On the nature of the psyche' (*CW*8 1947/1954) concerns the image of *scintillae* or sparks. According to alchemical and Gnostic traditions, the *scintillae* represent the spirit of God in the multiplicity of natural forms. This ancient idea ran through the history of alchemy whilst having similarities with the Platonic ideas of *formae rerum essentiales* from which Jung derived his own concept of archetypes. Jung cites Khunrath (1597), who described the *scintillae* as visible seeds of light in the Chaos, the arcane mud of the world essence, which is animated by them. Jung also cites Dorn, who, he says, wrote about the 'sparks' as if they were analogous to consciousness, both human and Divine:

> Thus little by little he will come to see with his mental eye a number of sparks shining day by day and more and more growing into such a great light that thereafter all things needful to him will be made known . . . for the life, the light of men, shineth in us, however dimly, and as though in darkness . . . it is in us and not of us, but of Him to whom it belongs . . . in this wise we are made like unto him, that he has given us a spark of his light.
>
> (Dorn, 1602: 275, cited in *Theatrum Chemicum*, p. 460, *CW*8 1947/1954 §390)

Jung connects Dorn's description with individual personality by interpreting the symbolic idea of the 'sparks' as an archetypal image, which, when singular, functioned as the archetype of the self, which is to say, also of the *imago Dei* – the image of God in the world. When it appears as multiple, as in Dorn's and in Paracelsus's writing, the sparks shining in the dark substance become a Divine 'firmament' within mankind (see p. 62). It was of great interest to Jung that Paracelsus attributed an active dynamic function to the spark of light in individuals: the star 'desireth to drive man toward great wisdom' (Paracelsus, *Fragmenta medica*, in Huser, V, p. 130, cited by Jung in *CW*8 1947/1954 §390), since this echoed Jung's idea that images formed by archetypes 'drove' the individual towards individuation. Jung also noted Paracelsus's belief that the *lumen naturae* taught human beings prophetic knowledge through dreams: 'as the light of nature cannot speak, it builds shapes in sleep from the power of the word' (of God; Paracelsus, *Liber de Caducis*, IV, p. 274, cited by Jung *CW*8 1947/1954 §391). One can understand Jung's excitement in discovering such close parallels with his own neo-Platonic conceptualisation of autonomous archetypes which influence the psyche from within, which can be discerned as 'shapes' in dreams, and imagined in the form of mandala symbols.

Mandala symbols and the self

An important group of studies published in 1950 brought Jung's alchemical and religious ideas together and emphasised the central concept of individuation in his personality theory. The first is a 'thoroughly revised and enlarged' version of an earlier (1934) Eranos lecture entitled 'A study on the process of individuation'. It is a study of the paintings (mostly in the mandala form) made by a woman who had studied with Jung in the late 1920s. In his detailed analysis of the 24 paintings, Jung identified symbols whose significance for alchemists pointed to a process of transformation towards wholeness and unity. His concluding remarks voiced his growing confidence in making the inner process of the mandala 'more intelligible': 'They are . . . self delineations of dimly sensed changes going on in the background, which are perceived by the "reversed eye" and rendered visible with pencil and brush, just as they are, uncomprehended and unknown' (*CW*9.1 1934/1950 §622).

His subsequent essay 'Concerning mandala symbolism' (1950) recounts the history of the mandala in Indian religious rituals and in Tibetan Buddhism and analyses fifty-four illustrations painted by different people, some of whom were patients of his. Jung's conclusion was that:

> Their basic motif is the premonition of a centre of personality, a kind of central point within the psyche, to which everything is related, by which everything is arranged, and which is itself a source of energy. The energy of the central point is manifested in the almost irresistible compulsion and urge *to become what one is.*
>
> (*CW*9.1 1950 §634)

Personality in relation to the problem of evil

In 'The spirit Mercurius' (1943/1948), Jung gives a rich and complex elucidation of the historical threads that run through the imagery and symbolism associated with the figure of Mercurius. Of interest in relation to personality theory is the Gnostic doctrine in which Mercurius is related to Saturn, is neither good nor evil but contains evil, and represents all opposites. Mercurius is described as 'dark, paradoxical and thoroughly pagan' and, in many ways, pointing to the devil (*CW*13 1943/1948 §289). Both God and the self are similarly paradoxical for Jung. Jung speculated that the split between the conscious and the unconscious was projected into the figure of Mercurius, in whom it appeared as a duality of the powers of light and of darkness. Just as the alchemists kept alive dark elements forgotten in Christianity, Jung's analytical psychology could serve a similar function, keeping alive knowledge of the dark elements within the personality. Jung questioned what Christianity's 'enlightened optimism' might serve to conceal about human nature (*CW*13 1943/1948 §293). 'Today as never before it is important that human beings should not overlook the danger of the evil lurking within them. It is unfortunately all too real' (*CW*9.2 1951a §97–98).

Jung believed that individuation as he conceived it healed this split by unifying opposites in the personality and potentially in the Western world. *Aion* (*CW*9.2, 1951a, written in 1950 and 1951) most fully explicates the connections among Jung's concepts of self, unity, and God. He had discovered in the concept of the *mysterium coniunctionis* of alchemical philosophy a potential for healing on two levels, material and psychic, which he expressed in psychological language as 'individuation'. He reframed individuation as a psychological *mysterium coniunctionis*, 'the self being experienced as a nuptial union of opposite halves and depicted as a composite whole in mandalas' (*CW*9.2 1951a §117). What was new in *Aion* was Jung's focus on the moral purpose of introspection. He stresses the social importance of accepting that evil is part of the human psyche and the global potential of self-knowledge for limiting its power: 'Only an infantile person can pretend that evil is not at work everywhere, and the more unconscious he is, the more the devil drives him. . . . Only ruthless self-knowledge on the widest scale, which sees good and evil in correct perspective . . . offers some guarantee that the end result will not turn out too badly' (*CW*9.2 1951a §255). At this relatively late stage in his life, Jung was making the strongest possible case for his conviction that individuation, the central concept of his transformational theory of individual personality, if realised on a wide scale, would improve, even save, the world.

Alchemy and the collective unconscious

Jung's last book, *Mysterium Coniunctionis: an enquiry into the separation and synthesis of psychic opposites*, written between 1941 and 1954, examined a number of alchemical texts in detail (*CW*14 1955–56). The most striking and salient fact from the point of view of this enquiry is that Jung sought to finish his life's work with a clear statement about the wider canvas that alchemy offered for the study of the collective unconscious. Jung needed a multitude of comparative examples to demonstrate that the core of the human psyche is the same for all. Acknowledging his debt to Herbert Silberer[10] in penetrating alchemy's psychological aspects, Jung explains that he had collected relevant material for more than ten years with the 'aim of demonstrating that the world of alchemical symbols stands in a real and living relationship to our most recent discoveries about the psychology of the unconscious'.

Jung completed 'Symbols and the interpretation of dreams' (*CW*18 1961) in the year of his death. His final words returned to the problem of opposites, the importance of symbols, and the unifying potency of the unconscious:

> Our actual knowledge of the unconscious shows it to be a natural phenomenon, and that, like nature itself, is at least *neutral.* It contains all aspects of human nature – light and dark, beautiful and ugly, good and evil, profound and silly. The study of individual as well as collective symbolism is an enormous task, and one that has not yet been mastered. But . . . a beginning has been made.
>
> (*CW*18 1961 §607)

It was no coincidence that Jung became interested in alchemy, in which immortality was a central concern. Jung's 'collective' unconscious is immortal in an unusual sense of the word. Jung's conception of immortality is not of the person as he or she has been in life. He drew on Paracelsus's vision, which affords immortality both to the *Astrum* (the Divine spark) and, to a degree, the *Iliaster* (the autonomous dynamic individualising principle). The Paracelsian way of envisioning a human form of immortality gave Jung an important new perspective, the 'third idea' that allowed him to answer his questions about opposites, about how to reconcile infinite diversity with oneness and death with immortality. He concluded that the unconscious represents the borderline between psyche and soma, mind and instinct, humanity and nature. This both precedes and continues beyond individual life, because it is the matrix, the *materiaprima*, from which individual life is formed. Viewed from this perspective, the unconscious includes an aspect that is part of the world-soul, part of the universe. In it, humanity and nature meet and melt into one another. Furthermore, Jung's collective unconscious, as nature, has generative power that individuals can access. By bringing this into conscious awareness, individuals can tap a creative source of which they are also a part. Thus the individual participates in its own genesis, having inside itself the source of its own being. It is both creature and creator. It may be said to mirror the Divine imagination as expressed in the idea 'as above, so below' in the alchemical vision. Through borrowing from alchemy's philosophy, Jung felt able to give an account of the collective unconscious that satisfied him, as well as of the dynamic, autonomous process of individuation. No other imagery or philosophy could have achieved this for him.

Alchemy helped give birth to and extended Jung's ideas on psychological self-development and his means of expressing them. He realised that anyone facilitating these processes could be understood as doing the Divine work of revealing God within the individual, and thence in humanity and civilisation. From his detailed study of Paracelsus, Jung was able to draw on the life-extending philosophy of alchemy, seeing within it a logical basis for his intuition of a timeless aspect of human personality.

Discussion

The historical accuracy of Jung's picture of alchemy

Jung's understanding of alchemy accords with recent scholarship that recognises the dual significance of alchemy both as an early practice of medical chemistry and as a philosophical religious practice. Historians of alchemy (such as Holmyard, Corbin, and Ball) have emphasised this point. We can regard Jung as one of the serious scholars of alchemy of his time. He carried out extensive researches into primary sources and acquired a vast knowledge of alchemical symbols. Whilst there are critical voices, his ideas on alchemy are treated with respect by historians of alchemy today, for example, by contributors to *Encyclopaedia Britannica*. There is, however, a significant problem with reflexivity of influence. Historians writing in the latter part of the twentieth century are themselves likely to have been influenced, directly or indirectly, by Jung's work on alchemy and his psychological interpretation of alchemical practice. Many acknowledge this. For example, Henry Corbin, a philosopher who sought to expound and explain pre–Islamic religious thought (Sufi-ism) to Western readers, met and conversed with Jung, as both men contributed regularly to the Eranos lectures from 1949. In the resulting cross-fertilisation, it is difficult to disentangle who influenced whom. Corbin uses the discourse of depth psychology and the concept of individuation to articulate mysticism, while Jung recasts the yearning towards the divine into a psychological discourse, as individuation.

Burckhardt's critique of Jung's psychological interpretation of alchemical practice

Titus Burckhardt, a publisher of ancient manuscripts, many of which he translated from Arabic, and a prolific writer on Sufi doctrine, alchemy, and Middle Eastern culture, objected to Jung's approach to alchemy on the grounds of reductionism, saying that: 'The alchemical work is not a treatment for mental illness' (Burckhardt, 1997: 101). Burckhardt felt that Jung reduced the profound mystical and religious philosophy of alchemy to a kind of practical psychotherapy, but, in this, he does Jung an injustice. Jung does not *reduce* alchemy to a psychological projection of the alchemist's mind. Rather, he says that there is a psychological facet buried in the alchemical philosophical system, which, if understood, can expand the arcane and esoteric symbolism in a new way and opens the field of psychology to a totally new vision of personality. I wonder if

Burckhardt entirely understood Jung, who, in his writing, was reaching for an understanding of belief in the sense of Gnosis: 'Either I know a thing and then I don't need to believe it; or I believe it because I am not sure that I know it' (*CW*18 1956/1957 §1589). Jung is looking *ahead* as well as *backwards*, envisioning a psychological future through links with the past. This was the task neither of Burckhardt nor of historians, though it was the task of the newly emerging twentieth-century psychology.

Burckhardt himself said that, although alchemists practised metallurgical procedures for the purification and transformation of metals and alloys, their real work was 'the transmutation of the soul' (Burckhardt, 1997: 23). It was through alchemy that Jung brought religious phenomena into the centre of the psychological arena, as universal, vital, innate properties of a mind/body/matter synthesis.

In his 'Reply to Martin Buber' (*CW*18 1952/1973), in which Jung defends his empiricism against the critique that he was a Gnostic metaphysician, and in his analysis of the Visions of Zosimos (*CW*13 1938/1954a), Jung argues that a projection by a second-century AD alchemist must be understood in the context of thinking peculiar to that time, and not in the context of twentieth-century post-Enlightenment thinking. In suggesting that the alchemists were projecting, it is unlikely that Jung, given the level of his understanding of the philosophical and religious background of alchemy, was seeking to diminish its profound religious meaning. Rather, he wanted to add a psychological perspective connecting alchemy with individuation. For Jung, projection's close link with imagination makes it part of 'the Divine' element in the psyche. In spite of the likelihood that some alchemists did not recognise or understand it in these terms, in Jung's view, projection transcended them. Ultimately, the critique of Jung's idea that alchemists were projecting their own unconscious contents into their observations hinges not on its alleged reductionism but on the empirical basis for the existence of projection. If his core constructs or intervening variables[11] were found to be demonstrably erroneous, his alchemical metaphor would be seriously flawed.

The accusation of 'mysticism'

Mysticism acquired a pejorative sense with the post-nineteenth-century development of an atheist scientific perspective, but it would not have appeared to Jung in a negative light. His work has a good deal in common with mystical thinking as understood by Happold (1964). The issue is not so much whether Jung's work has elements of mysticism – it evidently has – as whether it can be called 'scientific'. In Jung's understanding, psychology is empirical in a broad sense. For him there was no reason why mysticism, which emphasises the experience of God, should not be approached empirically. Perhaps what is implied by Jung's critics is that he is worse than mystical, he is 'religious'. This is indeed true. I have aimed to show why religious, mystical, and alchemical elements in his theory are essential for understanding his concept of individuation. Jung is concerned with 'the occult', that which is hidden from view. This is also the quest of alchemy. One might say that, while alchemy is mystical (in that the adept seeks a direct experience of the divine), it is also experiential, experimental, metallurgical, and medical. In addition, it has been used as a metaphor and was used by Jung as a powerful metaphor for the process of psychotherapy (Samuels, 1989: 175–193). Through his association with alchemy, Jung demonstrates that investigating the nature of individual personality requires considering questions that occupied philosophy and religion. Jung made this explicit and did not consider it unscientific.

Conclusions

This chapter demonstrates that Jung's alchemical project led to major developments in his theory of personality and provided a rich metaphor for the psyche's potential for self-transformation and for the stages of psychotherapy. Alchemy provided Jung with evidence for the existence of dynamic archetypes. In the alchemical literature, Jung found that others had expressed in pictorial form the transformational processes that he had expressed both verbally and in images in *Liber Novus.* His alchemical studies were a kind of meditation on ideas and images that Jung allowed to 'react on him' and affect him so as to enable his own ideas to form and to emerge. He used alchemy and its rich imagery rather like a complex mandala symbol as a source of meditation and amplification that helped his own vision to crystallise in his mind and in his writing. This vision centred on personality, the individual self.

We have seen in this chapter that, from his earliest adult years, Jung was aware of alchemy and initially used its images as literary allusions and in a comparative way, but later, in the late 1920s and early 1930s, he began to collect alchemical texts and to study them systematically. Discerning similarities between Paracelsus's view of healing and his own, he began to describe psychotherapy in terms of goals and stages similar to those of the alchemical project. Jung's mature years focussed on the dynamic role of images such as the mandala in the formation of the new self, and he explored and developed the religious aspects of the concept of individuation, extending his concept of self to include aspects of immortality. In his late life, he completed and published extensive alchemical research and explored further the problem of opposites in the personality and the potential for individuals' reconciliation of opposites to have a positive impact on society in terms of healing the split between good and evil in the world.

In addition, we have seen that Jung's studies of Gnosis and then of alchemy required him to understand logic in a way that was very different from Greek and Roman reasoning as developed in the legal systems and political structures of the Western world. He realised that to understand alchemy, you have to make a mental leap to a time and a way of thinking that preceded our own and learn to follow reasoning by analogy and by correspondences, which Jung recognised as similar to the logic of dreams. He became aware of the existence of a kind of 'pragmatic logic', older than rational logic, that explained how the psyche could make use of and benefit from the images and ideas that emerged from the unconscious. Jung was to use this way of thinking as part of his own emerging epistemological position.[12] That alchemy opened up new ways of thinking for Jung may have been a particular value. Through alchemy, Jung was able to form important new ideas such as that individuation is *both* distinctiveness and oneness, a concept that derived from alchemical writings.

At the same time, in showing how the thinking of a historical figure like Paracelsus could be understood as a kind of science and by insisting that he was himself engaged in scientific work, in the way that he saw science, Jung challenged and unsettled conventional views of science in the first half of the twentieth century. It was a facet of Jung's project to bring science and religion together, thus healing a second split in the twentieth-century psyche (Main, 2000). This is why Jung, who had trained in empirical science and made use of experiments in his early years, chose, after 1916, to follow a more metaphorical route. We have seen in Chapter 2 how closely Jung's thinking on personality is linked with religious ideas. In addition to this, Jung showed that alchemy and its way of thinking can, if understood sympathetically, provide an interesting and fruitful link among personality, science, and theology.

Alchemy continues to hold value for many psychotherapists as an important metaphor for the transformative processes in psychotherapy and has ongoing potential as a metaphor for the interpersonal, intrapsychic, and productive aspects of the therapy relationship, in the images of the king and queen[13] and the product of their union, the newly developed 'soul' image of alchemy. It may be suggested that all psychotherapists use a nonspecific alchemical 'theory' to understand transformative processes in psychotherapy, whether these are understood as social, interpersonal, educational, or biological processes, when they emphasise transformation from a kind of 'base material' to the fully developed person.

By the end of his life, Jung had enriched the subject of alchemy by revealing its psychological perspective, viewed through his particular psychological lens, and he had demonstrated in rich detail how psychology, alchemy, and religious traditions look at the same questions of diversity and wholeness and point to the possibilities of transformation within the individual and in human civilisation.

Notes

1 There are more than 3,000 alchemical references to 114 alchemical authors and to 118 alchemical texts in Jung's *Collected Works*. By comparison, references to God, the Bible, Christ, Christian, Church, and religion, taken together, total almost 3,600, whilst there are a few more than 1,000 references to the unconscious and only slightly more (1,300) to dreams.

2 See Roob (2006) for a comprehensive collection of examples of cosmological art drawn from libraries, museums, and galleries from all over Europe and from Israel, India, and the New World.

3 These were the *Ars chemica* 1566, *Artis auriferae* 1593, *Aureum vellus* 1598, *Bibliotheca chemica curiosa* 1702, *De alchemia* 1541, *De alchimia* 1550, *Musaeum hermeticum* 1678, *Theatrum chemicum* 1602–61, and *Theatrum chemicum Britannicum* 1652.

4 Burckhardt cited Artephius (pre–1250, mentioned by von Lippmann 1919) as saying 'ours is a cabbalistic art', meaning that it is passed on orally and 'full of secrets', *cabbalistic* having an etymological sense of 'handed down orally' (Burckhardt, 1997: 28 and footnote 6).

5 See the chapter on Corbin's expositions on angels and their function as guide and on the protective roles of a human spiritual master in Islamic mysticism in Cheetham (2003: 98–111)

6 Jung painted his Mandala of a Golden Castle (Jung, 2009: *Liber Novus* p. 163) after receiving the text of *The Secret of the Golden Flower* from Richard Willhelm in 1928.

7 Jaffé quotes Jung as saying that he regarded his work on alchemy as a sign of his inner relationship to Goethe, who 'was in the grip of that process of archetypal transformation which has gone on through the centuries', saying 'I myself am haunted by the same dream, and from my eleventh year I have been launched upon a single enterprise which is my "main business". My life has been permeated and held together by one idea and one goal: namely to penetrate into the secret of the personality. Everything can be explained from this central point, and all my works relate to this one theme' (Jung & Jaffé, 1963: 232).

8 For examples, see Jung's Systema Munditotius (*Jung History* 1.2. 2006 Front cover); Jung's Mandala of a Golden Castle (Jung, 2009: *Liber Novus* p. 163), and, for comparison, the eighteenth-century Tibetan Kalachakra Mandala in *The Hermetic Museum: Alchemy and Mysticism*, Roob, 2006: 275. See also Figures 1 through 48 with which Jung illustrated 'Concerning Mandala Symbolism' (Jung, 1950, *CW* 9i, § 627–712).

9 In 1931, Jung sent out a questionnaire via friends and acquaintances to determine whether people in spiritual distress preferred to consult a doctor rather than a clergyman. The questionnaire was answered by Swiss, German, and French Protestants and a few Catholics (*CW*11 1932 §511). In 1950, Jung collected and analysed the horoscopes of 580 married couples in connection with his investigation of causality and the principle of synchronicity (*CW*8 1952a chapter VII Pt 2 and *CW*18 1958b §1174–1192).

10 Silberer, H. 1914, *Problems of Mysticism and its Symbolism*, cited by Jung in his Foreword to *Mysterium coniunctionis* (*CW*14 1955–56).

11 Assumed processes which are based on fact (see Chapter 8, pp. 153–154).

12 See Papadopoulos (2006b) for an analysis of Jung's use of Gnostic and other ways of thinking in forming his own epistemological stance, and also Rowland (2010: 112), who notes that alchemy was of interest to Jung because it was a non–Newtonian theory in which God, nature, and the psyche are linked in a world that is an interconnected web, not separated by the subject–object division of Newtonian science.

13 The *coniunctio* stage of the alchemical process was often illustrated by images of the sexual union (*hieros gamos* or sacred marriage) represented by two figures or personages, such as a king and queen who symbolise opposites but who are at the same time related in terms of their rank and their marriage and through their sexual intercourse with one another (Samuels, 1989: 184).

Chapter 5

The role of the archetype in personality

Introduction

This chapter concerns Jung's most debated concept, his theory of archetypes. It shows the development of the concept from his original conception of *primordial ideas* and its importance for understanding Jung's conceptualisation of the process of thought formation. This is the last chapter in Part I, in which the focus has been on exposition and understanding, while Part II focuses on the value of Jung's theory and its treatment in textbooks.

Archetypes

In *Memories, Dreams, Reflections* (Jung & Jaffé, 1963: 182–185), Jung is reported to have said that a dream he discussed with Freud in 1909, of a house with two storeys, a cellar, and a prehistoric cave, made him aware of successive layers of consciousness, the foundations of which consisted of an impersonal layer that reflected earlier modes of functioning, which he recognised as forms of instinct. It is these forms that later he called *archetypes.* His personal discovery that he had the ability to generate vivid waking fantasies convinced Jung that those vestiges of old experiences that could be found in the unconscious were not inert but took an active part in our living being (Jung & Jaffé, 1963: 197).

In 1938, Jung used the example of a crystal to illustrate how archetypes could exert influence without themselves having content or form. He noted that the axial system of a crystal is inherent in the liquid from which it forms. It adopts the subsequent crystalline structure without that structure having any previous material existence of its own. Jung thought that the archetype, similarly, has no material existence. It is pure form, a 'possibility of representation, of which only the form is inherent, not the actual representation'. This was true of instincts as well as the archetypes, since instincts are determined as to form but not as to actual expression (*CW*9.1 1938/1954b §155). Neither archetypes nor instincts manifest themselves directly, and although the archetype has a nucleus of meaning, it has many variations of potential forms of manifestation (*CW*9.1 1938/1954b §155).

Background to Jung's *archetype* concept

Whilst it was important to Jung to see himself as belonging to a long line of thinkers who have taken notions similar to archetypes seriously, including anthropologists,[1] he made strenuous efforts to distinguish between an anthropological understanding, in which archetypal ideas are transmitted through the influences of tradition and migration, and his own claim that archetypal ideas can be transmitted by heredity (*CW*11 1938/1940 §88). Jung's contribution, as he saw it, was to have shown that archetypes can arise spontaneously, at any time, at any place, and without outside influence (*CW*9.1 1938/1954b §153).

Jung took from Kant the idea that the cognitive capacities of the mind impose limits on our access to the external world, which in any case can only be experienced indirectly though our sense organs. For Kant, the object is primary, although we are incapable of taking in all its aspects. But, for Jung, empty forms in the mind determine the way we see. So, in Jung's case, mind is primary. It dominates the object and organises the world. The thinking of the abstract thinker, he says, is not *based on* sensory experience but *uses* sensory experience to make ideas representable (see *CW*9.1 1938/1954b §148–151).

Jung extended Kant's idea of inherited *a priori* categories of logical thinking to all types of thought, since he held that the human mind contains *a priori* unconscious contents (archetypes) that give the individual a preformed functional disposition to arrange experiences in particular ways. His observations led him to believe that archetypes could be experienced as 'stage managers' of the thinking process. According to Jung, abstract thinking occurs when attention is turned inwards, such that external objects cease to be the focus of attention and irrepresentable primordial images become active. Jung thought that when this shift of attention occurred, energy that would otherwise be directed towards external objects accumulated to the thinker in whom content-less images began to act dynamically as operative factors in the thinking process. Thought then uses empirical facts and objects to clothe preexisting 'empty' ideas rather than directly representing what it sees. Hence, for Jung, '[ideas] represent themselves *in* facts rather than representing facts' (*CW*6 1921 §513).

How archetypes function

Jung's first answer to the question 'How does the archetype function?' was 'through dreams'. In *Symbols of Transformation* (1911–12/1952), he made public his discovery that dreams contain impersonal mythological themes as well as material of a more personal nature (*CW*5 1911–12/1952).[2] A series of dreams and fantasies were amplified with parallel symbols drawn from mythological and religious sources. He called these symbolic ideas *archetypal symbols* to indicate that these images were the symbolic form of the archetypes (instincts) that gave them form.

Jung saw that the same or similar archetypal symbols were repeatedly generated by successive generations and by diverse and widespread cultural groups. He surmised that archetypal symbols form a framework of images representing universal human characteristics. He held that they constellate energy (that is to say, they are experienced as drawing energy towards themselves) and that they express libidinally charged psychic structures common to all humans. He understood these structures to reflect human instinctual patterns and thought that they must correspond to the concept of patterns of behaviour in biology (*CW*5 1911–12/1952 §224). These images had power, which individuals feel, because they are related to instinct. Hence, the images gripped people in the same way as the power or drive of a strong instinct (*CW*5 1911–12/1952 §225). 'It is a psychological fact that an archetype can seize hold of the ego and even compel it to act as it – the archetype – wills' (*CW*5 1911–12/1952 §101). He warned that, in letting oneself be possessed by an archetype, one forfeits one's humanity. The archetype acts as an amplifier, for example, of the power and effects of the real parent whose image combined with the archetypal representation becomes a divine or daemonic imago (*CW*4 1909/1949 §744. It was the internal representations of the parents, not the real parents, that Jung thought could become overpowerful when infused with the energy of instinct. The drama took place within the psyche, where affect-laden figures and forms behave like parts of the personality (*CW*5 1911–12/1952 328 §505).

Archetypes and personality

The concept of the archetype was important to Jung inasmuch as it is a hypothesized construct whose function within his personality theory is to account for observed phenomena that are not accounted for in other ways. The archetypes are the link between soma and psyche, instinct and mind, species and individual. Innate archetypes are assumed to have direct influence on character and on choices made in individuals' lives. Jung insisted that archetypes are not themselves patterns or images but proclivities whose tendency is to create symbolic images.

We have seen that, early in his writing, Jung insisted that individual personality is at least partly derived from the personalities of our internal archetypes:

> [M]an derives his human personality only secondarily from what the myths call his descent from the gods and heroes; or, to put it in psychological terms, his consciousness of himself as a personality derives primarily from the influence of quasi-personal archetypes.
>
> (*CW*5 1911–12/1952 §388)

What can a twenty-first-century psychologist make of this as an approach to understanding personality? As I mentioned in Chapter 1, Jung maintained that individuality disappears in the deeper instinctual levels of the unconscious

(*CW*5 1911–12/1952 §258–259). What differentiates the individual is his or her conscious personal adaptation to instincts. For Jung, on the one hand, personality development is a matter of conscious adaptation to the external world via acculturation. On the other hand, potent forms and images spontaneously produced by the unconscious are instrumental in bringing about a less conscious process of adaptation: individuation (*CW*18 1916/1970 §1084–1106).

Jung believed that during the process of individuation, internal forms experienced in dreams and conscious fantasies (for example, the circular mandala symbol of the self) could exert a potentially strengthening and sometimes godlike influence on the personality. In 'The Origins of the Hero', for example, Jung referred to inversion as a source of contact with the divine. He explained, 'What we seek in visible human form is not man, but the superman, the hero or god, that *quasi-human* being who symbolizes the ideas, forms and forces which grip and mould the soul' (*CW*5 1911–12/1952 §259). He suggested that, by turning back to oneself, to the psyche, one might gain conscious contact with this source, which could be understood as a kind of 'mother of humanity' which existed before consciousness. By *inversion* Jung seems to be obliquely referring to the practice of active imagination, which was occupying his attention at this time (1912) and to which he attributed his personal experiences of individuation that he documented in *The Red Book* (Jung, 2009). In this way, something of that mysterious and irresistible power which comes from being part of the whole could be regained (*CW*5 1911–12/1952 §259).

However, Jung acknowledged that gaining freedom and wholeness necessitates sacrifice, which he understood to be itself an archetype with significance for personality development. He held that individuation requires a sacrifice in the form of separation from the mother and renouncement of childhood ties. He drew attention to parallels in the Upanishads where the concept of sacrifice is given cosmic importance. Other ancient epic myths and stories told how the power of sacrifice created the world and a new state of man which is 'beyond human' and 'can be described as immortal' (*CW*5 1911–12/1952 §657). The implication is that individuation, the core concept in Jung's theory of personal development, carries something of the superhuman potential of the archetypes.

In *Psychological Types* (*CW*6 1921), Jung addressed the question of the function of symbolisation in the prehistory of human beings. He thought that symbols draw energy away from objects and into the observing subject, depriving objects of the power that would otherwise be invested in them through the process of identification. This would free the human, as subject, to develop an inward, introverted attitude. Jung's picture of the emergence of individual consciousness in mankind as a whole was based on the work of Lévy-Bruhl, whose influence on his own work Jung acknowledged on many occasions.[3] From Lévy-Bruhl Jung derived the idea that prehistoric primitive people identified so completely with significant objects in their external environment that cognition was rendered impossible. This was because 'if the object had an absolute value, it would be an absolute determining factor for the subject and would abolish his freedom of action absolutely' (*CW*6 1921 §402).

Symbolisation meant that libido was invested in the mentalised symbol which drew energy into the internal world of the subject:

> It draws libido away from the object, devalues it and bestows the surplus libido on the subject. The surplus exerts its effects on the unconscious so that the subject finds himself placed between an inner and an outer determinant, whence arises the possibility of choice and relative subjective freedom.
>
> (*CW*6 1921 §404)

Thus individual personality only became possible when identification with the external world was balanced by the creation of an internal representation of the world that incorporated significant meaning and value and drew energy and affect towards itself. That is to say that personality developed when individuals found themselves a middle position, midway between inner and outer realities, with the option to go in either direction. This idea of an optimal midway position is also found in Jung's description of individuation as a process of adaptation to both inner and outer realities (*CW*18 1916/1970 §1084–1098) and is important for understanding the significance of an essential balance between extraversion and introversion in Jung's typology (see Chapter 3).

Of interest too is Jung's claim that the archetype always begins to function when there are no conscious ideas present or when conscious ideas are inhibited, for conscious or unconscious reasons (*CW*6 1921 §625). Here it seems Jung was drawing on his personal experience of active imagination, using his own self-experiment as empirical evidence for his otherwise unsubstantiated statement. He appears to say that you can access archetypes if you succeed in reducing the activity of the conscious mind. You may then become aware of the archetypes clothed in shapes and forms and figures derived from remembered experiences. However, he states that archetypes are also represented in the unconscious as preferences or tendencies to look at things in a certain way, which is to say as unconscious archetypal structures which determine one's approach to life and, hence, personality. This, he felt, was particularly so in the case of introverts, whose characteristic is that they give greater value to their psychic life than to objects in the external world, whilst extraverts believe themselves to be more directly influenced by external objects and influences.

We can now begin to see how, in Jung's way of thinking, archetypal structures are thought to underlie *differences* of personality. They do so by superimposing a set of preferred orientations and attitudes which are expressed as personality types. More than any other concept in Jung's theory, the concept of the archetypes is a radical antibehavioural approach to the psychology of personality. Furthermore, at a deeper level, the ancient idea of the Divine Imagination underlies Jung's approach to personality. Divine Imagination, believed to be the creator of form in the cosmos, is reflected in the human microcosm in the power that the 'empty' forms of archetypes have to form dynamic images in the psyche and, consequently, to influence the expression of the individual proclivities of personhood.

Archetype as *idea*

In considering the origins of the *idea*, Jung stated that it had a precursor, the primordial image. Earlier, he had spoken of both ideas and images as products of archetypes. In his operational definition of the term *idea*, however, he seems to say that archetypal images precede and dynamically drive the formation of an idea: 'It derives this [*a priori*] quality from its precursor – the primordial, symbolic image' (*CW*6 1921 §736). He clarified this further by calling on his theory of personality differences and proposed that the idea has a dual meaning as both a primary determinant (as in *primordial ideas*) *and* as a product. In Jung's typology, different personality types emphasise these meanings differently. An introverted thinker would be likely to emphasise ideas as determinants, while extraverts would give greater emphasis to ideas as products. He admitted that he often personally slipped 'promiscuously' into using the term *idea* for the primordial image itself, falling momentarily, as he put it, into an extraverted attitude (*CW*6 1921 §737).

The list of operational definitions that appears towards the end of *CW*6 is Jung's attempt to clarify his usage of terms in that volume, which is to say, the terms he was using at an early stage when he was working out his theory of psychological types. At that time, he rarely used the term *archetype* and did not define it, speaking mainly of *idea* and *image* and the intrapsychic relationship between these two. That primordial images could precede the idea and determine it while not being known to consciousness was something that emerged when Jung was thinking about character types and how they might differ. It would seem that, at this time, Jung saw these differences as being primarily intrapsychic and having to do with the individuals' attitudes towards their own mental products (*CW*6 1921 §737).

Archetype as *image*

Unsurprisingly, given the importance Jung gave to the power of imagination, he gave the image great psychological value since, in his view, it functioned as a condensed expression of the psychic situation as a whole (*CW*6 1921 §745). He speaks of the image as part conscious, part unconscious – a momentary constellation of elements of the activity of both. The image, then, is a kind of bridge that transcends the conscious and the unconscious. An interpretation of its meaning can only come from understanding the reciprocal relationship between the two (*CW*6 1921 §745). He distinguished between *primordial images*, which have an archaic character and are collective in that they correspond with mythological motifs, and *personal images*, which do not. Personal images express unconscious personal contents and reflect personal situations (*CW*6 1921 §747). It was specifically the primordial archaic image with mythological parallels that Jung was to term *archetype*.

Archetype as instinct

In *Psychological Types*, Jung ended his definition of *image* by clarifying its relation to instinct. The primordial *image* was instinct's source of energy and vitality and its self-activating generating power. It was the psychic background and counterpart to instinct (*CW*6 1921 §754). Jung's 'Instinct and the Unconscious' (1919) drew on Bergson's understanding of intuition as an instinctive act of comprehension, differing from instinct in that it is not conscious sensory action but unconscious apprehension. It is in relation to instinct that Jung is first known to have used the term *archetype*. The unconscious, he said, holds inherited qualities, such as instincts, to carry out actions without conscious motivation, and *a priori*, inborn forms of intuition, namely, the archetypes of perception and apprehension which force individuals' ways of perceiving life into specifically human patterns. Instincts and archetypes together formed the collective unconscious (*CW*8 1919 §270).

In the early years of the twentieth century, instincts were a focus of interest for all disciplines studying animal and human behaviour, including personality. It is likely that Jung wanted to position himself within this field. He maintained that there was a plurality of instincts that motivate human behaviour (Shamdasani, 2003: 242), disliking restriction to a very few which, he felt, reduced instinct to the level of reflex (*CW*8 1919 §271). It followed from his conceptualisation of *a priori* ideas that there must be a similar number of primordial archetypal images for instincts. His occasional use of the term *primordial image* to refer to both the *a priori* idea and its image-product (*CW*6 1921 §737) has caused considerable confusion, as readers have felt that it is left unclear whether Jung's *archetype* is a capacity for forming images or the image itself.

Jung noted that physical experiences and dangerous situations arouse affect-laden fantasies that give rise to archetypes or myth motifs inasmuch as they repeat themselves (*CW*8 1927/1931b §334). He suggested that a group of these, representing mankind's ancestral experience of father, mother, child, husband, wife, and dangers, had been exalted and transformed into the principles of religious and political life in recognition of their psychic power (*CW*8 1927/1931b §337). In the course of the growth of civilisation, the divergence of consciousness from the unconscious left people with the problem of how to adapt to the demands of instinct as well as those of the environment. This problem was to become Jung's lifetime preoccupation, his view that people need to reconnect to their instincts as their source of vitality and creativity, since 'From the living foundation of instinct flows everything that is creative' (*CW*8 1927/1931b §339).

Archetype as symbol

In 1950, Jung claimed that mandala symbols were comparable with their ethnographic parallels in both form and meaning (*CW*9.1 1950 §711). He emphasised that knowledge of the common origin of these and other symbols has now been lost to us, and so it is necessary to read texts from old cultures to understand and elucidate their functions for psychic development. He spoke of historical layers below the surface of the psyche that are alive and continuously active in everyone: perhaps to a degree that we cannot imagine in our present state of knowledge (*CW*9.1 1950 §712).

Jung's preformed ideas also limit what our creativity can create. He thought that preformed ideas that determine form could explain why myths, legends, and fairy tales and all creative ideas, including scientific theories, tend to have similar themes and patterns. He concluded that fantasy 'can never roam to the infinite' but is restricted to the range of themes and patterns that *a priori* Ur-patterns in the unconscious can generate (*CW*6 1921 §512).

Because of their archaic origins, archetypal symbols open a door to understanding archaic modes of thought. In 1948, Jung asserted that 'the archetype did not ever come into existence as a phenomenon of organic life, but entered into the picture with life itself' (*CW*11 1942/1948 §222 n.2). Discerning what he may have meant calls for some unravelling of the close connection he made between archetypal ideas and the phenomena observed in dreams. According to Jung, archetypal dream images reveal the raw material of the psyche and its archaic reasoning. In a footnote to the Terry Lectures, Jung quotes from Nietzsche:

> As a man now reasons in dreams, so humanity also reasoned for many thousands of years when awake: the first cause which occurred to the mind as an explanation of anything that required explanation was sufficient and passed for truth . . . this atavistic element in man's nature continues to manifest itself in our dreams, for it is the foundation upon which the higher reason has developed and still develops in every individual. Dreams carry us back to remote conditions of human culture and afford us a ready means of understanding it better.
>
> (Nietzsche, *Human, All too Human,* 1909 1: 24–25, trans. Zimmern & Cohn, modified by Jung and cited in *CW*11 1938/1940 §89 fn 17)

One important feature of archetypes for Jung was that they afford the means by which the psyche can reflect on its own nature. Jung believed that the psyche needs to know the meaning of its own existence, 'not just any meaning, but the meaning of those images and ideas which reflect its nature and which originate in the unconscious' (*CW*13 1945/1954 §476). This need was as important as the need for food. Jung (and Nietzsche) assumed that in dreams we find relics of the stages of psychological development that humankind has passed through in aeons of existence. Similarities between archetypal images and individual dream symbols pointed to the possibility that an unconscious substructure within the psyche, like that of the body, is common to all (*CW*13 1945/1954 §478).

At other times, Jung referred to *a priori* ideas as the result of repeated and accumulated experiences, the effects of which are handed down through the ancestral line (*CW*6 1921 §659). This and similar statements have led to the criticism that Jung espoused a Lamarckian view of evolution in which characteristics that developed as a result of environmental pressures could be directly inherited by descendants, sidestepping Darwin's natural selection based on survival to reproduce. The question of whether Jung really leant towards a Lamarckian view of inheritance has not been resolved, though Jung always denied it. Instead, he referred to Kant's concept of the *noumenon* as a formative influence on his thinking. 'The archetype would . . . be, to borrow from Kant, the noumenon of the image which intuition perceives and, in perceiving, creates' (*CW*6 1921 §659). This suggests that Jung understood the archetype itself to be the driver of the evolution of thought.

Archetypes, personality, and religious experience

In Chapters 3 and 4, I emphasised the strong connection Jung makes between the archetypes of the unconscious, personality development, and religion. The link is the psychological process that Jung called *individuation.* In a passage in *Symbols of Transformation* (1911–12/1952) in which he analyses the dreams and fantasies of Miss Miller, he applied the technique of amplification to Miss Miller's dream-poem 'The Moth to the Sun'. In the poem, intense longing is expressed through the image of a moth fatally drawn to the light and heat of the sun. Jung concluded that psychic energy (libido), expressed as yearning, both creates and is the God-image. That is to say, Jung understood the God-image as the archetypal image of psychic energy and at the same time an image of the vital energy or living essence of the human self. He explained that energy expresses itself in form and thus creates its own image, which, discerned psychologically, is experienced as God, the self, or both (*CW*5 1911–12/1952 §128–129). He concluded: 'I am therefore of the opinion that, in general, psychic energy or libido creates the God-image by making use of archetypal patterns, and that man, in consequence, worships the psychic force active within him as something "divine"' (*CW*5 1911–12/1952 §129). Naturally, Jung was aware of the potential consequences of this for the personality. He continued: 'To carry a god around in yourself means a great deal; it is a guarantee of happiness, of power, and even of omnipotence, in so far as these are attributes of divinity. To carry a god within oneself is the same as being God oneself' (*CW*5 1911–12/1952 §130). Jung deduced that the main psychological purpose of this increase in power must be to strengthen individuals against their 'all-too-human' personal weaknesses and insecurity in life.

Archetypes and death

In 1939, Jung amplified his definition of archetypes so as to include not only instincts but also dynamic instinctual complexes, which, he believed, could, like *Karma*, determine life and character and may also drive the psychic process of death. Jung interprets Karma as psychic heredity-traits of character and gifts, a special class of which are the universal dispositions of the mind (*CW*11 1939/1954 §845), in accordance with which the mind organises its contents. Their specific content, he said, only appears through the course of life when personal experience is taken up in these forms. Jung understood these forms to be inherent, dynamic, instinctual ways of organising individual psychic life, a 'fact' which is understood by the dead whom *The Tibetan Book of the Dead* instructs. The dead are exhorted to surrender to the 'Karmic illusion', a visionary, irrational, internal world of *images*, in which an order of gods and goddesses is arranged in four directions with four colours representing the four light-paths of wisdom,[4] which the dead recognise as radiations of their own psychic faculties. The dead have to recognise that gods and spirits are nothing but thought forms which take on the character of reality in images, which arise from the collective unconscious in the individual. That is to say that the path of the soul after death is one of individuation in reverse, no longer differentiating into increasing diversity and complexity but converging into unity, restoring to the soul the divinity it lost at birth. Even in death, the archetypes, as dynamic thought forms, organise and shape the personality. Now they guide it to turn in a reverse direction, to embrace the end of all conscious, rational and morally responsible conduct of life (*CW*11 1939/1954 §842–855).

Moral aspects and consequences of archetypes

Jung held that archetypes have an influence on the psyche even if the individual remains totally unaware of their presence. For example, in 'The Significance of the Father in the Destiny of the Individual' (1909/1949), Jung referred to parental images in the psyche, of parenting and of being parented, as inborn systems that are organised and ready to function in a specifically human way. These powerful images, he said, are like the migratory and nest-building instincts of birds, which are not acquired or learned but are present at birth as a ground plan, a congenital and preexistent instinctual model or pattern of behaviour (*CW*4 1909/1949 §728–729). He was concerned that these preformed aspects of the psyche may exert an influence that fascinates. As pure unreflecting instinct, they could be dangerous forces. Humans needed to make these influences conscious to avoid being enslaved to them. Jung gives the example of the archetype of the father, which is capable of exerting both beneficial and destructive effects on both parent and child, and acts on consciousness rather as Yahweh acted towards Job – powerfully but ambivalently (*CW*4 1909/1949 §741). Because of the potential for archetypal forces to 'grip' an individual and exert unthinking power, Jung concluded that unconsciousness (the failure to develop awareness of unconscious influences in oneself) is the original sin (*CW*4 1909/1949 §729–730).

Consciousness needs to be in touch with the primordial images that connect it with the source of its own vitality. From his own experiences Jung discovered that the practice of exercises that allow free rein to unconscious fantasies can be a path to personality development. He puts this idea into a historical perspective, suggesting that the earliest human mentality was neither fully conscious nor individualised and was subject to projections of intrapsychic fantasies of powerful archetypal figures. Until a higher consciousness was developed, human consciousness was in thrall to primordial fantasies generated by the unconscious (*CW*13 1929d §11–26). For Lévy-Bruhl (1966), whose work Jung cited, the development of consciousness enabled higher-order concepts to develop. On the other hand, Jung felt that too much consciousness could lead to neurosis in a too-rational society. It followed that healthy adaptation for modern people must involve a stage of personality development that rediscovers unconscious values and potentialities through integrating activated archetypes.

At the same time, Jung recognised the potential for individuals and nations to become dangerously inflated by the power and numinosity of activated archetypes. In a lecture in London in 1936, Jung warned that what civilised humans thought was archaic and primitive seemed to be very much alive in modern times: 'The man of the past who lived in a world of archaic *représentations collectives* has risen again to very visible and painfully real life . . . in many millions of people' (*CW*9.1 1936b §98). When a situation occurs that corresponds to a given archetype, the archetype becomes activated and a compulsiveness appears which lacks reason and will, in the same way as a strong instinct will cut across will and dominate action. The remedy Jung offered was to promote individual awareness and integration though the message of his personality theory.

Developmental and therapeutic functions of archetypes

Jung also emphasised the transcendent influence of archetypes in his 'Commentary on *The Secret of the Golden Flower*' (1929d). Patients could grow 'beyond themselves' because of unknown potentialities sometimes expressed in dynamic archetypal symbols like the mandala. He used the intentionally nonspecific term *new thing* to describe a new attitude or new possibility that emerged which, once accepted, helped this growth to come about (*CW*13 1929d §18–19). Moreover, he emphasised that developmental growth occurred because of inaction (acceptance) rather than as the result of effort. Where effort was required, it was for actively preventing consciousness from interfering, helping, correcting, and negating. The psychic process could, however, be fantasised as an image that might be drawn or modelled, as a means of giving it concrete form. In this way, something that had been excluded and which was now capable of bringing about a reversal that enriched and enlarged previous values would come to the patient (*CW*13 1929d §21–23).

The Chinese idea of acceptance leading to Tao seemed to offer Jung the authority of a whole civilisation as a basis for believing that what he had observed in his patients was a universal means of gaining integrity and achieving wholeness. A crucial point, of relevance for Jungian psychotherapies and all approaches that encourage the use of art forms in therapy, is that Jung believed that the whole personality is initially expressed in a symbol before it becomes a reality. That is to say that first there is the idea of the future personality expressed as symbol. If the symbol is allowed to have an influence, it will enable many people to develop beyond their original potential. Jung conceded that a Taoist concept of personal development was not identical with what personality development meant to a twentieth-century person in the West. But for him, there was value in the idea that conflicts between psychic opposites might be resolved and transformed as a result of the emergence of a new development initially expressed as a symbolic idea (*CW*13 1929d §25–26).

Levels of development of archetypes

In 'Psychology and Alchemy' (1944a), Jung stated that an archetype could itself be more or less developed and that it was capable of endless development and differentiation. He explained that an archetype that is projected is unconscious, hence cut off from participation in and influence on the conscious mind. In its projected form, it is prevented from exerting a formative influence on consciousness. Furthermore, once unconscious, the archetype might regress to lower and more archaic forms (*CW*12 1944a §12). The assimilation of projections is therefore a means of enabling the archetype to develop with the effect that its influence becomes beneficial.

Jung was interested in symbols that seemed to express opposites and paradoxes. He speculated that by existing in paradoxical forms, archetypal images could spur consciousness to a higher level. This is because logical contradictions that are impossible on one level become possible when understanding is lifted to a higher level, from which it can 'see the scope of' the paradoxical truth. In this way the psyche comes to understand its own paradoxical nature and thus contributes to the development of the self. Once the conscious mind experiences the images of the unconscious and is confronted with the contradictions of its own human nature, wholeness (of the self or the personality) becomes possible through a new understanding of contradictions and opposites (*CW*12 1944a §23).[5]

Thus for Jung, the paradox of good and evil was a developmental force influencing the growth of the self, which is at once an archetype of unity and of conflict because of its conscious/unconscious split. The emergence of archetypal symbols of wholeness, a centre or goal, signified the development of a healing process within the psyche and constituted a kind of 'salvation'. Hence, Jung concludes that, as the archetype develops, it influences and develops us by drawing the psyche in towards its own centre. Dreams, Jung said, rotate around this centre, the self, drawing closer to it. He envisioned the self and its development as a circular motion aiming towards its own centre, drawn to this by the need to encompass oppositions, conflicts, and paradoxes (*CW*12 1944a §34).

Different types of archetype – differentiating pure symbols from personified figures

From 1934, Jung, in his published work, began to discuss dream images in terms of active personalities,[6] such as the figure of the 'child', the 'wise old man', the 'shadow', the 'anima', and the 'enlightener' or 'psychopomp' as exemplified in Nietzsche's figure of Zarathustra (*CW*9.1 1934/1954 §71–80). Jung observed in himself and his patients that these personified forms of archetypes arose under certain psychological conditions such as a loss of direction or in times of psychic conflict. He proposed that processing such experiences involved the activation of another class of archetypes, archetypes of transformation. Transformational archetypes would not be experienced as personalities but as symbols of typical situations, places, ways, and means that symbolise the kind of transformation in question and are paradoxical in nature (*CW*9.1 1934/1954 §80). Jung notes that, as true symbols, these forms are ambiguous and cannot be exhaustively interpreted as signs or allegories can. Instead, symbols and transformational archetypes are experienced as full of half-glimpsed meanings because of their wealth of reference, their manifold meaning, and their inherent paradoxicality. Jung gave an alchemical example to illustrate this quality of paradoxicality, the alchemical 'spirit, which is at the same time a youth and an old man', and he elaborated this point with reference to the *I Ching*, whose symbolic process, he says, is an experience in and of images, in a rhythm of loss and gain, dark and light, negative and positive. Its goal was enlightenment, illumination, or higher consciousness (*CW*9.1 1934/1954 §80–81).

In Jung's understanding, because of its autonomy and its paradoxes, the transformational image urged and pointed towards the formation of an intuition of a new realisation, an illumination of significance for the person's development. The process could either be compressed into a single dream or short moment of experience, or it might extend over months and years (*CW*9.1 1934/1954 §82). The entire self-making, self-development process is thus driven by the necessity to create new syntheses from paradoxical positions. In Jung's view, this synthesis could not be achieved by a process of reasoning alone but by a gradual process of making conscious the symbols and personified figures of the activated unconscious contents and, ideally, engaging in a dialectical procedure such as an actual dialogue, resulting in a real coming to terms with them (*CW*9.1 1934/1954 §85). Jung proposes active imagination as an effective means by which an individual brings into consciousness her/his inherent nature and, as a result, 'becomes' what s/he always 'was'.

Summary

This chapter traces the meaning and functions of the concept of the archetype in Jung's psychology and its particular significance within his personality theory and shows why a description of Jung's theory of personality that fails to consider the concept of archetypes, as some authors have done (see Chapter 6), has failed to engage adequately with Jung's total approach to understanding the human personality.

This chapter is the last in the series of chapters that explore and discuss the meaning of constructs that are essential for understanding Jung's theory of personality. We turn now to Part II, which focuses on issues of evaluation and considers how the merit of the theory has been or might be judged.

Notes

1 In 1934, Jung provided a long classical lineage for the term *archetype*, tracing it to the first-century Jewish historian and religious writer Philo Judaeus's *De opificio mundi* (I, 69, Whitaker trans, 1, p. 55) as a reference to the *Imago dei* in man and to the second-century Christian Bishop of Gaul Irenaeus's *Adversus haereses* (11, 7, 5, Roberts/Rambault trans. 1, p. 139), who states that the creator of the world did not fashion things directly from himself but copied them from archetypes outside himself. In the *Corpus hermeticum* collection of alchemical (Hermetic) texts dating from the early Christian era, God is called archetypal light, and Jung notes that the term occurs in the work of the fifth-century mystic Dionysius the Areopagite as *immaterial archetypes* and *Archetypal Stone* (*CW*9.1 1934/1954 §5). Jung attributes the idea, though not the term, also to St Augustine's *De diversis questionibus LXXXIII* in his *ideae principales*, which are themselves not formed but are contained in the divine understanding, and that it occurs as a paraphrase of the Platonic *eidos*. Jung also mentioned that the anthropologist Lévy-Bruhl (1837–1939) used the term *représentations collectives* (*CW*9.1 1934/1954 §5–6) and added Cicero, Pliny, Nietzsche, the anthropologist Bastian (1826–1905), and Usener, scholar of comparative religion (1834–1905), to the growing list of authorities who had made use of the term or the idea of archetypes (*CW*9.1 1938/1954b §153 and *CW*11 1938/1940 §89 and footnote 15).

2 Some references to archetypes in this early volume may have been inserted as part of Jung's 1950 revision (*CW*5 1911–12/1952, p. xxv).

3 But see Segal's critique (2007: 635–658) arguing that Jung may have misread Lévy-Bruhl and psychologised his notion of primitive identification, which Lévy-Bruhl explained sociologically, and that Lévy-Bruhl saw modern thinking as an advance in consciousness, whereas Jung emphasises the primitive thinking that has been retained in the unconscious psyche of modern people. My understanding is that Jung saw Lévy-Bruhl's *représentations collectives* as having a psychological origin but as being subsequently transmitted by tradition and migration (*CW*11 1938/1940 §88), and it could be argued that Jung's notion that older types of thinking can be discerned in the dreams of modern people is a further development, not a misunderstanding, of Lévy-Bruhl's original ideas.

4 One can see parallels with Jung's typology and its four functions.

5 In this passage, the self is compared with the Christ-symbol, which, unlike the self, is not a union of opposites but can be shown historically to represent the opposition of good and evil, darkness and light. For Jung, it is the self that can become whole and thus influence the development of the Christ-symbol. The self heals the Christ-image and unifies *it*.

6 See *CW*9.1 chapter IV (1940) and V (1945/1948); *CW*9.2 chapters II and III (1959). See also the work of von Franz (1988, 1997) and Hillman (1985, 1990, 1996), who explore the rich meanings of these archetypes.

Part II

Evaluating and reappraising Jung's personality theory

For a theory to be evaluated, it has to be understood. Jung has to be reconstructed as a personality theorist. We can then see what academic psychologists have used to 'construct' Jung's theory and can understand some of the difficulties they have had. Part I concentrated on understanding. Chapter 1 defined personality theory, discussed the reasons for including Jung's work in this category, and established which parts of Jung's work should be regarded as his personality theory. Chapters 2, 3, 4, and 5 explored the religious and alchemical ideas that have a bearing on personality, his use of *active* imagination as means of facilitating personal development, and his concept of archetypes in relation to individuation and the self.

The next three chapters take this book in a different direction, one which is concerned with theory evaluation. The academic world has found Jung difficult to evaluate, partly because of the nature of the theory itself and partly because of the way the academic world meets his theory. This has hindered people from seeing the value for them in Jung's ideas. Chapter 6 looks at the theory's reception and dissemination by psychologists of personality. Chapter 7 asks how personality theories are evaluated and proposes new criteria. Chapter 8 discusses Jung's theory in the light of these criteria and shows how fresh criteria and openness to a cross-disciplinary approach can transform the critical evaluation of Jung's standing as a personality theorist.

Chapter 6

Jung's theory in sixty-five years of personality textbooks

[T]he public reputation of outstanding psychologists . . . may be more substantially influenced by textbooks than by their own writings.

(Hobbs & Chiesa, 2003: 50)

Introduction

C.G. Jung's approach to personality has been neglected by academic psychology, particularly in the United Kingdom. This has had the effect of restricting Jung scholarship to Jungian circles. Meanwhile, opinions, criticisms, and controversies, whose source is often not acknowledged, have circulated freely in academia and have become 'common knowledge' about Jung's ideas. Undergraduate textbooks written by psychologists have an important role in creating an image of Jung in the academic world. This chapter reviews the treatment of Jung's theory in textbooks and supplementary texts of personality theory over almost seventy years. I consider how the image and place of Jung has been constructed and transmitted in texts that are likely to have had a formative influence on the psychological professionals of today.

Although there has been little research on the treatment of Jung in textbooks, it has been shown that the work of some other major figures in twentieth-century psychology is inadequately described or misrepresented. For example, Todd and Morris (1983), Jensen and Burgess (1997), and Hobbs and Chiesa (2003) reviewed the treatment of B.F. Skinner's work in recent introductory textbooks of general psychology. They found a number of errors, omissions, and misrepresentations of Skinner's ideas. Buys (1976) reviewed six decades' treatment of Freud in introductory psychology texts (from 1908 to 1969) and found many contradictory statements about his work and its value. Buys concluded that authors whose orientation to the study of psychology was empiricist-experimentalist were more likely to write negatively critical summaries of Freud's theories than were nonempiricist and nonexperimental authors. These examples suggest that textbooks offer conflicting rather than balanced reviews of eminent figures in psychology's history. Whether it is best to provide a balanced view as opposed to taking a particular perspective on the field is a matter for debate, and future texts may adopt different approaches. However, in the majority of twentieth-century introductory texts, the authors state that they seek to offer an impartial view.

Todd and Morris (1983) make the important point that public policy is shaped by individuals whose exposure to psychological theories is through psychology textbooks and through educators who assign them. They warn that, where textbooks contain errors, misconceptions, and unsupported criticism, the resulting policies and decisions are unlikely to reflect important conceptual and applied contributions that the theory could offer (Todd & Morris, 1983: 158). Advisors in education and mental health policy are likely to have formed their views of Jung's work and its value from the books they read as undergraduates. Thus texts published thirty years ago still have a pervasive influence today. Furthermore, views expressed in earlier texts are repeated subsequently by later writers who were influenced by or taught by the earlier authors; hence the influence of academic textbooks on generations of students should not be underestimated. As Hobbs and Chiesa point out, 'textbooks may be the only way a student gets to know about a particular theory or prominent figure' (Hobbs & Chiesa, 2003: 50).

My focus is on the construction of Jung and his work and on how the picture of Jung has been handed down to generations of psychologists. The textbooks I have reviewed can be seen to have contributed to the perception that Jung was mystical (Sullivan, 1953–1964; Feist, 1985) or psychotic (Stolorow & Atwood, 1979), that his therapy approach is exclusive and elitist (Hjelle & Ziegler, 1992), that his writing style is arcane (Schultz, 1976), and that his ideas are vague (Schultz, 2001). While it is reasonable to ask what in Jung's own work may have led to these misconceptions, such perceptions will have had negative consequences on the provision of Jungian psychotherapy in contexts dominated by experimental values and stringent economics.

There is no established methodology for reviewing textbooks. Some reviews such as that of Buys (1976) are largely descriptive, while others such as Todd and Morris's (1983) attempt to explain the processes by which errors, distortion, and misrepresentation occur. Their starting position is that students need to be able to balance criticisms with informed argument and to have well-referenced information if they are to get an accurate picture from the introductory literature.

Textbooks of personality theory developed slowly from the 1930s, as personality became established as one of the subdisciplines of psychology and was taught in undergraduate courses in psychology mostly in the United States. I examined university undergraduate texts presenting personality theories and theorists focussing on texts from the United States and Britain, from 1937 when the first textbooks of personality began to appear until 2002. Some textbooks are clearly aimed at the introductory level, while other texts are directed towards more advanced students. Many went into several reprints and editions spanning several decades. Where possible, I examined more than one edition to see how authors updated their information and views on Jung over the years (for example, textbooks by Schultz, Maddi, Hall & Lindzey, and Monte). Not all the books published in each decade are included. Some have been omitted because they did not mention Jung's theory or did not cover psychoanalytic theories.

This sample, which is comprehensive but not exhaustive, comprised almost the entire stock of personality textbooks of a UK university library (University of Sussex) in 2003. It includes a small number of texts that are not textbooks in the conventional sense but functioned as such. Comparative checks with three other UK university library catalogues, those of Essex, Liverpool, and University College London, suggested that almost all of the better-known texts stocked by the other libraries were included, plus a range of lesser-known books. Essex, Liverpool, and University College London libraries held a smaller number of undergraduate textbooks in personality than the University of Sussex did. The majority of the texts were U.S. publications, many of which are extremely well known. Thus there is no reason to suppose that UK universities prioritised UK texts or that the Sussex selection was atypical.

Four specific considerations guided my consideration of the adequacy of the coverage of Jung:

1 Is the presentation well informed and well researched using primary sources and reliable secondary sources?
2 Does the presentation cover the significant concepts and ideas in Jung's theory accurately and sufficiently broadly to give a sense of the theory as a whole?
3 Is the presentation sympathetic? What position does the author prefer, such as empiricist/experimentalist, trait-oriented, holistic, behaviouristic, cognitively oriented, or psychoanalytic, and is this information made available to the student reader?
4 Does the author explicitly aim to be impartial, and how successfully is that achieved? Are references given for critiques, and are references to counter-arguments offered?

Based on the understanding of Jung's theory that I outline in Chapters 1 to 5 of this thesis, an adequate account of Jung's theory of personality should include at least:

- an accurate statement of Jung's position on hereditary aspects of personality and the nature/nurture balance in his theory
- an account of Jung's concept of the unconscious that reflects Jung's own statements
- an exposition of Jung's archetypes that includes their dynamic involvement in shaping the personality, in the process of thinking, and in creativity
- an exposition of the concept of individuation that reflects Jung's own statements and acknowledges the centrality of a transformative developmental process in adulthood in his theory of personality

- an account of Jung's mystical approach and of the relevance of his comparative studies of cross-cultural symbolism in religion and alchemy for his concept of individuation
- an account of Jung's own aims and his postwar concerns about the unacknowledged potential for violence in human nature
- a well-informed and impartial biographical account, where such accounts are included for all theorists within the framework of the textbook

In this chapter, I selectively focus on elements that are either particularly misleading or noticeably comprehensive and well informed. The textbooks and their treatment of Jung are presented chronologically, to reflect changes in style, aims, and values from decade to decade and to allow themes to emerge over time. For example, there are differences between introductory texts published before and after 1980. Major differences can be seen between North American and British publications, with British authors tending either to be hostile or to omit Jung. There are two stories to tell. One is a historical account which sets the presentations of Jung in a wider context within the developing field of personality psychology, and the other is a thematic account which identifies errors and distortions and contrasts these with more reliable accounts.

The 1930s

Textbooks published in the United States

Before 1930, textbooks used for teaching psychology were of general psychology, psychiatry, education, and abnormal psychology. Two strands already discernible in the 1930s were to become the two main twentieth-century approaches to personality. Factor analysis was incorporated from statistics into psychology to become the hard-science trait approach, while the holistic personology pioneered by W. Stern was carried into academic psychology by G. W. Allport and Henry Murray.

The first real textbook of personality was Allport's *Personality: A Psychological Interpretation*, published in 1937. It was hugely influential and is still read today. Allport was critical of psychoanalysis for having 'made virtually no contact with any other branch of psychology' (Allport, 1937: 13), a criticism that was to be repeated by Eysenck twenty years later in the UK. Allport's treatment of Jung was more sympathetic than his treatment of psychoanalysis, possibly because Jung's preference for personology over elementarism corresponded with Allport's own. Allport's account of Jung's work was fair and well informed from the primary sources available at that time. (See Appendices 3 and 4 for the primary and secondary sources cited by the authors of the texts reviewed.) Much of Jung's later work was yet to be written. Allport acknowledged the influence of Jung's introversion and extraversion traits on the work of others and the enduring impact of these as common language terms but had reservations about

Jung's hypothesis of the collective unconscious, to which he refers incorrectly as 'racial unconscious'. For Allport, such theories 'deny the basic tenets of empiricism', being, in fact, 'extreme varieties of intuition' (Allport, 1937: 356). 'Racial unconscious' is not a term Jung used. For him, the *collective unconscious* is species specific, not 'race specific'.

Thorpe was more hostile towards Jung's work. In *Psychological Foundations of Personality* (1938), he gives a superficial overview with a focus on the typology and instincts as drives. The text contains an important misrepresentation of Jung's type theory. Thorpe suggested that Jung's theory of introvertive and extravertive types was similar to Kretschmer's physiological types (Thorpe, 1938: 317). However, Jung's type theory is markedly more psychological than Kretschmer's and is not based on physique. Thorpe's comparison with Kretschmer was unfortunate for Jung because Kretschmer could be associated with theories which Allport regarded as dubious, such as physiognomy, graphology, astrology, and phrenology (see Allport, 1937: 65–77). A further example of misrepresentation based on misapprehension occurs in Thorpe's critique of the dual classification implicit in Jung's typology, based on Jung's alleged linking of introversion with schizophrenia and extraversion with manic depression (Thorpe, 1938: 322). Thorpe claimed that evidence from questionnaires given to groups of psychiatric patients and 'normals' had disconfirmed Jung's hypothesised link between extraversion and manic depression (Thorpe, 1938: 324). However, since Jung actually linked extraversion with hysteria rather than manic depression (*CW*6 1921 §566), it was not Jung's hypothesis that the questionnaires tested. Criticism based on this particular misperception of Jung's typology continued to have influence for many years as the misrepresentation was repeated by later authors.

An important later criticism of the religious elements in Jung's theory can be traced back to Thorpe's use of the term 'doctrine' to describe psychoanalytical and other schools of thought. Thorpe's reference to Jung's and Adler's theories as 'doctrine' (Thorpe, 1938: 360) may reflect a desire to distinguish between schools of thought and research-based theories. The term was used earlier by McDougall (1933), who used it nonpejoratively in *Energies of Men: A Study of the Fundamentals of Dynamic Psychology* to mean 'teachings', as did Allport in relation to behavioural theories (Allport, 1937: 248, 255). Notwithstanding this usage, McDougall likened the psychoanalytic schools of Freud, Jung, and Adler to the 'narrow doctrines' of physicians (McDougall, 1933: 27). He described Jung's school as 'a very speculative doctrine' (McDougall, 1933: 316) but one which 'contains less of fundamental error [than Freud's] and, perhaps, more indications of the lines of progress of psychology in the future'. It is the words 'narrow' and 'speculative' rather than the word 'doctrine' that carry the weight of McDougall's critique, but with every subsequent use, the term 'doctrine' carried echoes of McDougall's remark.

Although Thorpe's textbook is unlikely to have been as influential as Allport's, textbooks on personality were few in the 1930s. Thorpe's was one of the first in the field and was influenced by the new behavioural theories of J. B. Watson; it marked a move to replace the use of case studies with the exclusive use of experimental research (Thorpe, 1938: viii–ix). Whereas Allport's (1937) text gave a more reliable and sympathetic picture of Jung's ideas, Thorpe's (1938) text contains and fails to correct distortions and misrepresentations that have been presented as truth in respect of Jung's theory. Thorpe's picture of Jung's work helped to sow doubts about the validity of Jung's theoretical concepts which endured for decades in the psychological academic world.

Textbooks published in Britain in the 1930s

There were no British textbooks from the 1930s in the sample and none were found subsequently.

The 1940s

Textbooks published in the United States

Two U.S. texts written in the 1940s, *The Collected Works* of Harry Stack Sullivan (1892–1949) (published posthumously 1953–1964)[1] and Murphy's *Personality: A Biosocial Approach to Origins and Structure* (1947), offered contrasting views of Jung's work and its value.

Sullivan admired Freud and became increasingly critical of Jung. In 1925, in *Schizophrenia as a Human Process*, he had acknowledged Jung as 'the primus in the field' of developing theories of schizophrenia in that he 'amplified Freud's repression theory' with his contention that dissociative processes could explain much of the bizarre speech and behaviour of schizophrenic patients (Sullivan, 1964: 32), but in 1948, Sullivan's tone was much more hostile:

> As you grow old in this game, you will discover that every system which has got any following among our fellow men has achieved astonishing results. Many of them, so far as I am concerned, are too preposterous to be taken seriously, such as the Jungian system with its racial unconscious, according to which you are a sort of bud on a great reservoir of God knows quite what.
>
> (Sullivan, 1964: 258)

A decade later in 1961, Allport made a similar point in *Pattern and Growth in Personality*, saying that, for Hegel and others, 'each person is but a single incarnation of a common life', stating that this similarity to 'islands [that] are connected by way of the sea bed' was the basis of Jung's 'racial unconscious and of archetypes' (Allport, 1961: 542), transmitting the remark onward to a new generation.

The second text from the 1940s, Murphy (1947), constitutes a unique theory in its own right while incorporating an overview of other theories. Gardner

Murphy's text did not explicitly compare Freud, Adler, and Jung, preferring to outline separately the contribution that each made towards understanding human nature. He drew on most of Jung's published works available at that time. Unperturbed by the statistical finding that most people fall between the types and seeing this as a consequence of the limitations of contemporary research, he was enthusiastic about Jung's 'valuable hypothesis on individual differences based on unconscious dynamics'. He expressed doubt that all schizophrenics are introverts and criticised the terms *introversion* and *extraversion* as 'foggy'. However, he saw these terms as clarifiable by further research. He argued that types in general are not pure, but like naturally occurring ore, they are full of impurities but should not therefore be thrown away (Murphy, 1947: 740).

Murphy also admired Jung's approach to dream interpretation:

> If the analyst wishes to determine the full significance of the dream, to read between the lines, to immerse himself in a world between heaven and earth in which everything tentative is real and impossibilities become possible, it may be better for him (at least for the time being) to dream along with his subject, to allow a certain tentativeness to lead him slowly into a semi-mystical world in which anything that happens to be a hypothetical possibility becomes an immediate reality. Exactly this path was trodden by Jung in his amazing *Psychology of the Unconscious.*
>
> (Murphy, 1947: 424)

He elucidated the logic of Jung's method of dream analysis and noted its value as a tool for understanding the nonlogical source material of dreams 'where the dreamer is a larger self than the waking man' and where 'methods that are different in every respect are called for from those of waking life'. Like Jung, Murphy held that 'the dream is often the most eloquent spokesman regarding personality' (Murphy, 1947: 432).

Textbooks published in Britain in the 1940s

Hans Eysenck's *Dimensions of Personality* (1947) primarily focused on the author's own developing trait theory and, selectively, on Jung's categories of introversion and extraversion (ignoring the rest of his theory). Like Thorpe in the United States in the 1930s, Eysenck linked Jung with Kretschmer and Kraepelin. He knew, however, that it was Kraepelin who, in 1899, established a dichotomy between schizophrenia and manic-depressive illness and corrected Thorpe's (1938) error, confirming that it was schizophrenia and hysteria that Jung regarded as opposites. Eysenck traced this confusion to Henderson and Gillespie's 1943 *Textbook of Psychiatry*, which asserted that Kretschmer's cyclothymic personality represented an extreme degree of extraversion. Eysenck cited Bowlby: 'a moment's reflection will show the serious confusion in these passages' (1940, cited in Eysenck, 1947: 14). Eysenck was aware that, for Jung, introversion and neurosis were different, and he stated that, where a more accurate questionnaire was used, the experimental results, taken with Eysenck's own, strongly supported both Jung's and his position that the two factors, introversion and neuroticism, are independent of one another (Eysenck, 1947: 52). In the 1940s, though not later, Eysenck's treatment of Jung's work was fair and accurate, although his emphasis on Jung's typology rather than his wider theory conveyed a partial picture, thereby limiting its perceived value.

The 1950s

Textbooks published in the United States

The sample includes five U.S. texts from the 1950s: Cattell's *Personality: A Systematic Theoretical and Factual Study* (1950), Blum's *Psychoanalytic Theories of Personality* (1953), McCary's *Psychology and Personality: Six Modern Approaches* (1956), Guilford's *Personality* (1959), and Progoff's *The Death and Rebirth of Psychology* (1956), which became an important secondary source for textbook authors, teachers, and advanced students, as well as for analytical psychologists.

We see that a trait-oriented psychologist, Cattell, took an evenhanded approach. The author of a psychoanalytical text, Blum, compared all other psychoanalytical theories, including Jung's, with Freud's, using the term 'neo–Freudians', though giving an accurate account of their differences from Freud. McCary's edited collection exemplified the negative effect of omitting Jung's theory from discussions of types and traits and of cross-cultural approaches, where it might be expected to appear. Guilford suggested a research programme that was never fully taken up by Jungian scholars, and Progoff balanced his enthusiasm for Jung's theory with an acknowledgement of Jung's shortcomings in clarifying some of his paradoxical and conceptually difficult ideas.

Cattell's (1950) treatment of Jung was brief but fair. Cattell's book mainly concerns his own trait theory; he describes Jung's introversion and extraversion traits briefly. Cattell criticised psychoanalytic theories in general on the grounds that they were constructed from clinical cases and so needed confirmation by other means. In fact, Jung did not make very much use of the case study. However, this is a reasonable general criticism.

Blum's (1953) exposition of Jung's theory is brief but accurate. Although he admits to using a secondary source (Jacobi, 1962), he consulted a range of Jung's pre–1935 work. Blum noted that Jung's view differed from Freud's in significant ways. He was one of many textbook writers who compared all other psychoanalytical theories of personality to Freud's, repeatedly using the term 'neo–Freudian', even though he acknowledged their separate and independent views.

J.L. McCary (1956) edited a collection of lectures from a symposium on personality held at the University of Houston in 1954. The book was aimed at advanced students. Jung's work is strikingly absent. For example, Leopold Bellack mentions Freud and Murray, but not Jung, as early psychoanalytic thinkers, and Jung's influence on Murray (see pp. 31–32 and 132) is not acknowledged. Jung is not mentioned at all in the 'types and traits' section, which is surprising given that Jung's work was in the forefront of the field at that time. Papers in this section focus exclusively on Freud's oral, anal, and phallic types. Margaret Mead's chapter on cross-cultural approaches to personality makes no mention of Jung, although Jung had been a pioneer in undertaking cross-cultural psychological work on myths and dreams. These omissions are significant since McCary mentions other psychoanalytic theorists and was attempting to bring together key figures and key ideas, seeing advantages in integrating theories.

Guilford (1959), who was interested mainly in traits and their measurement, focused exclusively on Jung's typology in his presentation of Jung's theory. He criticised Jung's introversion/extraversion concept on the grounds that trait concepts 'created by fiat' should be regarded as hypotheses, subject to verification or rejection on the basis of empirical tests (Guilford, 1959: 88). There was also the problem that two types were not enough (1959: 91). Guilford put forward the suggestion that types are like syndromes, combinations of qualities, or attributes which are interrelated and can ultimately be specified, then subjected to testing (1959: 98). Guilford's suggestion pointed the way to a potential research programme that has only partially been taken up by Jungian scholars.

Progoff's comparative review of the theories of Freud, Jung, Adler, and Rank in *The Death and Rebirth of Psychology* (1956) was read by advanced students and became an influential secondary resource that is cited by several textbook authors (Bischof, 1964; Schultz, 1976; Smith & Vetter, 1982). Progoff took the position that 'psychological work only fulfils itself when it goes beyond psychology' (Progoff, 1956: 262). He argued that psychology requires a theory and practice that approaches the human personality with an awareness of its magnitude and that uses psychological concepts as instruments with which to develop man's spiritual and creative aspects. In Progoff's view, Jung's religious ideas, together with his concept of the self as both the source and the culmination of the desire for fulfilment, offered a conception of man as an organism that was of inherent psychological depth and spiritual magnitude, setting the task of personality development beyond that of adaptation to a competitive world.

Progoff was close to Jung and was both well informed about his ideas and sympathetic to them. Nevertheless he raised an important criticism of Jung's concept of self. Progoff acknowledged that the fact that Jung spoke of the self differently at different times had led to misconceptions. He recognised that, in Jung's schema, individuation was a paradoxical process, being both natural and inherent, *and* a psychological discipline that seeks to work with that process (Progoff, 1956: 180–181). He held, though, that Jung's failure to make these distinctions clear led to problems of misunderstanding. However, he felt that this shortcoming in Jung's explanatory style was, in part, due to the conceptual difficulty Jung encountered.

Textbooks published in Britain in the 1950s

I reviewed three British texts from the 1950s, Eysenck's *Uses and Abuses of Psychology* (1953), Notcutt's *The Psychology of Personality* published in the same year (1953), and Eysenck's *Sense and Nonsense in Psychology* (1957). Only Notcutt's text can be precisely described as a textbook, but Eysenck's paperback volumes fulfilled a similar function and had significant impact, being read ubiquitously by students and intellectuals. All were negatively critical of Jung's theoretical ideas.

Eysenck maintained that psychoanalysis was not a science since psychoanalytical thinkers preferred a goal of understanding to that of explaining. He cited Jung as a particular example since he understood Jung to have explicitly rejected scientific methodology in favour of subjectivity. In fact, Jung recognised that there were limits to what psychology could achieve. He valued empiricism and always represented his comparative methodology as scientific and based on empirical observation. Eysenck was strongly critical of anti-empiricism, arguing that writers who rejected the methods of science should not then claim the results. Quoting Humpty Dumpty in Lewis Carroll's *Through the Looking Glass*, he suggested that psychoanalysts (including Freud) 'turn meaning inside out', using words to mean what they choose them to mean. Psychoanalysis, he said, is strong on hypotheses and weak on proof and verification. 'Its hypotheses are almost impossible to test' (Eysenck, 1953: 228–229).

It was in this publication that Eysenck remarked that all Freudians have Freudian dreams whilst all Jungians have correspondingly Jungian dreams (Eysenck, 1953: 231). Here too he made the much-quoted observation, based on his research, that two out of every three patients suffering from neuroses improve without being given any psychotherapy at all (Eysenck, 1953: 233), adding that in schools of psychoanalysis, 'criticisms from outside are ignored, [and] utterance is dogmatic. . . . These are the mental mechanisms associated with the growth of a religious orthodoxy, not with the progress of science' (Eysenck, 1953: 240). None of this was specifically directed at Jung, and Eysenck's remarks were equally hostile towards Freud, but the general criticism that psychoanalysis was practised like a religion discouraged people from looking at Jung's ideas and still does so.

Notcutt's (1953) text appeared in a Methuen series of 'Manuals of Modern Psychology', which included Eysenck's *The Structure of Human Personality.* Notcutt was interested in the emerging trait theories. His comments on Freudian psychoanalysis echo Eysenck's almost word for word:

> In spite of official opposition [psychoanalysis] has shown an astonishing power to win adherents, and for many of them it has had the force of a religion or way of life. But an unfortunate result of all the abuse to which the psycho-analysts have been subjected has been their tendency to form

> a sect, to pursue their own meditations in sympathetic company, protected from outside criticism, and reading only one another's works.
>
> (Notcutt, 1953: 16)

Citing no specific examples in support of his view, he added that 'At times, psycho-analysts appear to have been content with standards of evidence that would hardly have satisfied anyone more critical than a palmist or a teacup reader' (Notcutt, 1953: 16). Concerning Jung's typology, Notcutt agreed with Jung's conclusion that introversion is a feature of schizophrenia. However, he stated that the fascination that Jung, McDougall, and Kretschmer had with the notion of a symmetrical antithesis of schizophrenic and manic depressive personalities 'has served for many years to obscure and confuse the picture of psychosis' (Notcutt, 1953: 70). As we have seen, this was Thorpe's (1938) error misrepresenting Jung's view, which Eysenck (1947) had tried to correct (see above, p. 127).

In his 1957 text *Sense and Nonsense in Psychology*, Eysenck repeated his criticism that, in obedience to the analyst, Freudian patients begin to have Freudian dreams, while Jungian analysands dream in Jungian dream symbols (Eysenck, 1957: 168). This was because the person being analysed begins to learn the symbolic language of the analyst and obediently makes use of it in their dreams. Eysenck's general point, that dream analysis is unscientific as no control group is ever used in experimental studies of dream interpretation, applied to both Jung and Freud. With respect to Jung's comparative mythological evidence for the universality of dream symbolism, Eysenck argued that it is easy to show that the symbols are actually related to the education and experience of the dreamer and are therefore not innate (Eysenck, 1957: 173). This was a criticism that Jung never adequately answered and should now be researched.

Overall, the treatment of Jung by British textbook authors in this decade tended to be restricted to his typology and was negative in tone. Notcutt reiterated the misrepresentation of Jung's position that had been made by Thorpe in 1938 but had been corrected by Eysenck in 1947, and Eysenck criticised Jung's use of comparative mythological evidence for the universality of dream symbolism.

The 1960s

Textbooks published in the United States

There were seven U.S. textbooks from the 1960s in the sample: Wepman and Heine's *Concepts of Personality* (1963), Bischof's *Interpreting Personality Theories* (1964), Sahakian's *Psychology of Personality: Readings in Theory* (1965), Byrne's *An Introduction to Personality: A Research Approach* (1966), Borgatta and Lambert's *Handbook of Personality Theory and Research* (1968), Mehrabian's *An Analysis of*

Personality Theories (1968), and Norbeck and colleagues' *The Study of Personality: An Interdisciplinary Appraisal* (1968). By 1961, the year of his death, Jung was acknowledged as an eminent figure with a worldwide reputation. The positive treatment of his work in this decade may reflect the respect in which he had come to be held at this time. For example, Ginsburg in Wepman and Heine (1963) proposed an innovative application of Jung's theory of archetypes. Byrne (1966) emphasised Jung's influence on others, quoting in full Murray's 1940 description of Jung as the first full-blooded, spherical, and Goethian intelligence he had ever met (Byrne, 1966: 286), while Stein in Borgatta and Lambert (1968: 930–931) listed research that lent support to Jung's type and creativity concepts. Sahakian's (1965: 48–49) biographical notes focus on Jung's career, his travels, and his many honorary degrees, and Bischof (1964: 178–223) provides insightful expositions of the most complex of Jung's theoretical terms and constructs drawn from a comprehensive range of primary sources and from relevant research.

On the negative side, Mehrabian (1968) expounded the ideas of Murphy and Murray without mentioning Murray's indebtedness to Jung. La Barre in Norbeck and colleagues (1968: 81) described Jung and others as neo–Freudians rather than as independent theorists. La Barre suggested that neo–Freudians including Jung 'projected and erected their own unanalysed portions into a system' which, though in a certain sense true (see Chapter 3 on the link between Jung's *Red Book* and his typology), is phrased so as to imply that this necessarily undermines its value. Repeating a term that had been in circulation since Glover published his scathing (1950) attack on Jung, Bischof (1964: 33) described Jung's disaffection with Freud as 'defection', which links him more strongly with Freud than was actually the case and suggests disloyalty where an allegiance is owed.[2] Nevertheless, Bischof, who met Jung and consulted with him in writing his chapter on Jung, condensed a great deal of material without distortion or loss of meaning and described Jung as 'an original and provocative writer whose theory is different from others' and whose theory is a hopeful one (1964: 180).

Textbooks published in Britain in the 1960s

In Britain in the 1960s, theorists exclusively followed the trait-theory approach. I reviewed two texts, Foulds, Caine, and Owen's *Personality and Personal Illness* (1965) and Eysenck's *Fact and Fiction in Psychology* (1965).

Foulds and colleagues (1965) were both supportive and critical of Jung's theoretical propositions. Their cogent criticism, based on an accurate account of Jung's position and evidence from research, was that there was virtually no support for the idea that a balance between introversion and extraversion was involved in neurosis (Foulds et al., 1965: 26–27). The opportunity for others to address this criticism via a programme of research was unfortunately not taken up.

Eysenck (1965) attacked Jung's conception of introversion-extraversion, saying, firstly, that it did not originate with Jung (Jung did not claim to have originated the terms) and, secondly, that 'what is new in Jung's typology is not true, and what is true is not new', without providing details to substantiate his claim (Eysenck, 1965: 58).

In the 1960s in academic psychology in Britain, the teaching of personality theory was almost exclusively concerned with trait theory and its research. There were increasingly divergent developments in personality theory and its teaching on either side of the Atlantic. In Britain, psychoanalytical thinking was marginalised from academia.

The 1970s

Textbooks published in the United States

A great number of textbooks on personality were published in the United States in the 1970s. In this decade, the two streams, scientific experimental and psychoanalytic, were equally represented. Towards the end of the decade, Monte (1977) and Stolorow and Atwood (1979) applied their theory of intersubjectivity to personality theories, suggesting that they should be understood as projections of the theorist's own personality.

In the 1970s, several authors provided well-informed and comprehensive accounts of Jung's ideas on personality. Arndt's *Theories of Personality* (1974), Maduro and Wheelwright's 'Analytical Psychology' in R. Corsini's *Current Personality Theories* (1977), Monte's *Beneath the Mask: An Introduction to Theories of Personality* (1977), and Hall and Lindzey's *Theories of Personality* (1978) drew from numerous references from every decade of Jung's career and emphasised the complexity of his theory. In 1977, Monte gives in-depth treatment to conceptually difficult aspects of Jung's ideas such as the concepts of equivalence and entropy, the symbolic linking of Christ with self, and the notion of antinomies and opposites as inherent in Jung's conceptualisation of the God-self. Hall and Lindzey consulted a large range of secondary sources not available to earlier authors (Cohen, 1975; von Franz, 1975; Hannah, 1976; Jaffé, 1971; Progoff, 1973; Stern, 1976). Arndt's *Theories of Personality* (1974) includes more references to Jungian texts than to those of other theorists he reviewed, suggesting a particular interest in Jung's work. Schultz, in *Theories of Personality* (1976), made use of a large range of primary and secondary sources. On the other hand, Levy's *Conceptions of Personality: Theories and Research* (1970) is less comprehensive, with few references to primary sources and none from Jung's later work. Mischel's description of Jung's theory in *Introduction to Personality* (1971) is fair but reductive in its brevity, being based on only two of Jung's most popular works, *Psychological Types* (1921/1977) and Jung and Jaffé's *Memories, Dreams, Reflections* (1963).

Complexity in Jung's theory is perceived differently by different authors. In *Personality Theories: A Comparative Analysis* (1972), Maddi noted that in Jung's theory, several core characteristics are involved which tend to oppose one another (Maddi, 1972: 84) and cautioned that the value in his theory is lost when it is tackled only with the tools of logic (1972: 75). Hall and Lindzey described Jung's knowledge and depth of understanding as 'probably unsurpassed' (Hall & Lindzey, 1978: 117). However, Levy in *Conceptions of Personality: Theories and Research* (1970) felt that Jung's principle of opposition was vague, diffuse, and lacking in explanatory value (Levy, 1970: 105), and the scientific basis of his concept of the collective unconscious 'so remote . . . that there is little point in dwelling on such speculations' (1970: 115). The accusation of vagueness dates back to Boring (1950). In his classic *History of Experimental Psychology*, Boring refers to 'the vagueness of [Jung's] theories' but cites no specific examples of vagueness (1950: 711).

Like Arndt (1974) and Monte (1977), Maddi saw the importance of spirituality in Jung's ideas and concluded that this accounted for his wide appeal (Maddi, 1972: 95), as did Schultz, who acknowledged that Jung's interest in the occult, the supernatural, and religion was both the source of most of the criticism levelled at him and the reason for his popularity in the United States (Schultz, 1976: 137). Hall and Lindzey agreed with Schultz and balanced this with Jung's own view that occultism, mysticism, and religion *should* be studied as evidence for archetypes (Hall & Lindzey, 1978: 142).

Mischel (1971), Lindzey, Hall, and Manosevitz (1973), Arndt (1974), and Schultz (1976) compare Jung with Freud. Mischel's brief description of Jung's theory is found under the heading 'Neo-Freudian psychoanalytic developments', and Schultz (1976) referred to Jung as a 'defector' from Freud, which, as I have suggested earlier, both casts Jung's work as a departure from an assumed orthodoxy and implies infidelity to a cause. Notwithstanding this, Schultz concluded that Jung's theory is 'unlike any other' and 'stands apart from all other approaches to personality in its complexity and unique emphasis' (Schultz, 1976: 119). Arndt's comparison of Jung's work with Freud's favours Jung.

Similarly divergent pictures are given of both the research value and the research basis of Jung's theory. Maddi criticised 'believers in Jung' for their lack of interest in research (Maddi, 1972: 360) but acknowledged that research support exists for Jung's introversion/extraversion dimension. Maddi's justifiable critique was that 'belief' leads to neglect other forms of validation, but his use of the word 'believer' has echoes of Thorpe's (1938) use of the term 'doctrine' (see here p. 95). Mischel (1971) agreed that the introversion-extraversion dimension has been 'extensively researched', and Lindzey, Hall, and Manosevitz referred to Jung's typology as research based, noting that it had produced a psychological test, the Myers-Briggs Type Indicator (1962). They also observed that systematic evaluation of Jung's personality theory was increasing (Lindzey, Hall, & Manosevitz, 1973: 37, 57–66). Maduro and Wheelwright give a long list of potential sources of validation for the existence of archetypes: psychedelic drug experiences, Levi-Strauss's structural theories ('binary oppositions'), the work of the ethologist Konrad Lorenz, Piaget's innate 'schemata', Spitz's 'innate organisers', Melanie Klein's 'unconscious phantasy' or 'unconscious knowledge', Chomsky's innate grammar, and modern ego psychology's archetypes in action as the unfolding of a genetic social character in response to the environment (Maduro & Wheelwright, 1977: 113). They emphasise that Jung was both the first psychiatrist to apply scientific methods to disturbed patients and the first to produce experimental data on unconscious processes (Maduro & Wheelwright, 1977: 106). Hall and Lindzey, on the other hand, caution that ingenuity would be required for hypotheses from Jung's theory to be tested (Hall & Lindzey, 1978: 149).

Maduro and Wheelwright emphasise the applications of Jung's theory, saying that his therapy is unique, offering an optimistic approach for older patients, patients suffering from schizophrenia, and people with borderline profiles (Maduro & Wheelwright, 1977: 108), and that it generated projective and other psychological tests (1977: 106). Some authors in the 1970s emphasised Jung's wide influence on others. Schultz called attention to the continuing growth in Jung's influence more than a decade after his death (Schultz, 1976: 119). Maduro and Wheelwright (1977: 106) mention Jung's influence on Murray, Rorschach, Binswanger, and Boss and the contribution of his ideas in education (Maduro & Wheelwright, 1977: 109). Hall and Lindzey mention Jung's influence beyond psychology, for example on the writer Herman Hesse (Hall & Lindzey, 1978: 146). They point out that by the end of the 1970s, Jungian institutes were established in many cities. They conclude that Jung's wide influence is incalculable. Hall and Lindzey were the only textbook authors who drew attention (1978: 148–149) to the possibility of the existence of unconscious, and therefore unacknowledged but discernible, influences of Jung's ideas on the work of others such as Maslow and Erickson.

In this decade more than any other in the United States, there was great emphasis on biographical material.[3] As in the previous decade, some authors, such as Schultz, selected biographical material that emphasised childhood pathology, failing to balance this with a sense of Jung's later achievements (Schultz, 1976: 119–121). In contrast, Maduro and Wheelwright (1977: 86–87) and Hall and Lindzey (1978: 114–115) focussed on Jung's career and emphasised that he had developed an independent orientation to the unconscious which differed significantly from Freud's before they met in 1906. Maduro and Wheelwright show how Jung's differences from Freud grew as he discovered evidence of unconscious contents that did not fit well within a Freudian framework (Maduro & Wheelwright, 1977: 85–87), and Hall and Lindzey note that the lines of Jung's analytical psychology were being worked on throughout their relationship (Hall & Lindzey, 1978: 114).

Three authors, Monte in *Beneath the Mask: An Introduction to Theories of Personality* (1977) and Stolorow and Atwood in *Faces in a Cloud: Subjectivity in Personality* (1979), maintain that personality theorists are not and cannot be objective and that their theories are the results of their projection of their own experiences. While Monte emphasised the creative aspects and saw the 1913 through 1917 period of Jung's life as a voluntary exploration of his own unconscious to which many of his later theoretical views could be traced (Monte, 1977: 140), Stolorow and Atwood took the view that personality theorists were not aware that they were not objective and that this made their theories questionable (Stolorow & Atwood, 1979: 22). Monte agreed with Stern (1976) that Jung's childhood was lonely but emphasised its positive outcome in that it enabled Jung to accept the rational and irrational as partners and to 'welcome the mysteries with relish' (Monte, 1977: 167). Stolorow and Atwood emphasised Jung's childhood defences against anxiety. They suggest that these drove him to propose a dialogue with the unconscious that led to a kind of symbiotic bliss in which the unconscious would supply all the conscious's needs like the symbiotic mother (Stolorow & Atwood, 1979: 77–78). This is a misreading of Jung's accounts of the conscious/unconscious confrontation, which he held leads to an awareness of 'divine conflict' with the result that one is at odds with oneself (*CW*11 1952b §659).

Stolorow and Atwood are inclined to distort Jung's ideas by representing them in object-relations terms. For example, they describe Jung's concept of the archetypes as 'primitive, highly aggrandised, omnipotent objects' (Stolorow & Atwood, 1979: 75), whereas Jung considered archetypes to be dynamic forms of ideas (see Chapter 1, p. 22; and Chapter 5, pp. 102, 106). They reinterpret Jung's dreams and important experiences in terms of their own theoretical approach which sees such experiences as signs of pathology.[4] Their analysis was prejudicial because the emphasis on these experiences as a defence against a childhood that was pathologically lonely helped fuel the myth of Jung's near-psychosis. Jung himself viewed these experiences as a subject for conscious reflection which led to the development of his later ideas (see Jung & Jaffé, 1963: 65).

Corsini in *Current Personality Theories* (1977) approached the problem of fairness and partiality by inviting experts on each personality theorist to contribute chapters and to critically evaluate the theory. As well as maximising fairness, this minimises errors, as the author of each chapter is by definition well informed and in sympathy with the theorist's ideas. Its disadvantage is its benevolence.

The U.S. textbooks of the 1970s contained both criticisms and significant evidence-based refutations and corrections of earlier errors. Maddi criticised Jung for inconsistency but concluded that there may have been good reasons for Jung's juggling with complexities and a paradoxical sense of unity (Maddi, 1972: 93). Schultz stated that Jung's writing was 'frustrating to read' and 'beset with apparent inconsistencies and contradictions' (Schultz, 1976: 137), though he gave no specific examples of poor writing, inconsistencies, or any indication that other views on these matters exist – for example, those of Progoff (1956: 177–187), who suggests that apparent inconsistencies could be the result of the fact that terms like the *self* have different meanings in other systems of thought, some of which differ from Jung's meaning, and some of which derive from traditions that have contributed to Jung's meaning.

On the other hand, Hall and Lindzey corrected errors made in earlier critiques. They took a critically reflective approach to earlier texts and identified the sources of critiques, such as Boring's (1950) dismissal of Jung's psychology, and Peters (1953), who found Jung's psychology 'so mysterious as to be almost undiscussable' (cited in Hall & Lindzey, 1978: 147). They also draw attention to examples of uneven treatment of Jung in earlier texts, such as Boring 'devot[ing] six pages to Freud and four *lines* to Jung' and Murphy 'devot[ing] six pages to Jung compared with a chapter of twenty-four pages given over to Freud' (Hall & Lindzey, 1978: 147).

Several of the texts I reviewed went into many editions and so are likely to have had and continue to have enormous influence on U.S. psychologists and psychological therapists of today. A number of U.S. authors were enthusiastic about Jung's project and gave accurate, comprehensive, and sympathetic summaries, while others were strongly critical. Some authors traced the origins of frequently repeated criticisms of Jung's work and provided counterarguments and refutations. Students reading textbooks from this decade get a very different picture of Jung depending on which text they read.

Textbooks published in Britain in the 1970s

While publications in the United States were numerous, there was only one British textbook in the sample from the 1970s, a short paperback by Peck and Whitlow published in 1975, which mentions Jung only briefly.

In *Approaches to Personality*, Peck and Whitlow (1975) dismissed Jung as a major influence on contemporary developments, which, from the vantage point of experimental psychology in the UK in 1975, was probably true. There is some unevenness with respect to the treatment of psychoanalytical theorists in this text. Peck and Whitlow outlined both Freud's and Klein's theories in detail, whereas other broadly psychoanalytical approaches such as Jung's are simply described as schisms from Freud which did not play a major role in contemporary theory of personality (Peck & Whitlow, 1975: 27). They mention Freud's but not Jung's influence beyond psychology: on anthropology, mythology, and education (1975: 30). The sparse treatment of Jung in this text is paralleled by an absence of references to Jung's work in the bibliography, which suggests that the authors did not have or did not make use of first-hand knowledge of Jung's work. They admit that they based their opinions of psychoanalysis on Rachman (1971) and Brody (1972), who claimed there were no unequivocal demonstrations of unconscious phenomena in controlled conditions (Peck & Whitlow, 1975: 32, 35). This seems surprising, since studies of memory for emotionally laden words had revealed the effects of unconscious emotional processing, and other studies suggesting that language and emotional processing is largely unconscious were well known by 1975.[5]

Peck and Whitlow's book may not be the best-known textbook on personality, but it was easily accessible to students as a short inexpensive paperback edition and filled a niche as a general introduction to personality from a research viewpoint.

It is interesting that there have been very few of the 'primary source reader' type of textbook published in Britain, the one exception being Lazarus and Opton's *Personality* (1977) that ran into many editions. This may simply reflect a different style of teaching in British universities, with textbooks being used more as supplementary resources than as the bases of courses.

The 1980s

Textbooks published in the United States

In the 1980s a developing sense emerged that personality theorists needed to find a way of synthesising ideas previously regarded as divergent. Whilst fair and positive treatment of Jung's ideas can be found in this decade, errors, distortions, and misrepresentations can still be seen. Ewen, in *An Introduction to Theories of Personality* (1980), for example, warns that 'Jung's model of the psyche is considerably more chaotic than Freud's' (Ewen, 1980: 78). By 'more chaotic', Ewen seems to mean that the Jungian unconscious can exert control over the personality, 'whereas the Freudian id remains entirely unconscious' and, in Jung's theory, 'unconscious components may fuse together, rather than remaining separate and distinct'; I wonder whether Ewen derives this from the greater fluidity and dynamism of some elements in Jung's theory. He adds that 'Jung conceives of the ego as a relatively weak entity that is often at the mercy of more powerful forces, tossed like a shuttlecock between the demands of reality and those of the unconscious' (1980: 78). This is not an accurate reflection of Jung's account of the ego and the unconscious as mutually enriching, enhancing one another. However, Ewen brings all of these aspects of Jung's theory into his description of Jungian psychotherapy (Ewen, 1980: 104) and summarises every aspect of Jung's theory, including religion and alchemy. His chapter is directly based on Jung's work and mentions a range of relevant research.

As in previous decades, authors used biographical material selectively. Smith and Vetter in *Theoretical Approaches to Personality* (1982) chose material that emphasised Jung's 'difficult childhood', his teenage spell of fainting, and his religious concerns and included only a relatively brief account of his adult life (Smith & Vetter, 1982: 89). Feist, in *Theories of Personality* (1985), also selected some of the most bizarre pieces of biographical information postulated about Jung (Feist, 1985: 99). Misreading Ellenberger, who mentions a rumour that Jung's grandfather was an illegitimate son of Goethe (1970: 660–661), Feist gives prominence to Jung's alleged belief that he was Goethe's grandson and a reincarnation of him (Feist, 1985: 96). Feist also states that, in his period of self-analysis (1913–1916), 'Jung suspended the formulation of new theoretical concepts' (Feist, 1985: 98), which, as we have seen in Chapter 3, was not the case. In contrast, Massey says that both Freud and Jung had a creative illness (Massey, 1981: 25) and that Jung continued to work and function in his large family during his period of self-exploration (1981: 84).

Some old charges were repeated without critical reflection or balancing views. Feist, for example, suggests a contradiction between Jung's belief that he was a medical psychologist and scientific observer of human behaviour and the view of 'many readers' who 'may regard him as a fantasy writer, a philosopher, or an introspective mystic' (Feist, 1985: 124). Though this illustrates a point of debate, there is nothing to guide the reader as to how to decide between these two views, and no evidence or arguments are given. Without an understanding of the arguments and counter-arguments, the student might well conclude that Jung was deluded.

Some criticisms were made on the basis of misinterpretation. Ewen states that Jung was irresponsible in suggesting that if ideas arise from the unconscious, they are not one's own, whereas Freud took the view that we are primarily responsible for our psyche and our actions (Ewen, 1980: 111). His judgement that Jung's position lacked morality overlooks Jung's point that individuation is achieved by bringing dangerous and aggressive instincts into conscious awareness and thus into the sphere of personal responsibility. Feist criticised Jung's theory for totally lacking operational definitions (Feist, 1985: 125), seeming to have been unaware that Jung was one of the first psychologists to offer a set of operational definitions (*CW*6 1921 §672–844). Feist also criticised Jung for lack of parsimony, saying that 'that part of the theory pertaining to the conscious and the unconscious is probably more unwieldy and esoteric than others which address themselves to the same topics' (Feist, 1985: 125); he does not say which other theorists he has in mind.

Both Ewen (1980) and Smith and Vetter (1982) listed criticisms and controversies around Jung, with references, although not necessarily the original sources. Ewen identified P. Stern (1976) as the source of the criticism that Jung's religious synthesis is 'shallow and unsuccessful' and as one of several sources of the criticism of conceptual confusion (Ewen, 1980: 110). Smith and Vetter not only give sources for critiques of Jung's theory but also give evidence and counterarguments (Smith & Vetter, 1982: 103–105). For example, they attributed to 'the Freudian School' the criticism that Jung's theory lacks developmental concepts, since the Freudian School[6] compared Jung's negatively with Freud's detailed treatment of the developmental process. Smith and Vetter argued that Jung offered social learning and adaptation as the mechanisms for development combined with natural growth (Smith & Vetter, 1982: 105).

The authors of the 1980s U.S. personality textbooks were well informed. They drew from a wide range of primary sources and gave substantial coverage of Jung's theory. Although Smith and Vetter (1982) based their description on a limited number of primary sources (eight essays from the *Collected Works*), the other U.S. texts, Ewen (1980), Massey (1981), and Feist (1985), are comprehensively referenced and researched. Feist's chapter on Jung was based on original sources spanning the whole of Jung's published work from 1916 to 1961. Ewen's (1980) references to Jung's work covered most aspects of his theory. Ewen used direct quotations to illustrate some of the more difficult terms, explaining that many were used by Jung in unique and special ways. Massey (1981) explored Jung's religious side more than any other textbook writer, presenting it as the centrepoint of Jung's view of self-development. Massey also fully explicated Jung's idea that the God-image included the animal instinctual side of human nature as well as the higher side, with all the disturbing and paradoxical implications of this idea. He included Jung's discussion of Christ as the archetype of self (Massey, 1981: 92–93). His description of the transcendent function is followed by a rare and useful attempt to pull out from Jung's work a sense of how the transcendent function might actually work (1981: 94). Few authors of general texts on personality have had sufficient grasp of Jung's thinking to enable them to attempt this.

More than in previous decades, the U.S. texts of the 1980s attempted to give a balanced view. Massey noted Jung's argument that psychology should involve a more comprehensive study than scientific materialism allows (Massey, 1981: 101). He is the only author to mention Jung's private publication of his *Seven Sermons of the Dead*, his unpublished *Black Books*, and the *Red Book* (1981: 84). Ewen appreciated that Jung had been the first to recommend that analysts themselves undergo analysis (Ewen, 1980: 106).

With respect to Jung's wider influence, Ewen noted that Jung's ideas on religion have been regarded by theologians as major contributions to religious thought (Ewen, 1980: 107). Smith and Vetter (1982: 106) mentioned Jung's influence on theorists who have modified and expanded his ideas – for example, Read (1945), Adler (1948), Wickes (1948), and Progoff (1953, 1956). Smith and Vetter also acknowledge his influence on the development of the Rorschach and Thematic Apperception Tests and the incorporation of his ideas into the theories of Maslow and Rogers. However, they contrast with this the relative lack of scholarship in the Jungian field and 'the small amount of space allocated to his theory in most histories of psychology and psychiatry', which has limited his sphere of influence, and link this with the concurrent development of behaviour theory. Smith and Vetter conclude that the very characteristic which may have led to his being neglected, namely, Jung's ability to deviate from the prevailing behaviourist influence in psychology at the same time as maintaining his differences from Freud, made him daringly and 'refreshingly different' (Smith & Vetter, 1982: 107).

Feist evaluated Jung's theory as a meaningful framework that organised known observations, added new dimensions, and was the broadest personality theory in scope. He regarded Jung as the only modern personality theorist to include such a broad scope of human activity within a single theoretical framework (Feist, 1985: 124). At the same time, Feist saw Jung's collective unconscious as his most controversial and distinctive concept (1985: 110). He believed the typology was verifiable but accepted that it is more difficult to generate hypotheses from the *archetypes* and the *collective unconscious*, though these might be seen as explanatory concepts (1985: 124). Feist appreciated that Jung looked beyond psychology in his search for data and that he believed that personality was not the prerogative of any one discipline (1985: 125).

It may be seen that a more critical evaluative perspective became apparent in the 1980s in the development of textbooks of personality in the United States. At the same time, the decade is primarily characterised by the recognition of a need to synthesise theories rather than to contrast competing theories. For example, Massey's text is organised chronologically to reflect cumulative developments in theories of personality. Each theorist is compared with those previously discussed. At the same time, each theory is presented in its own terms, respecting its integrity as a perspective on human existence. Feist (1985) took the position that each theorist has a unique philosophical orientation shaped by experience, so that diverse and divergent theories may all contribute to a holistic model or synthesis. Evaluation of a personality theory should be based on its usefulness rather than its 'truth' (Feist, 1985: 6). The emergence of a synthesising attitude in the United States had a positive influence on the treatment of Jung's ideas in this decade.

Textbooks published in Britain in the 1980s

The synthesising attitude that was developing in the United States in the 1980s was not prominent in the UK in this decade. The sample included Hampson's *The Construction of Personality: An Introduction* (1988) and the second edition of a text published earlier in the decade in the United States, Ewen's *An Introduction to Theories of Personality* (1984).

Hampson's research-based textbook looked at personality from three angles: psychologists' theories, lay theories, and the self-perspective. Her treatment of Jung is confined to a single paragraph (Hampson, 1988: 47), in which she noted that Eysenck was influenced by Jung's theory of personality, and offered a simplified summary of the terms *introversion* and *extraversion*. The single primary source cited is Jung's *Psychological Types* (1921/1977), and her brief summary focuses on one part of Jung's theory as if it were the whole. However, her book is short relative to some of the American texts of the 1980s.[7]

Robert B. Ewen's *Introduction to Theories of Personality*, first published in 1980 in New York, came out in the UK in 1984. As we have seen, Ewen's coverage of Jung's theory was substantial and lists the sources of some of the criticisms and controversies surrounding Jung (see above). That this edition was published in the UK may be an indication that American approaches to personality theory were becoming established in British universities alongside the trait-theory approach.

The 1990s

Textbooks published in the United States

During the 1990s, the field of personality theory in the United States continued to develop a synthesis approach. At the same time, textbooks which featured major historical figures remained popular. Several reprints and new editions of previously published textbooks were circulating and had wide influence. These included editions from Hall and Lindzey, Hjelle and Ziegler, Maddi, Monte, and Schultz, whose textbook life spanned two and in some cases three decades.

As well as some very thorough accounts, some misrepresentations and unsupported negative criticisms can be found in the 1990s texts as in the sample texts from previous decades. For example, Hjelle and Ziegler selected biographical material for *Personality Theories: Basic Assumption, Research and Applications* that emphasised Jung's childhood fantasy that he was two different people. They suggest that his period of 'severe mental crisis' had 'brought him to the edge of madness', becoming 'so debilitated that he resigned his lectureship at the University of Zurich' (Hjelle & Ziegler, 1992: 170). Hergenhahn was the only textbook author to observe in *An Introduction to Theories of Personality* (1994/1999) that biographical accounts of Jung appear to be contradictory, pointing out that while Stern portrayed Jung as a prepsychotic (if not psychotic) opportunist with anti–Semitic and pro–Nazi leanings, Hannah portrayed him as brilliant, sensitive, humanitarian, neither anti–Semitic nor pro–Nazi, nor a madman, in biographies which were both published in 1976 (Hergenhahn, 1994: 63). Hergenhahn decided to stick to biographical facts over which there was little disagreement and commented that Jung emerged from his period of self-reflection with a theory of personality that bore only a remote resemblance to Freud's (1994: 72).

Some 1990s authors explain Jung's terms and concepts so briefly as to verge on the misleading. For example, in *Theories of Personality: Understanding Persons* (1996), Cloninger's succinct descriptions of most of the important terms and postulates in Jung's theory, while accurate and objective, are sometimes so brief as to lose meaning and complexity. For example, the statement that 'Jung encouraged people to participate in the religious traditions in which they had been raised' fails to do justice to the theoretical complexities in Jung's blending of personality theory and religion and its place in psychotherapy (Cloninger, 1996: 81).

The criticism that Jung's writing style is unclear and difficult to read, suggested by Schultz (1976: 137), is reiterated in this decade by Hjelle and Ziegler, who warn that 'the breadth of intellectual study coupled with Jung's arcane writing style makes his theory one of the most difficult to understand in the entire discipline of psychology' (Hjelle & Ziegler, 1992: 171), and by Ryckman in *Theories of Personality* (1993), who states that Jung's analytical psychology is 'complex, esoteric and obscure' (Ryckman, 1993: 68), adding that since few readers could grapple with Jung's wide range of reading, many found it easier to dismiss the theory (1993: 68–69).

The criticism that Jung's theory lacks testability was made in this decade by Hjelle and Ziegler, who concluded that his theory remained 'at the level of conjecture', that his concepts were 'not defined precisely enough to validate', and that 'far more research is needed if Jung's theory is to have a lasting impact on the field of personality' (Hjelle & Ziegler, 1992: 177). Hergenhahn too observed that Jung's theory had been criticised as unfalsifiable but argued that Jung sought validation in human experience and intuition, not in the laboratory (Hergenhahn, 1994: 91). Ryckman concluded that Jung's theory fails in precision and testability because of the ambiguity of its concepts and the 'inherent vagueness' of his metaphysical concepts such as archetypes (Ryckman, 1993: 93). The precise nature of the vagueness is not indicated. Conversely, he noted that scientists were becoming 'increasingly interested in testing some of Jung's complex and original ideas' (1993: 94). He referred to research such as Carlson's in the 1980s on the types as providing considerable support for the Jungian scheme of the types (Ryckman, 1993: 86). Cloninger identified a substantial amount of relevant research from the 1980s and 1990s, including that by Rosen, Smith, Huston, and Gonzalez (1991), who developed an Archetypal Symbol Inventory for use in an empirical study of associations and archetype (Cloninger, 1996: 84). Monte (1995) concluded that Jung's theory is refutable in some respects but not in others: the hypothesis of emotional complexes is refutable by means of the Word Association Test; the typology is empirically testable, but the hypothesis of the *collective unconscious* is not.

Cloninger notes that Jung conducted therapy 'face to face', not on a couch, and that this 'reflected his conviction that the therapist should not hide behind authority and a guise of scientific objectivity (Cloninger, 1996: 82). While Hjelle and Ziegler acknowledge Jung as 'the forerunner of the human movement in personology', they put forward their view that individuation requires 'considerable leisure time' and hence 'excludes the vast majority of humanity' (Hjelle & Ziegler, 1992: 176–177). Hergenhahn repeats various criticisms of Jung's theory (being friendly towards occultism, spirituality, mysticism, and religion) without giving sources but in some cases outlines counterarguments – for example, that Jung defended his interest in occultism on the grounds that he studied these things to gain information about the collective unconscious (Hergenhahn, 1994: 92). Ryckman's statement that Jung's personality theory 'comes close to matching Freud's' in its comprehensiveness implies that Freud's theory is the benchmark (Ryckman, 1993: 93).

Despite the uncritical repetition of earlier criticisms, American textbook authors of the 1990s confronted the complexity of Jung's ideas and recognised his continuing influence thirty years after his death. Ryckman, for example, stated that Jung's theorizing about the nature of psychopathology and its treatment had had a highly positive impact on the work of many therapists and that his ideas had been useful to members of many disciplines (Ryckman, 1993: 95). Balancing criticisms with an appreciation of Jung's contributions, Hergenhahn acknowledged the importance of religion in Jung's theory as the major vehicle for self-actualisation and noted that self-actualisation was taken up by other theorists. He recognised that Jung was the first personality theorist to emphasise the future in determining human behaviour, that Jung placed great emphasis on meaning and purpose, that Jung's is an optimistic theory, and that selfhood rather than sexuality is seen as the master motive for human behaviour (Hergenhahn, 1994: 91–93). He concluded that 'Jung's theory creates an image of the psyche that is believable in the light of the times in which we live; an image of a psyche that is pushed by the past, pulled by the future, and is attempting to make sense of itself in the present' (1994: 93).

Before turning to British texts, I will mention a U.S. text from the 1990s that marked a sea change in the way personality is conceptualised and may help open the way for a scholarly reappraisal of Jung's approach in the twenty-first century. Hogan, Johnson, and Briggs edited a *Handbook of Personality Psychology* (1997), in which Runyan's chapter places personality theories within a broad framework of criticisms of 'soft science'. Runyan explores the uses of a hard-soft continuum for understanding the different traditions and methods in psychology, with some groups preferring the traditions and methods of 'hard science' and others preferring a social and experiential 'soft science' approach. He concludes that these differences historically led the two groups to severely criticise each other's research (Runyan, 1997: 46) and argues that personality psychology needs to attend to several different objectives if a person's life is to be understood (1997: 49–50). The psychoanalytical tradition is concerned with understanding particular lives and relies on interpretive and historical or case-study methods rather than quantitative methods, whereas research at the 'hard end' of psychology, in cognitive science, raises some important questions but does not address other important questions about the understanding of persons, lives, and inner subjective experiences (1997: 59–61).

Runyan's vision for the future of personality theory was that an emerging 'soft synthesis' study of lives in social and historical contexts could integrate the social and personal with clinical and developmental psychology. Runyan's 'soft synthesis' emphasises the overlap of psychology with social sciences and the humanities, in contrast with 'hard synthesis' which emphasises the overlap with biological and computer sciences. A 'soft' science draws on philosophy of mind, philosophy of the social sciences, and consciousness. Runyan argued that a 'soft' synthesis approach has the potential to integrate 'previously disparate and unconnected lines of work' and to turn back to the study of persons and lives (Runyan, 1997: 61–64). Since Jung's work must be classified as 'soft science', elevating the status of 'soft synthesis' approaches has positive potential for the discussion of Jung's ideas in the next generation of textbooks.

Textbooks published in Britain in the 1990s

Although there were no new UK textbooks on personality that covered Jung's theory, the sample from this decade included the second edition of Cook's *Levels of Personality* (1993), previously published in the United States in 1984. The preface to the first edition included Jung only as one of the theorists mentioned by Hall and Lindzey (1957) in relation to conceptual drift from Jung's concepts of introversion and extraversion to Eysenck's (Cook, 1984: 178). The 1993 edition makes no reference to Jung's work. Cook's chapter on Freud, however, is critical of psychoanalytical explanations generally. For example, he remarked that:

> Freud's critics often say that psychoanalysis is more like a religion than a science; certainly deriving a theory of personality from the twenty-four volumes of Freud's *Collected Works* [sic][8] is more akin to biblical criticism than scientific activity.
>
> (Cook, 1993: 150)

Although this is a criticism specifically of Freudian psychoanalysis, the reiteration of strongly phrased attacks on psychoanalytical theories in general by research-oriented trait theorists must have had a negative effect on the perception by psychological professionals in the UK not only of Freud's work but of other psychoanalytical theorists including Jung.

The beginning of the new century

At the turn of the new millennium, a new publication, Magnavita's *Theories of Personality: Contemporary Approaches to the Science of Personality* (2002), seemed to be moving personality theory in the United States in a completely new direction. In addition, there were new editions of older texts. I reviewed Carver and Scheier's *Perspectives in Personality* (2000), Pervin and John's *Personality Theory and Research* (2001), and Schultz's *Theories of Personality, 7th edn* (2001).

Carver and Scheier present Jung as a contemporary rather than a follower of Freud and observe that his theory differed from Freud's in many ways and is one of great complexity (Carver & Scheier, 2000: 254). Schultz reported research supporting the application of Jung's ideas of the midlife crisis to women and cited John and colleagues' (1988) findings, in a twenty-year follow-up study of college women, that individuated personalities (rated by independent judges) were the outcome of a midlife crisis (Schultz, 2001: 114–115). Schultz described Jung as 'less deterministic that Freud' and saw him as more hopeful than Freud, though pessimistic about Western culture, materialism, reason, and empirical science, adding that 'Jung's hopefulness about human nature was of a watchful, warning kind' (Schultz, 2001: 109). Schultz's critical comment on Jung's writing style, which was repeated in previous editions of his book (see above, p. 106), reappears in the seventh edition together with a comment by Richard Noll that Jung's major books are only partly intelligible since 'the connection between one thought and the next is not clear and there are internal contradictions' (Noll, 1994: 109, cited in Schultz, 2001: 116). Subsequently, Shamdasani (1998) strongly disputed Noll's critiques. Pervin and John's coverage of Jung's theory extends to only two pages under the title 'Related Points of View' (*sc.* to those of Freud). There is only one reference to a primary source, Jung's 1939 *The Integration of the Personality*, while the sole biographical event mentioned is the split from Freud.

The coverage of Jung by Magnavita (2002) is brief and uneven, in that discussion of Freud's theory extends to thirty-two pages while Jung's is covered in one. *Psychological Types* (1921) is the only work of Jung's cited. With the exception of Freud, the 'great men of psychology' no longer dominate. Instead, the sweep and scope of Magnavita's book is panoramic, especially with respect to present-day theories informing contemporary models of personality. Magnavita includes the human genome, biopsychosocial models, attachment theory, chaos theory, root metaphors, personality change, resilience models, cross-cultural approaches, the 'consumerised self', social policy, economic development, organisational behaviour, and the politicisation of personality and of psychopathology. His much broader approach signals major changes in the field of personality psychology. At the same time, new editions of older texts remain in circulation.

Conclusions and discussion

British and American differences

There are striking differences between the North American and British textbooks in their treatment of Jung. A large majority (two thirds) of the U.S. textbooks in the sample treated Jung fairly, and at least half of these were well informed. Some of the best-known frequently reprinted texts were evenhanded in their comparison of Jung's ideas with other theories. Although errors and misperceptions of Jung's ideas were present in every decade, only a minority of the U.S. texts I examined were unsympathetic or hostile. In contrast, the majority of the British textbooks were unsympathetic or hostile towards Jung's ideas. No British textbook on personality gave substantial space to Jung's theory or described it comprehensively. British textbooks that were not hostile were selective, tending to expound exclusively the concepts of introversion and extraversion.

By far the most noticeable difference between the United States and Britain was the dearth of British textbooks on personality in the twentieth century. In the United States, some textbooks ran into seven or eight editions spanning thirty years. Nothing comparable existed in Britain. The majority of undergraduate courses on personality were in North America, while those in Britain relied less on textbooks than in U.S. universities or made use of U.S. texts (as evidenced by the fact that large numbers of U.S. texts could be found in an English university library).

Use of primary and secondary sources

The most frequently cited primary source was *Psychological Types* (1921), which suggests that the typology is considered by many authors to be the central, most important part of Jung's theory, if not *the* theory. It is also the construct that has attracted the most research, so it is not surprising that research-oriented psychologists are interested in the typology. Even so, a number of authors drew from a very wide range of sources and acknowledge the theory's multifaceted nature. As an early work, *Psychological Types* might be expected to appear in the references of more authors. However, other early works such as 'The psychology of dementia praecox' (*CW*3, I) and the word-association tests (*CW*2) were cited far less frequently (see Appendix 3).

The most frequently cited secondary source was Jung and Jaffé's *Memories, Dreams, Reflections* (1963), which the authors regarded as the most reliable and most autobiographic source.[9] Whilst earlier authors had fewer secondary sources to draw on, most authors cite more than one secondary source, and some draw readers' attention to the existence of conflicting sources. Critical evaluation of the quality and reliability of the secondary sources used was strikingly absent, even though both sympathetic and hostile sources were drawn on by the same author. The use of secondary sources and their background, context, and rhetorical purpose is an area for future historical research in relation to reappraising Jung as a personality theorist.

Conflicting views

There was striking inconsistency in the authors' evaluation of Jung's work. In line with the paradoxical nature of Jung's personality theory, his ideas have evoked conflicting responses. What some authors liked about Jung's theory is exactly what other authors criticised. Every theme of critical evaluation can be matched by a more favourable view relating to the same aspect of his work and vice versa. The position authors took in relation to Jung's value as a personality theorist seemed to depend on the extent to which he adhered to the conventions of science or on their view of his success or failure in going beyond this. This depended on the individual author's attitude to the prevailing view of psychology as a science.

Authors who express strong hostility to Jung's ideas, such as Thorpe (1938) and Levy (1970), listed fewer references to primary sources, provided scant or reductive descriptions of Jung's work, or included inaccurate material. Eysenck (1947, 1953, 1957, and 1965) was well informed on introversion-extraversion but not on the later developments of Jung's ideas judging from the references given in these examples of Eysenck's work.

Sympathy for Jung was independent neither of breadth of knowledge of his ideas nor of the authors' own values, aims, and orientations. Some of Jung's most hostile critics are trait theorists or authors with a strong preference for Freud's ideas (Thorpe, Sullivan, Eysenck, Notcutt). Runyan's (1997) application of a 'hard science' versus 'soft synthesis' distinction to the field of personality psychology is useful in offering another possible route to understanding these facts, as it suggests that differences between the personalities of the authors go deeper than a mere choice or fashion. Runyan portrays two opposing groups, neither of which finds the insights that come out of the other group's work appealing or helpful: they reject it whilst engaging in rhetorical persuasion and attempt to negate the value of the other group's contributions. This difference of 'hard' and 'soft' values may be one reason it has been difficult for people to conclude that Freud and Jung both made significant and valuable contributions to personality psychology. Freud could be described as being more on the 'hard science' side and Jung a 'soft synthesis' psychologist in that he attempts to bring together ideas from anthropology, religion, and philosophy as well as from medical and scientific psychology. As with all dichotomies, this cannot account for all differences, but the 'hard science–soft synthesis' distinction usefully captures the sense of difference coupled with animosity that has split the field of personality theory for fifty years.

Various rhetorical moves have been noted in this review. One author, Monte (1977), contrasts Freud's and Jung's ideas, with the effect of presenting Jung in a positive light as someone who took Freud's ideas further. In other texts, the use of rhetorical style has a negative effect. For example, sparse description, as in Mehrabian (1968), Mischel (1971), or Peck and Whitlow (1975), creates an impression of a lack of comprehensiveness and depth in Jung's theory. Selection of biographical material as in Schultz (1976), Stolorow and Atwood (1979), Smith and Vetter (1982), Feist (1985), and Hjelle and Ziegler (1992), can create an impression of psychopathology, while eulogies about Jung as a Goethian figure, such as Murray's quoted in Byrne (1966), may be interpreted as biased and exaggerated. The use of the terms 'disciples' and 'doctrine' by Thorpe (1938) and Eysenck (1957, 1965) carries implications of religious dogma and cult formation. Sullivan's (1964) 'bud on a reservoir' remark was obvious sarcasm, as was Eysenck's (1965) 'what is new about Jung's typology is not true, and what is true is not new'. Failure to mention Jung in contexts where his work is relevant, for example by Mead and by Bellack in McCary (1956), conveys the message, even if unintentionally, that Jung's theory has no importance. Dismissing Jung's concept of the unconscious as unscientific speculation and his principle of opposition as too vague to be of any value in a science of personality, as in Levy (1970), is to imply that Jung's theory has no validity. It also suggests that this opinion has become a truism and needs no justification. Comparing Jung with Freud is commonplace, for example in Bischof (1964), Mischel (1971), and Ewen (1980), and implies that Freud is the standard of orthodoxy. Using Freud as a stick with which to beat Jung is a denigrating device – for example, in 'For Freud, there is an abundance of primary sources and research from which to choose. For Jung there is only an abundance of primary sources', however much it is qualified in the rest of the paragraph (Lindzey, Hall, & Manosevitz, 1973: 37).

It is reasonable to expect the evaluation section of a textbook of personality theories to be similar to that of a scholarly journal in respect of modelling for students the practice of weighing up evidence. Smyth's analysis of two textbooks of general psychology found multiple referencing when authors discussed a theory and the criticisms that were made of it (Smyth, 2001: 623–625). This was generally the case where validity was being evaluated, though not in relation to other aspects. For example, when Schultz expressed his view that Jung's writing style is difficult to read, he did not offer references to other opinions or any alternative balancing views. Rather, this was an example of 'fact making' from opinion, which occurs when one's own opinions or those of others are passed on with no specific references to their origin. Opinions about Jung, his theory, and his writing style have been treated as if to suggest there could be no differences of opinion or any grounds for debate.

The influence of time and place

The style and orientation of introductory books and textbooks of the psychology of personality evolved over time. Authors of the 1950s were comfortable with the contribution of psychoanalysis to the development of the field of personality, which was still emerging from a multiplicity of roots. The 1960s saw the rise of behaviourism in psychology and, in the personality field, consolidation of the trait-person split. The 1970s saw the publication of several extremely influential textbooks, suggesting a rapid growth of courses in personality in undergraduate degrees in the United States, not paralleled in Britain. From 1980 onwards, a critical leaning towards evaluation of theories and of research generated from them characterises the texts.

Psychology in the United States after World War II was enriched by the many European psychologists and psychological therapists with diverse interests who settled in the United States in greater numbers than in Britain. The influence of a wider range of theoretical approaches to psychology in North America led to doors being opened to Jungian ideas in universities in a way that did not happen in Britain. In addition, the establishment of privately financed universities and institutes in North America in the first half of the twentieth century may have allowed for a freer development of ideas and interests than could occur in Britain in a state system. Jung made several visits to the United States and lectured there. He visited Britain, too, but briefly. His personal influence in America was far greater than in Britain. By contrast, the presence of Freud in residence, however briefly, in London seems to have led to psychoanalysts in Britain being predominantly Freudian or neo-Freudian and to academic psychologists being anti-Freudian and anti-psychoanalysis. In attempting to champion a scientific approach to psychology and to challenge what he saw as bigotry in psychoanalysis, Eysenck created a climate in which a professional psychologist with an interest in psychoanalysis risked being regarded as unscientific and hence being professionally marginalised. All British authors of personality textbooks were predominantly focussed on trait approaches to personality. In the United States, although positivist and statistical approaches to personality were popular, they were not exclusively dominant.

One favourable influence in the United States that should not be underestimated was the huge popularity among U.S. psychologists of the work of William James. James wrote in a philosophical style, and his work created a climate in American psychology that was more receptive to Jung's ideas. It is also conceivable that the existence of a strong 'mental hygiene' movement in the United States, with its emphasis on personal adjustment and development, also created a climate into which Jung's notion of a necessary balance between social and personal adaptation could fit.[10]

A contemporary historical perspective

In a history of psychoanalytical theories of personality, Taylor (2009) proposes a threefold classification of parallel streams in American psychology – (1) experimental, (2) clinical, and (3) experiential – noting that the second two streams have always been subject to criticism from psychologists in the first stream (Taylor, 2009: 5). He suggests that different epistemologies of consciousness underlie the models of personality that have developed within the streams: the positivistic (consciousness is equal to awareness and there is no unconscious), the psychodynamic (everyday consciousness is controlled by a vast and more primitive unconscious that is partly accessible to rational awareness), and the transcendental. In the transcendental epistemology, awareness and consciousness are not the same. Both inferior and superior states can control rational awareness. Waking consciousness can be transformed by developing intuitive insight and by the experience of higher, more expanded states of awareness (Taylor, 2009: 14). The implication for evaluation of personality theories, Taylor suggests, is that 'the critic is almost always of a totally different mindset' and that consequently, one has to be aware of the critic's position in the streams and epistemological assumptions regarding personality (2009: 15). I find Taylor's classification of the three streams and their epistemologies a helpful perspective for understanding some of the misrepresentations of Jung's ideas I have identified in introductory textbooks of personality.

We await a thorough exploration of the effects of the many differences in the history of psychological ideas between the United States and Britain, and indeed between Britain and the rest of Europe. Differences between philosophical and intellectual cultures may have contributed to the hostility found in British textbooks of personality towards Jung. A strong empiricist tradition had existed in British philosophy since the eighteenth century through Hume,

Berkeley, and Mill. The post–Darwinian secularisation of psychology in Britain was built on preexisting rationalist-empiricist traditions. That Jung centred his concept of individuation in a religious framework and sought to reassert the importance of religion and spirituality did not resonate well in a culture predominantly concerned with the secularisation of ideas. Perhaps because religion had a more important place within secular American culture in the second half of the twentieth century, the religious vector in Jung's work aroused less hostility to Jung in textbooks of personality in the United States.

Notes

1 The psychiatrist Harry Stack Sullivan did not publish a personality textbook as such, but his journal papers and lectures, including his own theory of personality, were collected after his death in the two volumes of *The Collected Works of Harry Stack Sullivan*. This collection had the status of a general textbook for psychiatrists and psychologists.

2 *Defect* 'to desert' (*The New Oxford Illustrated Dictionary*, 1980); 'to become a rebel or deserter, e.g. from a party, a country, or a cause' (*Oxford English Dictionary* at oup.com); 'to desert one's country, cause or allegiance, esp. in order to join the opposing forces' (*Collins English Dictionary*).

3 The inclusion of biographical material in textbooks is selective, with items chosen to reflect particular aspects of a person's life and work. Numerous biographies have been written about Jung, from different viewpoints. Readers unfamiliar with Jung's life could consult Papadopoulos's *Chronology of Jung's Life and Work* (1992), which can be found in his two-volume compilation of critical assessments and interpretive papers on Jung's work (Papadopoulos, 2006a). Critically aware of the limitations of earlier biographies, Papadopoulos attempts to present as objective a biographical list as possible of the undisputed dates and milestones in Jung's life and work.

4 See, for example, their interpretation of Jung's childhood dream of the 'man-eater' and other childhood experiences (Stolorow & Atwood, 1979: 90–95).

5 See Bargh and Chartrand (1999) for an interesting overview of this area that includes studies from the early 1970s and before.

6 This was probably derived from E. Glover (1950), whose polemic against Jung emphasised this particular criticism. Glover's aim was to extirpate divergence from 'pure' Freudian theory in London.

7 Brevity of description is sometimes, though not always, related to the length of the text.

8 Cook is apparently referring to the *Standard Edition* of Freud's works.

9 Shamdasani (2005a) reexamined Jaffé's claim that this was an autobiography of Jung and cast doubt on the authenticity of some of the contents.

10 Danziger has suggested a possible link between the mental hygiene movement and the development of personality psychology in American psychology (1997: 127).

Chapter 7

Criteria for evaluating personality theories

It is extremely difficult to evaluate Jung's position. If the usual procedures of scientific, analytical thought were to be applied, the position could be easily faulted. But I have the nagging feeling, that, by tackling Jung's theory with the tools of logic, we are missing what there is of value in it.

S.R. Maddi (1996) *Personality Theories: A Comparative Analysis*, p. 95

Introduction

A frame of reference is needed that allows Jung's theory to be evaluated in a manner appropriate to its character. In the preceding chapter, I traced the appraisal of Jung's theory through twentieth-century textbooks on personality showing the lack of consensus, with some authors appreciating the qualities that others deplored. This chapter critically suggests a possible basis for a twenty-first-century evaluation of Jung as a personality theorist. The chapter has three sections, covering the historical background in which criteria for evaluating personality theory developed, Jung's own criteria, and the criteria I propose.

Standards used for value judgments are often not made explicit, and disagreements exist about what a theory of personality should include. Criteria for judging theories have been given the most explicit consideration within the philosophy of science, in which a very high epistemological status for scientific values and methods is assumed. To evaluate Jung, one has to be willing to question this.

Historical background to the development of criteria for evaluating personality theories

The criteria against which personality theories have been evaluated in academic psychology in the UK and the United States evolved in the context of the early twentieth-century struggle to establish psychology as a discipline separate from philosophy and to gain 'the spoils of scholarship' (Boring, 1961: 253). Jung's writing spans the period from the 1890s to the end of the first half of the twentieth century, the whole period during which psychology was emerging as an academic discipline and establishing itself as a science. Wundt in Germany and, later, Titchener in the United States, set out a programme for a laboratory science of psychology. Reviewing these developments in his autobiography, one historian of psychology, E. G. Boring, noted psychology's lack of self-criticism of its drive to 'make psychology a science'. Boring recalled his own indoctrination into Titchener's view that psychology needed to be brought into the scientific circle and rescued from the philosophers who still dominated it and describes the principles of textbook writing thus: 'The book was to be science . . . Facts . . . stressed. Controversy . . . left out. Dubious truths . . . omitted' (Boring, 1961: 56–57).

It was inevitable that the judgments of his academic contemporaries would reflect the degree to which Jung's work was congruent with the scientific community's current views on what would advance psychology's progress in the academic world.

In the twentieth century, some personality textbooks tended simply to describe personality theories without comparing them against specific criteria or with one another. Others, for example, Maddi (1996, and in earlier editions from 1975), attempted to set standards with lists of criteria. Most personality textbooks have a section in which the authors state their positions on what a good theory should include. Standards of judgement are also implied in authors' choice of focus, expressed aspirations, and critical remarks.

Foundations of developing theory criteria

W. McDougall, one of the earliest psychologists to publish a textbook of general psychology in the United States, indicates that a theory of personality should emphasise the organisation of character traits and their direction towards higher goals or ideals. Determination (free will) and creativity are also important, and a theory should offer an account of the stages of both biological and psychological development. For McDougall, an account of moral development was essential, and the term *personality* should be used to imply unity. 'The totality is not the mere sum of the distinguishable parts; it is the organic whole of which they are parts' (McDougall, 1933: 369). McDougall simultaneously promoted the adoption of methods of investigation borrowed from the physical sciences, such as classification and analysis of features and function, whilst also proposing a blueprint for a more philosophical psychology, one that is concerned with morality, free will, and higher goals. His values hint at underlying religious ideas. His widely read and frequently reprinted textbook reveals that, in the academic world of the United States in the 1930s, not only had psychology not yet moved away from philosophy, but it is precisely the philosophical features that are being used as points of comparison between theories.

A similar and stronger statement of the desirability of a close relationship between philosophy and psychology can be found in the UK. In Isaiah Berlin's

1936 evaluation of contemporary psychology in a letter to the Warden of All Souls' College (Berlin, 2001), he describes the main areas of achievement in the field, mentioning 'philosophical psychology', experimental psychology, behaviourism, social psychology, and the psychology of the senses. He regarded the last of these as the most cultivated field of psychology, as he approved of its close connection with philosophy. Berlin gave the highest value to the branch of psychology that engaged with philosophical issues and points of debate 'combining specialisation in a field with a broad informed attitude to the surrounding country', adding that only those psychologists with philosophical training could critically consider the methods of their own science; he implies that there is a hierarchy of disciplines based on epistemological criteria with philosophy at the top. Judgements of psychological theories would involve asking how theory contributed to questions of morality, ethics, and epistemology and to the progress and welfare of humankind. The meaning and value of the results of psychological investigations are to be judged philosophically, and a good psychological theory is one that investigates philosophical questions by other means.

Gordon Allport criticised psychoanalytical theories for their focus on the past (Allport, 1937: 13). Personality theories, he believed, should reflect a direction of growth and development, that is, upwards and towards the future. He considered typologies to be limited, describing them as halfway approaches to personality, preferring an emphasis on totalities and patterns of mental life, as in the Gestalt approach. Elementarism destroyed the meaningful totalities of life (Allport, 1937: 16–17). Allport's position that the study of personality should be the study of *individuality*, not laws of behaviour, lends value to 'grand theories' like Jung's, as he proposed a criterion of breadth of subject matter and prioritising the goal of understanding. Allport's own theory proposes that unity resides in a core of self-consciousness, a point of self-reference through which coherence between memories in the past and plans for the future is experienced (Allport, 1937: chapter XIII). The guiding principle that a personality theory should include both 'core concepts' such as the self-concept and 'peripheral characteristics' such as traits and elements of behaviour was reasserted much later by Maddi (1972: 644–649), resolving the tension of the comparative importance of elements of personality, behaviour, and the unity of the self-as-experienced.

One important point Allport made in relation to theory judgement is that theories that are out of fashion may nevertheless be valuable (Allport, 1937: 536), even though they appear to deny the basic tenets of empiricism. He was referring to ideas of innate knowledge or identity, such as may be found in the theories of the Gestalt psychologist W. Kohler (1887–1967), Jung, and one of the founders of the Society for Psychical Research, F. W. H. Myers (1843–1901). He argued for the value of intuition as the means by which facts are interpreted and understood (Allport, 1937: 536–548). In his list of 'concepts in psychology that have marked individualising value', he includes configuration, guiding image, integration, life history, trait, and unity and contrasts these with the concepts of sex drive, id, superego, factor, and dimension, which he felt lacked individualising value (Allport, 1937: 561). The set of criteria that Allport put forward fell out of favour in subsequent decades. It took more than half a century for personality psychologists to return to the holistic values popular earlier in the twentieth century.[1]

Themes in personality theory evaluation

Core themes endorsed by a substantial number of authors over the last century concern how whole persons are constructed and viewed, tending to favour a holistic view of the person; an emphasis on the person as individual and unique; an emphasis on selfhood; an account of development, a focus on life histories, case-studies, and biography; an awareness of the role of environmental, social, and cultural factors; and organising and coordinating principles and concepts, such as motivation and will. Less frequently endorsed but nonetheless important themes are a sense of the person as actively creative and inclusion of a harmonising and unifying construct that can hold together a diversity of factors and oppositions within the person. Several authors (Arndt, 1974: 474; Massey, 1981: 15–19; Maddi, 1996: 489) endorse the need for complexity in a good personality theory. Others (Allport, 1937: 549–566; Mischel, 1999: 9) emphasise the value of incorporating the elements of stability and consistency which make the person operate as a single person. Some authors (notably Maddi, 1972: 646–649) value the elaboration of core tendencies (as common to human species) as well as those traits and behaviours that are individual. Pervin (1996, cited in Mischel, 1999: 5) states that the roles of past memories, present situations and concerns, and construction of the future should be elaborated. In Murray's view, personality is expressed gradually over the whole life span, so, for him, an emphasis on life history is important (Kluckhohn & Murray, 1949: 32).

Unsurprisingly, as far as specific criteria used in evaluating personality theories are concerned, the criteria that are most frequently endorsed are the standard criteria for judging any theory in any discipline – that is to say, objectivity, validity, verifiability, quantifiability, generalisability, and predictive power. Many authors endorse links with known facts and research data, research emphasis, capacity to generate hypotheses and testable predictions, parsimony, utility or applicability, clarity, precise definition of terms and constructs, adherence to the rules of logic, coherence of structure, and capacity to organise and integrate complex data in a meaningful way. However, it is not the case that any author endorses all of these, or even that a majority of authors endorse most of these. Most authors mention a specific subgroup they find particularly important and then add one or two criteria of their own.

Few authors identify just what attracts the reader in an encounter with a theory, despite acknowledging that there is a subjective element in theory evaluation. Carver and Scheier (2000: 9) acknowledge that a theory must appeal to the reviewer's personal preferences and values. They cite William James, who said people valued the theories that are the most interesting and have strong aesthetic and emotional appeal (Carver & Scheier, 2000: 9–10). Some marginal criteria are among the most interesting. For example, Maddi (1996: 493), Hall and Lindzey (1978: 13), and Carver and Scheier (2000: 10, 312) think that a theory should be judged on its capacity to stimulate interest and thought, even disagreement, as well as research. Schultz (1976: 3–4) values distinctiveness of ideas.

The issue of the epistemology of theorising is raised by Maddi (1972: 11), acknowledging that theories are subjective, arising out of personal interest, that they are intuitive in the early stages, that intuition is an essential aspect of theoretical thinking, and that theories are also socially influenced. Others (Monte, 1977: 19; Massey, 1981: 13–15) have emphasised the positive value in terms of profundity and insight when direct personal experience is incorporated into personality theory. On similar lines, Allport (1937: 555) and Kluckhohn and Murray (1949: 9–11) imply that personal experience (phenomenology) should be included in the broad focus of personality theorising.

Others raise more explicit issues of ideology: Ewen (1984: 111), Hergenhahn (1994: 93), and Schultz (2001: 117) value optimism in personality theories. Maddi (1972: 4) and Mischel (1981: 8) feel that personality theories should challenge the process of living and facilitate social change, and Cloninger (1996: 408) suggests that a theory may be judged on the basis of the morality of the picture it presents of human nature and in the morality of its applications.

A number of textbook authors mention the theorist's writing style evaluatively. Maddi (1972: 2) prefers the writing not to be rhetorical, persuasive, polemical, or one-sided. Ewen (1984: 4) values the theory's provision of 'convenient descriptions'. A number of authors emphasise clarity and are critical of vagueness and ambiguity. Recent commentators on Jung, such as Rowland (2005), have begun to give attention to his style of writing and see its apparent ambiguity as essential to his meaning, opening up a promising area.

Jung's views on evaluating theories

Jung's view of science was that it is too limited in its values and methods to be really useful to psychology. He became doubtful about psychology's rush to imitate physics. For one thing, the historical roots of psychology, prior to Fechner's psychophysiology and Wundt's experimental psychology, were deeply embedded in philosophy and religion, and secondly, he thought that scientific approaches, borrowed from physics and transferred to psychology, were too narrowly focused to be applied successfully to psychology. In his review of Carl Wernicke's work, he says, 'Wernicke's ideas, for all their brilliance, are too narrow: brain anatomy and psychiatric clinics are certainly important, but psychology is more important still' (*CW*18 1906 §892).

Kotsch (2000) says of Jung that he viewed science as practice in the community. He identified, not with a body of established truths or with an infallible method of discovery, but with an evolving tradition – 'a tradition of seeking;

of doubt, indecision, and scepticism; of individual investigation, critical argument, and consensual validation' (Kotsch, 2000: 227). At the same time, Jung treats empirical methods with respect, even excitement, but he is talking about empiricism within an essentially inductive approach to theorising. His was not hypothetico-deductive science of the later twentieth century. In 1912, Jung was enthusiastic about the promise of Wundt's introspective laboratory studies and admired Wundt's erudition and genius for devising new methods of research. He described the ideas of Fechner, Wundt's senior contemporary, as 'a fertilizing force' (*CW*7 1912 §407). Even in 1946, although his own ideas had moved along another path, he remarked that Christian von Wolff was 'the first to speak of "empirical" or "experimental" psychology in the eighteenth century, when it became clear that philosophy had insufficient general validity, so that philosophical argument had to be replaced by experience and psychology became a science' (*CW*8 1947/1954 §345).

Despite his enthusiasm for and early use of experimental methods in the word association tests, Jung expressed numerous reservations throughout his life about the wisdom of applying scientific approaches to psychology. Kotsch concludes, 'Jung's scientific activity embraced a methodology consistent with his epistemology. . . . In his methodology there is no clear separation between the activity of the inquirer and the object under investigation'. His quest for knowledge involved an inseparable mixture of both methods of inquiry and findings. These findings 'are not final products establishing objective truth' but 'represent new data and assumptions from which to begin further enquiry' (Kotsch, 2000: 227). The methods Jung chose, the arguments he raised against a scientific psychology, his admiration for a certain kind of empiricism, and his attitude to inquiry can, by implication, be used to construct a picture of *his* intellectual values and hence of the criteria by which he might have judged theories of personality, including his own.

Firstly, Jung took the position that sensory perception is not the only or the most immediate experience.

> My sense impressions are psychic images, and these alone constitute my immediate experience. My own psyche transforms and falsifies reality to a degree that I must resort to artificial means to determine what things are like apart from myself. Then I discover that a sound is a vibration of air.
>
> (*CW*8 1931b §680)

Jung considered absurd the assumption that the intellect can comprehend the psyche. He viewed the intellect as a part and a function of the psyche, which is the mother and maker of conscious rationality (*CW*11 1938/1940 §141). Psychological ideas are original and 'naturally present'. They are 'essentially real' and far older than any philosophy (*CW*18 1938 §742–743).

Secondly, Jung held that the goal of science should be the description of the natural world, of which ideas are a part. Ideas are natural data and empirically real. 'Without this idea it is unavoidable that we should explain our psychic experiences in a way that does violence to a good half of them' (*CW*8 1931b §683). He revealed the religious basis of this particular view nineteen years earlier, in 1912, when he interpreted Jesus's words 'except that a man be born of water and of the Spirit, he cannot enter into the Kingdom of God' as: 'Do not think carnally or you will be flesh, but think symbolically, and then you will be spirit' (*CW*5 1911–12/1952 §332–335). For Jung, ideas are primary, older than consciousness, and cannot be totally comprehended by logical analysis. Furthermore, the attempt to restrict psychological knowledge to that which can be comprehended by the senses was morally dangerous, as it 'failed to give its due to that side of psychic life which expresses itself in superstition, and mythology, religion and philosophy, and above all, feeling which can be decisive in matters of good and evil' (*CW*8 1931 §683).

Thirdly, a scientific emphasis on simplicity would severely limit the scope of psychological enquiry:

> The experimental psychology of today . . . tries to isolate the very simplest and most elementary processes which border on physiology. . . . It is ill-disposed towards the infinite variety and mobility of individual psychic life.
> (*CW*7 1912 §409)

Jung came to regard this approach to psychology as inherently elementarist and atomistic rather than holistic. It was also materialistic. 'Modern empirical psychology was cradled in an atmosphere of rank materialism . . . viewing the psychic process exclusively from the outside' (*CW*17 1926/1946 §128). We can deduce that Jung valued complexity and that he saw rationalism as secondary to other prerational psychic processes. Furthermore, he thought that science is suspect because of its total reliance on sensory data observed 'from the outside'. This raises the possibility that, if the psyche is prior to philosophy, it can question philosophy (of which science is a product). Jung is saying something quite radical: that, however useful science may be, its ultimate judge, beyond philosophy, is the irrational psyche itself. Ultimately, you can only know the psyche by including the unknowable. Here we enter the world of paradox, another essential element in Jung's values to which I shall return later; but first I want to consider Jung's position on objectivity in psychology.

In addition to questioning the primacy of sensory information and asserting the natural reality of ideas, giving them equivalent if not higher status than empirically established facts, Jung asserts the inevitability and the necessity of subjectivity, expressing the strong conviction that psychology could never be objective. Not only is science too limited to encompass the complexity and 'infinite variety' of the human psyche, but it is also unavoidably caught in a reflexive problem that cannot be solved. 'Psychology lacks the Archimedean point outside and hence the possibility of objective measurement' and finds itself in a similar position to atomic physics 'where the process to be observed is modified by the observer' (*CW*17 1926/1946 §163). The problem of reflexivity, he says, is nowhere as important as in psychology, where its implications fundamentally undermine the assumption of the existence of absolute truth (*CW*17 1926/1946 §160–161). 'In no field of experience is the eye for facts so myopic as in the psyche's perception and observation of itself' (*CW*17 1926/1946 §160). He concludes that there is no knowledge *about* the psyche but only *in* the psyche (*CW*17 1926/1946 §161).

Jung's scepticism about objectivity in psychology is expressed in various ways throughout his life. One can find allusions distributed through the *Collected Works* from the period immediately following his development of word association tests. In 1914, for example, he says: 'Of course it is possible to understand the psyche objectively. . . . In this lies the whole worth and worthlessness of current experimental psychology . . . though this kind of understanding is undoubtedly scientific, it misses the point'(*CW*3 1914a §397).

The point is to understand not what something is but how it comes to be so and, from this, what it might be in the future (*CW*3 1914a §399). In 1921, Jung reminds us that 'science is not the SUMMA of life . . . it is only one of the psychological attitudes, only one of the forms of human thought' (*CW*6 1921 §60). One sees what one can best see oneself, which will be the mote in one's brother's eye rather than the beam in one's own. He adds that it is difficult to be self-objective except in a very limited way, such as by confining observations to 'the eye-pieces of chronoscopes, tachistoscopes and suchlike "psychological apparatus"' (*CW*6 1921 §9).

In 1939, Jung spoke of the prevailing fear of 'uncontrolled subjectivism' and of its defence, 'an enthusiasm for *facts* – mountains of facts'. He points out the folly of this:

> We have the pious hope that this incidental accumulation of facts will form a meaningful whole, but nobody is quite sure, because no human brain can possibly comprehend the gigantic sum total of this mass-produced knowledge. The facts bury us, but whoever does speculate must pay for it with a bad conscience – and rightly so, for he will constantly be tripped up by the facts.
>
> (*CW*11 1939/1954 §767)

In 1951, writing about the Self, Jung anticipates Heidegger's reflections on the nature of thinking (Heidegger, 1968) when he describes the difference between reading about a severe illness and actually having it. 'A pure intellectual insight is not enough because one knows only the words and not the substance of the thing from inside' (*CW*9.2 1951a §61). Elsewhere he states that theories come from oneself and are subject to personal prejudices that are rarely subjected to criticism.[2] He adds, 'to make absolute statements is beyond man's reach' even though he may be 'bound by his conviction to apply [his subjective truth] as a principle of his actions' (*CW*18 1956/1957 §1584). I conclude that Jung's views of the status of theory include the following:

- that truth is relative
- that there is no absolute validity or certainty
- that a theory is speculative and personal in nature, no matter how great the body of data that has been amassed
- that meaningful links should be made between theories, and
- that a theory, no matter how comprehensive, is just a single contribution with a limited life.

Looking back on his life from 1949, Jung admits that his own theory had false starts, adding that a second generation has the advantage of a clearer picture and that his theory was, in any case, incomplete (*CW*18 1949/1954 §1234). 'I cannot claim to have reached any definite theory explaining all of even the main part of the psyche's complexities; my work consists of a series of different approaches, or one might call it a circumambulation of unknown factors' (*CW*18 1953 §1165). As early as 1929, he had written: '[E]ach of us can carry the torch of knowledge but a part of the way, until another takes it from him' (*CW*16 1929a §157). One interesting aspect of Jung's approach to theorising is his attitude to causality, since he believed that it is more useful for psychology to ask about purpose rather than to seek to establish origins. This Jung called the 'constructive standpoint'. General laws about purpose can only be extrapolated when there have been very many similar cases (*CW*3 1914a §424). This is similar to quasi-judicial case-study research, an inductive method of building up case law that persists today both in law and in some areas of psychology such as personality.[3] Jung attributed to the unconscious a prospective function that was capable of expressing symbolically the coming phase of psychological development and which was oriented to a goal or purpose (*CW*6 1921 §701). The constructive method is based on single individual cases. It gives value to complexity and diversity and is not amenable to collective or group descriptions that are derived by 'leading back' from the individual to deduce collective attitudes or facts (*CW*6 1921 §704).

From very early in his work, Jung was caustic about scientific 'facts'. Take, for example, his 1912 dismissal of modern rationalism as 'sham enlightenment' based on the belief that 'What I do not know does not exist' (*CW*5 1911–12/1952 §113). Jung's desire to be viewed as an empiricist but not an empirical scientist can be understood in the light of his constructive method. It may seem curious that in 1952, in his reply to Martin Buber on religion and psychology, Jung quotes defensively from a description of himself in the *British Medical Journal* which states, 'Facts first and theories later is the keynote of Jung's work. He is an empiricist first and last' (*CW*18 1952/1973 §1502). To understand this apparent contradiction, it should be remembered that this refers to data collected in the service of inductive rather than the now familiar deductive methods, which were not given their modern form until the 1930s by Karl Popper, by which time Jung had formed his views and his empirical method.

Jung's insistence on his empiricism also raises the question of what he did consider to be facts. He explains that he is referring to the reality of the psyche as a hypothesis. His data are the facts of the symbolic output of the unconscious, expressed in dreams, fantasies, rituals, and practices (*CW*4 1929b §777–778). Twenty-three years later, he added that he formulated these not into a theory as such but into concepts which serve as tools (*CW*18 1952/1973 §1507). He had reservations about the status of theory in psychology, believing that psychology's similarity to philosophy was that 'both are systems of opinion about objects which cannot be fully experienced and therefore cannot be adequately comprehended by a purely empirical approach' (*CW*6 1921 §659). This, he felt, distinguished psychology and philosophy from disciplines like mathematics, geology, botany, and zoology.

Jung's use of the term *concepts* is itself interesting in connection with his simultaneous rejection of rationalism whilst defending empiricism. As a broadly empirical, though inductive, psychologist, in his early years, Jung was one of the first personality theorists to offer a list of carefully elaborated operational definitions for his concepts, taking on board the problems of imprecision and ambiguity in psychology, attempting 'to give them fixity and precision so that everyone is in a position to see what he means by them' (*CW*6 1921 §674). Later, however, he referred, somewhat denigratingly, to concepts as 'coined and negotiable values', 'finished and complete', in contrast with archetypal images which, though inapprehensible to the intellect, 'are life' (*CW*14 1955–56 §226).

From these various positions, I conclude that Jung understood a theory of personality to be a form of speculation based on empirical (in the broadest sense of the term) data concerning the conscious and unconscious psychic life of individuals, seen in the context of the wider aims of understanding the natural world. Jung was also motivated by his sense of himself as a healer, 'a struggle forced upon me by daily psychological experience of the sick' (*CW*7 1917/1926/1943 §200). His heart was involved as much as his head, although, as he put it, the two are inseparable, and 'practical knowledge will always seek a more philosophical level of understanding'. There is a very practical aspect to Jung's ideas on personality, perhaps best exemplified by his preference for posing 'prospective' questions about the future direction 'in acknowledgement of the fact that tomorrow is of more practical importance than yesterday, and that the Whence is less essential than the Whither' (*CW*4 1909/1949 §759).

One final point, leading back to Jung's metaphysical 'take' on psychology, is the prominence and value he gives to the notion of paradox. As with so many of his concepts, the religious origins of Jung's thought are revealed when, in 1931, he speaks of the danger of 'intellectual freedom from the opposites' and suggests that the solution to the logical problem of apparently giving value to two contradictory hypotheses lies in the nature of life itself:

> The conflict between nature and spirit is itself a reflection of the paradox of psychic life. This reveals a physical and a spiritual aspect which appear a contradiction because, ultimately, we do not understand the nature of psychic life . . . we must, if we are honest, be willing to contradict ourselves, we must pull this something into its antithetical parts in order to be able to deal with it at all.
>
> (*CW*8 1931b §680)

Jung's view was that it was the rise of the post–Enlightenment 'petty reasoning mind', intolerant of paradox, that had made things 'go down hill' philosophically (*CW*12 1944a §19). Only the paradox comes anywhere near to comprehending the fullness of life: 'A religion becomes inwardly impoverished when it loses or waters down its paradoxes'. This is because nonambiguity and noncontradiction are one sided and thus unsuited to express the incomprehensible (*CW*12 1944a §18). This statement is quintessentially characteristic of Jung's values and of his critique of psychology as a natural science.

Based on Jung's own views on science and on theorising in psychology, I surmise that Jung's criteria for a good personality theory would include validity, morality, aesthetic value, complexity and scope, explanatory value, and therapeutic value, but not objectivity, parsimony, or orthodoxy. Uniquely, he would emphasise the limits of rationality, since he held that the psyche can never be understood by rational means alone, and he valued ambiguity, fluidity, and paradox rather than precision. For Jung, a theory, like an archetype, is a living thing and only useful when it has the dynamism of life.

Values and criteria for evaluating Jung's theory of personality

The framework in Table 7.1 is envisaged as a way of making a beginning. It is a possible starting point for developing what could become a significant collaborative project among experts across relevant fields. In respect of most of the criteria, there is as yet insufficient data for the criterion to be applied at this time. Hence I am outlining a way forward rather than a completed evaluation. I see the framework as having several potential applications. For example, it could be used by existing organisations such as the International Association for Jungian Studies (IAJS) to develop an agreed-on programme of evaluative research. A specific programme aimed at enabling Jung's theory to be evaluated through the validation or falsification of its significant components is distinct from the broader aim of the IAJS of promoting Jungian research across disciplines and organising scholarly contact through exchange of views at conferences, an aim that does not exclude evaluative research. I see the framework as promoting the

Table 7.1 A framework for evaluating the personality theory of C.G. Jung

Alternative criteria for evaluating personality theories		
Aesthetic value	Influence	Originality
Complexity and scope	Influence on others' work	Orthodoxy/nonorthodoxy
Durability	Literary style	Persuasiveness
Empiricism	Logical coherence	Researchability
Generativity	Morality	Therapeutic value
Heuristic value	Objectivity/reflexivity	Utility
Impact on people's lives	Openness to exploitation	Validity
Applied to the following key concepts in Jung's theory of personality		
Alchemy	Ego consciousness	Psychosis
Archetypes	Individuation	Rationality/irrationality
Child development	Instinct	Religious instinct
Complexes	Life stages	Self
Creativity	Personal/collective unconscious	The typology
Dreams	Personal/species inheritance	
Considered in relation to evidence from		
Anthropology	General psychology	Philosophy
Biology/neuroscience	Genetics	Social and disciplinary history
Cognitive psychology	Other psychoanalytic approaches and research	Sociology
Developmental psychology	Personality research	
And compared with:		
Jung's evaluation of his own work		

work of the IAJS by focussing on the fundamental need to evaluate the theory itself. Or the framework might serve as a basis for setting up a new Foundation for Jung Research supported by voluntary donations, similar to the Philemon Foundation, with the aim of promoting the research that is currently lacking, since the Philemon foundation itself exists to publish Jung's unpublished work and historical research about Jung and his ideas. The framework could also form the basis of an academic research programme for which a university department might seek Research Council funding for the employment of research assistants and to attract research students.

The following paragraphs give an idea of the background to my thinking in relation to some of the criteria from the framework. I have focused mainly on the less conventional criteria (soft science) I have introduced and on some of the standard criteria where there are important issues to discuss. As there is considerable overlap between criteria, I have indicated where points made about one may be applicable to others.

In this chapter, the purpose of the discussion is to indicate why the new criteria are important and what needs to be considered in relation to Jung's work in applying more scientifically conventional criteria such as therapeutic value and researchability. The focus is on the theoretical question of how to approach evaluating Jung's theory as a personality theory. In Chapter 8, the focus is on the outcome of evaluation. There, the value of Jung's theory is explored more fully and programmatically against two of the most important and challenging criteria.

Aesthetic value

Aesthetics may be considered as a standard of comparison for personality theories because these theories conceptualise people in a particular way. Some people find Jung's ideas uplifting and inspirational, because he suggests a beautiful and inspiring picture of people as creative, innately spiritual, and capable of unifying conflicting tendencies and desires. However, a theory may have apparently elevated aims whilst concealing less elevated aims of social control or hidden forms of inequality such as racism. Kirsch (2000: 133) asks whether Jung's theories actually promote racist tendencies and whether the hypothesis of the collective unconscious is a racist hypothesis. If so, this would throw into question its aesthetic as well as its moral value. Moreover, the presence of a hidden and discreditable social or moral agenda causes aesthetic judgement to collapse into one of morality.

Literary style is important as an aesthetic value. Jung's highly metaphorical style is full of pictorial images evoked verbally. He uses a wide range of vocabulary reflecting the diversity of his reading and the diversity of his audience. In many ways, Jung could be compared with William James, whom many regard as the psychologist with the strongest claims to literary talent in the nineteenth and twentieth centuries. Strangely, James does not appear to have been the target of as many hostile responses as Jung, which may be because of differences in their styles of writing. Both used a mixture of everyday and technical language. Jung's style is characterised by his use of a word in all its meanings and connotations. It is a philosophical style of writing such as is used also by Levinas, Kierkegaard, and Derrida, who avoid closing off meaning, preferring to leave words open to all their potential interpretations and thus preserving a plurality of semantic nuances.

Quality of literary style is a matter both of preference and of debate. It invites further discussion of what defines the literary quality of a personality theory and how that can be judged. Undoubtedly, the value one might put upon the aesthetic judgment of a personality theory must be relative to other criteria which may be more crucial. Aesthetic judgment of style must depend on the appropriateness of the style of delivery to the theory's concepts and to its goals, aims, and assumptions. Jung's writing style has provoked criticism (to the point of derision) over the years, but Jung, like Levinas and Derrida, chose to present his ideas in the particular way he did in order to reduce misunderstanding and not to obscure meaning. The issue is whether he succeeds in his own aims and, if so, with what degree of aesthetic value.[4]

Complexity and scope

Complexity and scope, as criteria for evaluation, are particularly important for evaluating Jung's highly complex theory, which stretches the scope of 'personality' more than any other. Acknowledging that methods associated with a theory should be appropriate to the theory defined in its own terms, de Waele and Harré (1976: 194) proposed that a personality theory must reflect the contrast between the essential unity of a person and the social and functional multiplicity that living demands. This multiplicity will be reflected in the many different personae called for by different social environments and situations and in the complex self-reflexivity that constantly observes and changes their expression in action. They argue for a competence/capacity distinction that allows for an innate basis of capacity that sets limits on what can be socially acquired and expressed behaviourally in the repertoire of competences. De Waele and Harré differ from Jung in seeing human behaviour as being influenced more by social interaction than by instinctual factors. Furthermore, they ground their theory in methodologies for observing, assessing, and predicting behaviour in the manner of Barker and Wright (1955),[5] who pioneered psychosocial research methods for observation and recording data in natural settings using field methods from natural history and tested out predictions in specifically devised situations, all of which differs profoundly from Jung's methodological approach. However, de Waele and Harré's basic position, (a) that a good personality theory should have something to say about both capacity and competence, (b) that a personality theory should not lose sight of the individual in seeking to describe general laws, and (c) that its methods should not be such as to mask individual complexity, takes the debate back to the principles set out by the twentieth century's earliest personality theorists, Allport and Stern. Their position is highly relevant in considering Jung's theory and methods.

Durability

The issue of durability is important because many theories fall out of currency – for example, because they have no relevance for the modern world, even though they may have been highly relevant in their day. Some of Jung's concerns may no longer be relevant. Others have never stopped being debated. The degree to which the issues he raised remain relevant and important has implications for the utility value of his ideas. Jung's theory needs systematic reappraisal in the light of this criterion, especially because its durability has been limited by the fact that it has been marginalised because of *perceived* lack of relevance. Nevertheless, there are reasons for thinking that Jung's work may be particularly relevant today. Main, for example, suggests that Jung's way of bringing science and religion together has great contemporary relevance (Main, 2000), while Tacey has shown the influence of Jung's ideas on 'new age' cultures (Tacey, 2001), but we do not yet have a way of examining Jung's continued relevance as a 'sideline' influence on the field of personality.

Heuristic value

Heuristic value has been given particular prominence in textbook discussions of personality theory. In the sense used by personality texts, heuristic value has been measured by the capacity of a theory to generate research. In its original meaning, the term 'heuristic value' has a much broader connotation: the value of an idea in contributing to understanding the phenomena in question. In comparing Jung's theory with Freud's, one often-cited remark is that the greater heuristic value of Freud's theory is exemplified by the larger number of research papers. But counting research papers as the sole measure of heuristic impact ignores the powerful effects of the social processes operating in the practice of science and academic investigation. It is easier to win research grants in some areas of research than in others. Some theories do not lend themselves to the type of investigation that attracts funding, and some theories lack current academic prestige without the theories being inherently faulty. The type of research should also be considered. A nonscientific (in today's terms) theory like Jung's is less likely to generate scientific hypothesis-testing research and is more suited to qualitative and phenomenological approaches.

Logical coherence

One important philosophical approach has been to look at how psychoanalytic theories can be verified by means of their internal logic, by examining their internal coherence. This criterion has frequently been used in evaluating personality theories, but internal coherence has limits as a potential 'gold standard' because internal coherence is difficult to distinguish from consistency. No theorist writing and thinking over a lifetime could possibly be totally consistent. Ideas change in response to new insights and new information. One may arrive at a different view that creates a discontinuity that is logical, and the new insight may result in a change of direction. A later version of an idea can make distinctions and connections not seen earlier. Thus new perspectives create differences between versions but not incoherence. In addition, one may emphasise different viewpoints depending on the audience being addressed and the formality or otherwise of the context. Hence, it is possible to derive a false impression of incoherence from reading selectively. Nevertheless, logical incoherence may indicate an unfinished train of thought, not fully followed through, and this may be a serious and telling criticism if it concerns a central construct, or if it is not resolved within the whole opus.

Ultimately, internal coherence depends on there being an overall consistency of direction in the theory's constructs and in their links with one another in the theorist's overall thinking. The notion of coherence within an overall structure has the potential to resolve the problem of apparent textual inconsistency as it allows for flexibility, change, and growth of ideas within an overarching framework of ideas (see Chapter 8, pp. 156–158).

Morality

A theory is unlikely to be valued positively if it is not congruent with the critic's own moral position, no matter how coherent. Evaluating a theory is, at least in part, a matter of making one's own position and preferences clear and justifying them, which is one reason trying to answer the question of how Jung's theory should be evaluated is a personal challenge as well as an intellectual task.

There are questions that, if asked, could lead to the systematic gathering of relevant data. For example, does Jung's concept of individuation lead to a self-centred amorality? Are the implications of his theory harmful to others? Does Jung's theory lead to the celebration of dubious causes? Jung takes a controversial position with respect to good and evil, arguing that the conflict cannot be resolved by 'doing good'. Instead, he recommends developing full self-knowledge, including of the extent of one's own evil. An evident if unconventional moral agenda motivates Jung's ideas. According to the standards implicit in his own theory, Jung's work should be considered against the criterion of morality.

Objectivity

Objectivity is an aspirational criterion limited by the fact that science is a social activity within a discursive field. Its methods of investigative practice carry a persuasive message.[6] There is a rhetorical aspect of the scientist's claim to objectivity which appropriates 'rightness' and preempts disagreement (Danziger, 1997). Rather than seeking a level of 'objectivity' that cannot be achieved, theorists and scholars ought to be self-reflective and as self-aware as possible. The amount and limits of Jung's self-reflection in his work on personality can be explored. This is much more likely to be achieved when his theory is viewed through a critical-historical lens than a scientific one.

Openness to exploitation and abuse

All theories and all ideas are open to abuse. A responsible theorist should try to minimise this potential. There are two ways of evaluating this. One is to look at the theory's principles, and the other is to gather empirical data about how the theory has been used. The Jungian concept of individuation is, on the one hand, potentially subversive but, on the other hand, does not lend itself to misuse by authoritarian regimes. The aims of individuation tend in the direction of selective nonconformism, peaceful dissent (ideally), and individual unorthodoxy. Constrained by the need to adapt to both inner and outer conditions, the individuating person is required to allow others to individuate too. In this respect, Jung's ideas have something in common with Quaker nonconformist values, ideally leading to tolerance of diversity and respect for pluralism. People are seen to be struggling with their own internal arguments and dialogues. One point on which Jung's theory might be judged is whether there is evidence that developing a high degree of specifically Jungian self-awareness protects people from negative social influences or whether evidence suggests that it does not make any difference. Of course, Jung's theory is not unique in emphasising the goal of self-awareness, and data concerning the exploitation or otherwise of Jung's theory could be compared with data on other personality theories.

Originality

Originality attracts recognition and judgements of merit and is expected in the development of new ideas, but to what degree? More often than not, new developments are revisions of old ideas. Darwin's original contribution to the theory of evolution was his insertion of the role of chance as the key factor in the evolutionary process. All other elements of the theory were based on preexisting ideas. Often the original contribution lies in the way the ideas are rearranged or in that a theorist has seen a new meaning in old ideas. The spark of originality may be small, but it must be there if the theory is to be more than a repetition. For example, Jung's originality may be that he was 'a newcomer in a very ancient tradition who brought to light in our time a key to another order of knowledge for scholars and intellectuals', as Raine (in Main, 2003: 136) suggests. The new element may be conceptual innovation. This can be a concept of relation – a new vision of how phenomena can be understood in relation to one another. It does not need to be research based if the new relation makes new sense, by making phenomena intelligible in a different, alternative way. Originality unsettles and stirs. It *does* something, has an effect. Jung's ideas should be considered in the light of this kind of understanding of originality.

Taken-for-granted notions can restrict the development of new ideas.[7] The capacity to create fluidity and movement through the presence of alternatives in the culture can be a significant contribution to the development and enrichment of thinking. Rowland (2003: 25), for example, construes Jung's anticausality and antitheory position as a strong theoretical position. The 'outsider' can become a driver for advancement in the history of ideas. Stenner (2002: 45–46) observed that while groups are in opposition to one another, they are gathered in on themselves and lack openness and curiosity. The marginalized groups and ideas remain valuable but on the margins. However, the excluded have characteristics that are in inverse relation to the included, and, when the excluded paradigm becomes needed, the marginalized ideas come back into focus. The marginalised ideas have an indirect heuristic value. This is achieved through influence rather than research. By remaining in the culture, they influence the generation of ideas.

Orthodoxy/Nonorthodoxy

An important criterion for evaluating a theory such as Jung's may be its courageousness in taking an unorthodox path in expressing original views and offering a personal picture of the world. Commentators who emphasise this aspect of Jung's work include Main (2003) and Rowland (2003). Jung was sceptical of scientific rhetoric while supporting empiricism, but he developed many of his ideas using largely nonscientific methods. The value in Jung's nonconformism may be his expression of a vision, more usually expressed as religion or philosophy, within a scientific-medical context.

Persuasiveness

A personality theory will have value if it has the power to *persuade* people that human beings can live fulfilling lives and make a difference to their world. This implies that, as part of its utility value, a good personality theory should have rhetorical value. This, however, may be independent of whether the theorist is right or wrong. Persuasive theories, like ideologies, may lead to living hell. Jung uses a number of rhetorical devices, such as presenting things as opposites to emphasise points and using biblical syntax and phrasing to lend force and weight to some of his statements. He uses many colourful and vivid images to illustrate his points. Questions arise then of whether his use of rhetorical devices distorts his arguments and of whether he misleads by making exaggerated claims. If a theory's success lies partly in the richness of its metaphors, the vividness and aptness of its ways of conceptualising psychological ideas may be its spark of originality. Images are aids to thinking. Jung's images are open. They invite amplification. One may consider to what extent this is productive and effective. Whilst the main focus of persuasiveness is on its effect, there is some overlap between persuasiveness and aesthetic value. The criteria mentioned here are not independent categories.

Researchability

Textbooks of personality tend to criticise theories on the grounds of their methods of research. Authors have generally favoured theorists who rely on 'hard science' experimental methods based on hypothetico-deductive reasoning. Recent critics of this approach, speaking in defence of the 'soft science' qualitative approaches to research, have put forward arguments that may be useful in evaluating Jung's comparative method. The 'epistemology of methodologism' that asserts that research is good only if it has been conducted by certain methods, usually those of the quantitative tradition in academic psychology, has been questioned by Salmon (2003), who describes this assertion as a rhetoric of methodological objectivity. Salmon points out that the epistemology of methodologism is usually asserted rather than argued or justified. He reminds us that methods of research should be related to the subject matter and that the researcher's aim may be discovery rather than demonstration of a hypothesis or 'proof' of an idea. 'Good' research is imaginative, playful, and creative. Most methods are chosen for historical reasons, because the researcher has learned to use a particular method or has experience in using it rather than simply because the research question demands it, Salmon notes. The rigidity of the research methods employed by personality theorists in the last fifty years, in part motivated by the need to produce rapid publishable results to meet departmental demands to produce journal articles at a high and steady rate, was reviewed and lamented by Mendelssohn (1993: 114). Mendelssohn suggests that this pressure encourages focus on immediate outcomes and justifies the oversimplification of complex processes and phenomena in order to make them amenable to short-term investigation. The methodological questions that need to be addressed in relation to Jung's theory are whether Jung's research methods were appropriate for his theory and whether they are sufficiently rigorous without being rigid and conceptually reductive. Whilst these are currently matters of debate, they could and should become the subject of future investigative research.

Some useful methodological criteria for qualitative research which may be worth considering in relation to Jung's methods are offered by Salmon (2003: 26). Salmon advocates rigour achieved through 'strenuous methods' and thoroughness with an intention to enrich rather than to degrade the subject matter. A good researcher, he says, is willing to go beyond the usual conventions in seeking appropriate methods, to seek to organise findings analytically in ways which will empower readers or participants, and to seek research that will yield results that are not trivial but can offer coherent and meaningful advances to understanding in areas that matter not just to the researcher but to others. The work's value should be a consequence of its capacity to produce and develop ideas and to open up possibilities. These are exactly the methodological aims Jung engaged with actively throughout his life. We might critically examine whether Jung succeeded in finding the method of investigation that was best suited to his theory while considering what alternative methods were available to him.

Therapeutic value

One way of evaluating a theory of personality is by gauging its practical benefit in its applied form as a therapy. Each therapeutic technique contributes to a personality theory's usefulness. Jung's specific techniques, amplification in dream analysis, active imagination, and his four-stage process of therapy, can be reviewed on the basis of their potential to contribute to therapeutic effectiveness and, ultimately, to psychological 'health'. Only if it were to be shown that fully trained therapists with experience in the use of his methods were nevertheless ineffective or demonstrably harmful could these techniques be said to have no value. However, the main therapeutic value of Jung's theory is possibly its application beyond cure, when it becomes a way of life. This is the way Jung would have seen it, since he compared therapy's purpose with religions, which are ways of life. Jung's theory of a beneficial way of life could be said to have no value if it can be shown that it is valueless or actually harmful to follow a Jungian path.

The dilemma for theories from which therapies are derived is that outcomes should be taken as evidence of the value of the theory, but it seems there is no really good evidence base for this. Edward Erwin (1997) considers that theories of personality are bundles of causal explanations and asks whether causal explanations lead directly to therapeutic effectiveness. Instead, Erwin suggests they are best considered as points of departure leading towards new ways of thinking about human beings and how best they might become themselves. Matching to evidence from therapeutic outcomes collapses into utility, and this prompts the question of how this particular sort of usefulness should be measured. Is a therapeutically useful theory one that leads to the amelioration of some kind of pathology or one that helps people to express themselves as autonomous individuals, empowers people, and facilitates creativity? Jung was interested both in cure and in personal development. These are perhaps two different but related aspects of Jung's work. The first aspect, 'cure', can be evaluated through the systematic collection and intelligent interpretation of outcome data. Evaluating the second aspect calls for longitudinal approaches and large-scale projects that are possible but have not yet been undertaken for most therapies.

Other types of utility

Theories of personality impact ordinary peoples' lives. A theory may be valuable largely as a means of helping people to understand how to live in the world and how to act in it. The study of personality is about the successful, adaptive, and fulfilling living out of personal lives. If psychological ideas result in the discovery of new ways of relating to oneself and others and facilitate rather than restrict, exploit, or oppress people, they may be said to have had a real, practical human value (Lunt, 2004). Ideally, as the pioneering personality theorists of the 1930s knew and later twentieth-century personality theorists began to rediscover, psychology should benefit people. We need to find ways of assessing a theory's contribution to human welfare as well as to intellectual understanding.

In doing so, we need to consider whether psychological theory should help people to express themselves and their desires. Psychology should not be a way of imposing a set path (someone else's desire) on others (Schatzki, 2004). The capacity to foster autonomy is especially important in theories of personality. The most difficult question in human society has always been who should decide what human welfare is and what it is not. Entitlement to judge lies with those affected by ideas. Jung's readership is not restricted to psychologists, psychotherapists, or counsellors. Research that establishes reliable data on the spread of his ideas through dissemination of his work in published form and translation[8] may be more indicative of their utility value than the responses of other psychologists.

Validity

Validity is an essential but deceptively simple concept when applied to theories and their constructs. A totally verified theory is no longer a theory. It has become a fact. At the same time, a theory is more than a hypothesis. It is a complex construction of premises and conclusions whose data can be verified but whose theoretical concepts cannot be validated directly. A psychoanalytic theory is not an explanation in the causal sense. It should be considered more as a set of possible reasons or motives for behaviour and psychological development (Toulmin, 1948: 25–28).

Whereas it is relatively easy to build up evidence and even to 'prove' hypotheses such as that people behave this way or that in a particular situation, it is much more difficult to establish the truth or falsehood of a construct like individuation. In fact, there has been a long history of antiempirical argument which proposes that a direct religious or psychological experience may be *more* valid than sensory experience, since information mediated by the senses can mislead and be false (Richards, 2004).[9] Nevertheless, the concept of validity can be used helpfully as a tool for critical analysis of the value and implications of research findings; see the section on Validity in Chapter 8 for two examples of how this criterion can be applied in relation to Jung's theory.

Inference to the Best Explanation

Before leaving this discussion of criteria for evaluating theories, I wish to mention a recent approach to evaluating scientific theories that derives from abductive reasoning – a form of reasoning that is closer to Jung's own than either induction or deduction. The criteria discussed earlier can be understood as moving towards Inference to the Best Explanation, and my proposed framework is concordant with its principles.

Inference to the Best Explanation (IBE) is a systematic way of choosing among competing hypotheses on the basis of a set of principles and criteria. This is a new field, especially in relation to psychology, and so references are limited to a few writers who have taken up the idea. The main researchers in this area are Lipton (2004) and Thagard (1978, 1992). Proctor and Capaldi (2006) and Haig (2009a, 2009b) review the method in relation to psychology.

IBE is an approach founded on abductive reasoning. Abductive reasoning generates causal or explanatory (not descriptive) hypotheses about observed phenomena and makes comparisons between them, accepting the hypotheses that are the best available.[10] Abductive reasoning is distinct from both inductive reasoning, which reaches generalisations on the basis of cumulative observations, and deductive reasoning, which generates hypotheses and tests them through observation and experimentation (Capaldi & Proctor, 2008: 617). The second stage of the abductive approach is known as Inference to the Best Explanation. It has been suggested as an alternative to the hypothetico-deductive method for evaluating theories in psychology (Haig, 2009a: 219–234). The appeal of this type of reasoning is that it is widely used in science and in everyday life, and even, for example, by Sherlock Holmes (Capaldi & Proctor, 2008: 618). Essentially, evaluation of theories by means of Inference to the Best Explanation requires establishing rational scientific criteria that are appropriate to the type of theory being evaluated, just as I am seeking to do with respect to Jung's theory, and then comparing the theory in question with other theories that address, explain, or solve the same problems. The 'loveliness' of a theory is said to comprise such virtues as unificatory power, scope, and precision (Lipton, 2004 cited by Haig, 2009a: 221).

'To the extent that psychologists draw on criteria to evaluate their theories, they are using IBE', that is, they are making inferences to the best explanatory theory (Haig, 2009a: 231). Because I agree with Haig that the use of criteria implies that one is already using an inference approach of this kind, I want to pause for a moment to consider the potential advantages and problems in applying this approach to evaluating Jung's theory of personality. It would be naïve to assume that evaluating Jung's theory on the basis of IBE is simply a matter of deciding on criteria and applying them. IBE does not evaluate theories in isolation; it requires comparison with one or several comparable theories that seek to explain the same phenomena. Jung's theory seeks to explain individual mental experience and personality development in relation to the collective. Few personality theories attempt this as comprehensively as Jung did. Finding comparators is thus no simple problem, and, furthermore, the process of comparison is expected to take a very long time, perhaps decades, for example, using the ECHO program described in following paragraphs (Proctor & Capaldi, 2006: 80).

IBE compares theories on multiple criteria of explanatory goodness (Haig, 2009a: 220). The value of the theory is not based on its truth value, about which no assumption is made; the first step is to consider explanations in the light of plausibility. A hypothesis is accepted if it is (a) more plausible and (b) more 'lovely' than its rivals (Lipton, 2004 cited in Haig, 2009a: 222), the *best explanation* being described by Lipton as an ambiguous combination of the most *likely explanation* and the most *lovely explanation*, as defined by other criteria such as simplicity. Because it is a comparative process, IBE does not directly identify the best or most perfect theory. Its purpose is to identify the best available theory amongst a group of competitors (Proctor & Capaldi, 2006: 89). It is acknowledged that several theories may provide satisfactory explanations, or that all of them may be known to have problems that have yet to be solved.

Thagard (1978) developed a method and a theory of IBE he called the *theory of explanatory coherence* and designed a computer program known as ECHO

(Explanatory Coherence by Harmony Optimization) for its implementation. Thagard's theory is founded on seven principles – symmetry, explanation, analogy, data priority, contradiction, competition, and acceptability – and three criteria: explanatory breadth, simplicity (making fewer assumptions), and analogy (Haig, 2009a: 223–224). Analogy is included as both a principle and a criterion (Thagard, 1992: 66–68). Analogy refers to the use of explanatory ideas such as the 'blank slate' of the behaviourists, the computer-mind used by cognitive scientists, or the solar system analogy for the arrangement of electrons around a nucleus in atomic physics (Proctor & Capaldi, 2006: 74).

Abductive principles provide firm criteria for determining exactly when and why theories should be accepted or rejected (Proctor & Capaldi, 2006: 623 and 638). For Proctor and Capaldi, scientific criteria for evaluating theories tend to fall into three categories: empirical, logical, and practical. That is to say that a good theory is superior if it better explains phenomena, has fewer disconfirmations or problems, solves long-standing difficult problems, and has wider scope, if it is logically coherent, and parsimonious, and if powerful applications come from it (Proctor & Capaldi, 2006: 623). One can see that, while there are similarities with criteria mentioned by the authors of textbooks of personality psychology mentioned earlier (see pp. 122–126), IBE is envisaged to be a long-term process of comparing theories that persist and survive and seeing how well a theory does over time in comparison with other views. Since it takes time for alternative views to emerge, it may take decades to identify the best available theory.

For the most part, ECHO has been used retrospectively on theories such as Darwin's theory of evolution and Lavoisier's theory of combustion, which replaced the notion of phlogiston with oxygen. It is really a model of the process of scientific change.

Two further notions that are recognised as impacting on theory evaluation are Whewell's 'consilience' proposed in the 1850s and Giere's (1985) 'satisficing'. Whewell (1794–1866) noted that a theory gains value when its (inductive) inferences are supported by evidence from a variety of different sources. The idea became known as the *consilience* of inductions (Proctor & Capaldi, 2006: 12). This was also the strategy advocated and frequently used by Charles Darwin and by Jung, who drew upon evidence from other disciplines to lend support to his ideas. Proctor and Capaldi, following Thagard, take the view that a consilient theory has unifying power, as it unifies several classes of phenomena and explains common principles (Proctor & Capaldi, 2006: 94). Haule had consilience in mind when reviewing cross-disciplinary evidence in support of Jung's concept of the archetypes (Haule, 2011), and it is one of the principles that underlies my evaluation in Chapter 8 of the validity of Jung's concept of the relationship between the conscious and the unconscious mind. Whewell also emphasised the value of a theory's predictive ability, but this was disputed at the time by Mill, who thought that explanatory theories were valuable as well as those that generate useful predictions (Proctor & Capaldi, 2006: 60–61).

'Satisficing' is a term used to describe scientists' practice. Giere observed that decision makers, when they are deciding between more or less satisfactory outcomes or models, keep revising their objections until a satisfying outcome can be achieved. Similarly, evaluation ultimately involves a continual process of comparison with other theories, some of which are rejected, until the best available theory remains. Proctor and Capaldi note that this contrasts with Rorty's (1989) notion of relativism, which proposes that theories are alternative stories or descriptions, all of which are equally possible (Proctor & Capaldi, 2006: 50, 52, 124). I agree with Proctor and Capaldi that this does not work, because the basis for accepting a theory is that it explains phenomena better than other theories do.

The crucial point is that criteria and standards are themselves matters for dispute. One reason for rejecting total relativism is that, as we have seen in the conflicting views expressed by textbook authors, the different groups within psychology make judgements based on their own standards, which inevitably introduces bias.

Why IBE is useful for evaluating Jung's personality theory

IBE moves away from predictive accuracy to explanatory value. It is also a qualitative approach to establishing explanatory worth, though it encompasses and values quantitative data. The criterion of explanatory breadth is given the highest importance (Thagard, 1992: 74). This means that a theory has more explanatory value if it explains a greater range of facts (or, in psychology's case, phenomena). This has particular relevance for a wide-ranging and complex psychological theory like Jung's. IBE also includes analogy (the theory's similarity to already understood processes that have high credibility) as a criterion. Thus it emphasises the value of consilience, that is, of theories tending in a similar direction and which are capable of unifying a field. As we know, Jung sought to do this and aligned his ideas with those of Semon, von Hartmann, and Kant, for example. Whilst Thagard suggests three criteria, it is acknowledged that other criteria need to be proposed and agreed on within the field in which the theory sits. I hope that my proposed criteria may generate wider discussion that would further the process of arriving at a consensus on appropriate and adequate criteria that could encompass Jung's empirically researchable statements *and* his visionary and metaphysical concepts.

Why it is not yet possible to apply IBE to Jung's theory of personality

One can use the abductive reasoning of IBE informally as a framework for evaluation, but the lack of a sufficient body of research on key Jungian constructs is likely to preclude a formal IBE evaluation. Furthermore, since judgement is made by comparing two or more theories in relation to the available evidence, there is also the problem of finding comparable competing theories. Few theories address the same questions as Jung did or prioritise the same concerns (see Chapters 2–5, in which I outline the issues that Jung theorised on). One might have to compare parts of the theory – for example, archetypes versus the 'blank slate' of the social constructionist theory of mind. Psychological theories that focus on particular processes generate more comparable data than those that generate holistic explanatory concepts. On the other hand, a psychology that is holistic may gain explanatory power by being complex, multifaceted, and focussed on the individuality in human nature rather than solely on those aspects that can be explained by general laws.

Concluding reflections on the value of IBE and its potential for evaluating Jung as a personality theorist

As a form of reasoning about the evaluation of theories, Inference to the Best Explanation (IBE) has a number of advantages over testing the predictive and applied value of Jung's theory. It is a form of reasoning that values explanatory breadth and includes qualitative data whilst also offering an empirically defensible and transparent process of evaluation. However, I have positioned Jung's theory as not yet meeting the formal requirements of IBE and noted that this is thought to be the case with other psychological theories. My suggestion is that IBE is a good motivating framework for future research and an appropriate path for development and growth in the Jungian field, especially if it were to function as a unifying force for gathering the evidence base for Jung's most esoteric ideas.

There is, however, a notable criticism of IBE, that the best explanation or the best theory evaluated by IBE may be the 'best of a bad lot' and all the competing theories may be false (van Frassen cited by Haig, 2009a: 225). Haig offers the defence that the first stage of IBE involves reducing the explanations to the plausible ones,[11] and so the outcome may be 'the best of a plausible lot', and more than one theory may be plausible. Moreover, much of the discussion about IBE and abduction is focussed on the question of how and whether scientific revolutions actually happen. The aim of IBE theorists has primarily been to understand the historical process of scientific change rather than to evaluate current theories. This may limit its applicability to current theories. It has also been suggested that personality theory is not a science but a field in which a variety of approaches and theories is to be expected. Alternative world views lead to a multiplicity of formulations about the plasticity and multidirectionality of individual differences across the life span (Lerner, 1992, cited in Proctor & Capaldi, 2006:134). I agree with Rychlak's suggestion that psychologists have tried to stretch their scientific understanding of the material universe to cover human actions that simply cannot be captured in the same terms (Rychlak, 2003, cited by Proctor & Capaldi, 2006: 137). However, I do not think that these limitations negate the potential gain in taking the principles of IBE as far as they can be taken to structure a much-needed reevaluation of Jung's important ideas.

Concluding comment

Theories are points of view. They cannot be right, but they can be useful. The real value of a theory may be that it makes propositions that are counter to our immediate experiences and beliefs. This is important for 'human' subjects like psychology and personality, as we 'know' a great deal about these subjects in our everyday lives (Craib, 1992: 9). We learn most from theories that are different from the ones we generate ourselves. We need 'outside' theories because we are challenged to consider new and different views from our own. At the extreme, theories can make us consider that there may have been times when we were really doing the opposite of what we thought we were doing (Craib, 1992: 10). The benefit of this realisation is an increase in our range of effective action, of freedom of choice. One would need an aggregate of data to evaluate this. Such a picture might emerge from a historical analysis of the reception, spread, and public impact of Jung's theory but could never be incontrovertibly established. This, in itself, is a sign that a theory is alive and active. The impact of a dead theory *can* be evaluated and 'put away'. It is evidently not so with Jung's theory, about which there is a great deal of argument and debate.

Summary

This chapter has considered the issue of theory evaluation from three different angles. Firstly, evaluation criteria that have been proposed by the authors of personality textbooks were considered. Secondly, Jung's own views were discussed; and thirdly, developing the tradition of evaluation criteria for personality theories found in the textbooks, I put forward a framework for a future programme of evaluation and offered some preliminary thoughts about the criteria I am proposing. Whereas this chapter has looked at criteria from a general theoretical perspective, Chapter 8 gives three programmatic examples of how such criteria could be applied.

Notes

1 See Carlson (1971) for a late-twentieth-century plea for the return of holistic values in academic psychology.
2 See Jung's criticism of Adler's theory in 'Fundamental Questions of Psychotherapy' (*CW*16 1951b §234–235).
3 See, for example, D. B. Bromley's (1977) *Case Description in Ordinary Language*, which proposed a case-study method for the study of personality.
4 See Rowland (2005).
5 Their project was recorded in their book *Midwest and Its Children: The Psychological Ecology of an American Town* (Barker & Wright, 1955).

6 See Danziger (1997: 184) in relation to the function of the scientific method itself as a rhetorical device in psychology's history.
7 See Boring (1961: 317) on the simultaneously positive and negative influence of the scientific community in constraining development via the establishment of orthodoxy.
8 A beginning has been made. See Vieljeux (2005: 16–18) for a report on a project which is gathering data about editions and translations of Jung's work in other languages, for the *Catalogue chronologique des écrits de Carl Gustav Jung, en allemand, anglais et français* (1996), and for its future editions.
9 Richards (2004) cites Martineau's *Types of Ethical Theory* (1885).
10 See Proctor and Capaldi (2006) for a full exploration of the philosophical and historical background to the abductive approach and Thagard (1992) for an account of its potential functions in relation to Thomas Kuhn's account of scientific progress and the idea of scientific revolutions as the means by which scientific change is brought about.
11 See Runyan (1981) for an enlightening demonstration of the evaluation of greater and lesser plausibility in a systematic comparison among thirteen different psychoanalytical accounts of why Van Gogh might have cut off his ear.

Chapter 8

An approach to evaluating Jung's personality theory

Introduction

For a full and comparative evaluation of Jung's theory to be undertaken, more data need to be generated in relation to key constructs and hypothesised processes. This will require interdisciplinary cooperation in a long-term project. Here I examine the value of two of Jung's key concepts – the relationship between consciousness and the unconscious, and archetypes – against the criteria of coherence and validity, as programmatic examples to demonstrate what can be done. For reasons of space, it has been necessary to make a selection. The reason for choosing these two criteria as examples is that these are the most challenging, and they are considered fundamental by almost all the authors whose textbooks I reviewed in Chapter 6. Validity is important because some have claimed that Jung's work lacks credibility – many psychologists think of Jung's ideas as akin to 'phlogiston', that is to say quaint, unusual, outdated, and mistaken.[1] Structural coherence is important because it underpins logic and because it enables Jung's theory to be considered from a scientific perspective.

The value of Jung's theory as a whole is then discussed, in the light of those criteria that I have selected as the most important within the overall evaluation framework – criteria that I believe best test the value of Jung's theory for the reasons outlined in the paragraphs that follow (see Chapter 7, Table 7.1, for the complete framework). These are:

- Complexity and scope
- Heuristic value
- Morality/ethical value
- Originality
- Therapeutic value

Complexity and scope are related to Thagard's 'explanatory breadth', which he considered to be of great importance for Inference to the Best Explanation (see Chapter 7, p. 144). Morality, originality, and therapeutic value are 'soft science' criteria that I consider to be both fundamental for all personality theories and especially appropriate for Jung's with its avowed moral and therapeutic aims. Jung's work has recently been reexamined against some of these criteria by authors who come from perspectives other than personality theory. Their views and insights are highly applicable; see, for example, the work of Rowland (2005) on Jung's writing style (aesthetic value) and Papadopoulos's (2006b) work on Jung's epistemology, which links to logical coherence and originality, as well as the work of Stevens (2002) and Haule (2011) on archetypes (see p. 166). I consider the theory against these criteria in a less detailed way. Even so, all of the criteria discussed in Chapter 7 should be included in any comprehensive long-term evaluation programme that I or others might carry out in the future.

I conclude that reconnecting Jung's personality theory with his religious and alchemical ideas, along with using a more appropriate set of criteria to evaluate it, refreshes Jung's theory of personality and lets its value be seen more clearly.

Criterion 1: Structural coherence

In Chapter 1, I defended the classification of Jung's work as a theory of personality. Here I focus on its structure. One way of making the structure of Jung's theory of personality visible is to lay it out schematically in the form of a network, pyramid, or tree diagram, which are common ways of showing the structure of personality theories (see Figure 8.4). Such structures, depicting a hierarchy of lower- and higher-order concepts, are considered to be essential ways of organising the elements of any personality theory (see Murphy, 1958: 57; Millon, 1969: 95; Maddi, 1996: 16). Following are three examples: the first is Millon's network diagram of the clinical picture which reflects the structure of personality (Figure 8.1); the second is Murphy's earlier example of the pyramid structure of his personality theory (Figure 8.2); and the third is Maddi's schematic representation of personality theory (Figure 8.3). Examples are chosen from these authors because they made the structure of their theories explicit. Millon has articulated the structure of personality theories more than any other author in the field of personality psychology has. His clinical work has mainly been focussed on the psychopathology of personality, for which he has put forward his own theory. Murphy was one of the first personality theorists to articulate and illustrate the structure of his theory. Maddi is arguably the foremost expert commentator and analyst of personality theory amongst the authors of textbooks of personality psychology whose work spans several decades.

Figure 8.1 reproduces Millon's schematic diagram of the clinical picture, which is to say, a clinical description of the basic elements of personality.

Murphy's conceptualisation of a pyramid structure of personality is reproduced as Figure 8.2.

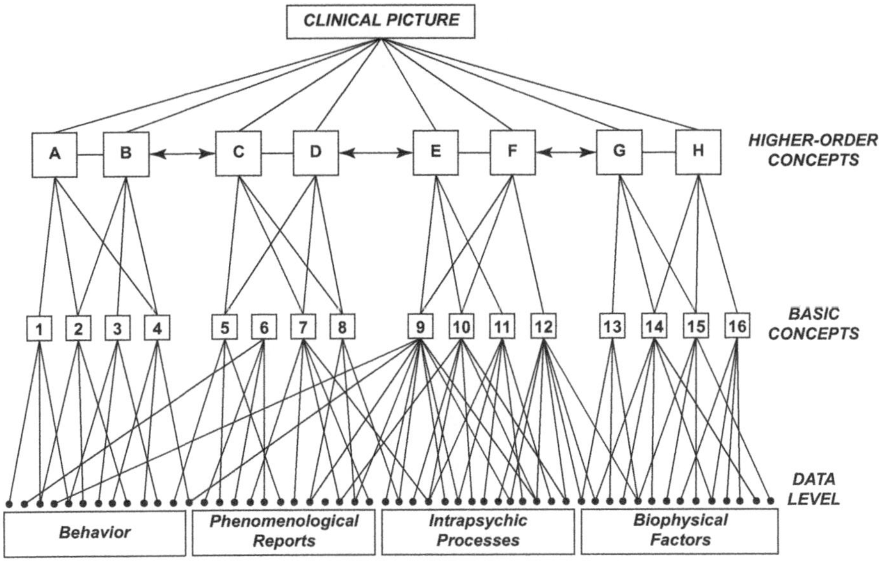

Figure 8.1 Describing the clinical picture. Inferences from the data level (usually overt signs) are formed progressively into basic and higher-order concepts. Behavioral, phenomenological, intrapsychic, and biophysical concepts are derived in large measure from different data sources, although they often represent the same data viewed from different theoretical orientations. The final clinical picture reflects a synthesis of several higher-order concepts drawn from each of the four data sources (Millon, 1969: 95, Figure 3-2).

Maddi's conceptualisation of the elements of a theory of personality showing the links between them is presented as Figure 8.3.

Maddi (1996) considers that, to be a scientific theory of personality, a conceptual network must have an underlying structure of linking statements or core constructs which are themselves arranged in levels of increasing abstraction and centrality. His view is that a personality theory which lacked any one of these essential elements would be structurally flawed. His schematic representation of a personality theory shows the hierarchical relationships between the data from clinical observation and the concepts used to represent them (Maddi, 1996: 16). By 'Statement on the nature of society' (centre right caption), Maddi refers to something akin to a cognitive schema, a composite picture of the 'societal world' that informs and influences the person's views and attitude to society.

In 1969, Millon also proposed a schematic diagram for the structure of a science, outlining its essential elements and specifying their linking relationships. These relationships form a set of rules by which the concepts of a scientific theory are integrated. For Millon, Murphy, and Maddi, the structure (which reflects the logical arrangements of the elements of a theory) maintains its coherence through the linkages that form the tiers of different types of data

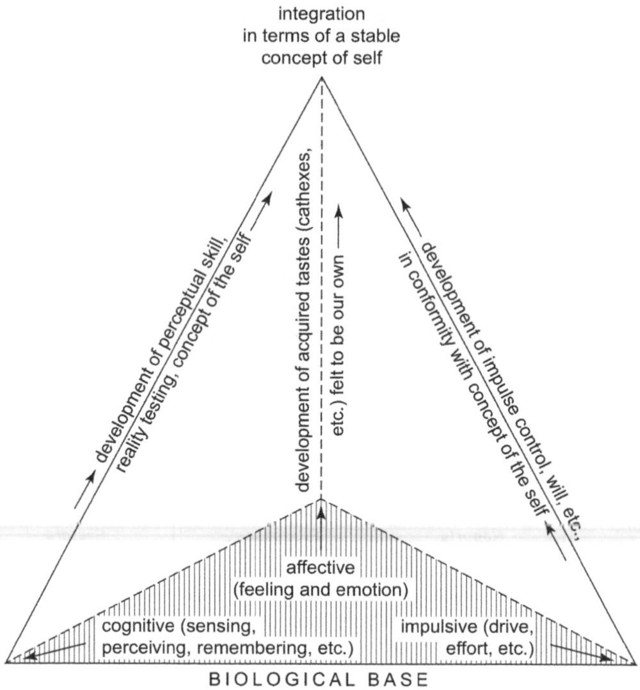

Figure 8.2 Pyramid structure of personality (Murphy, 1958: 57)

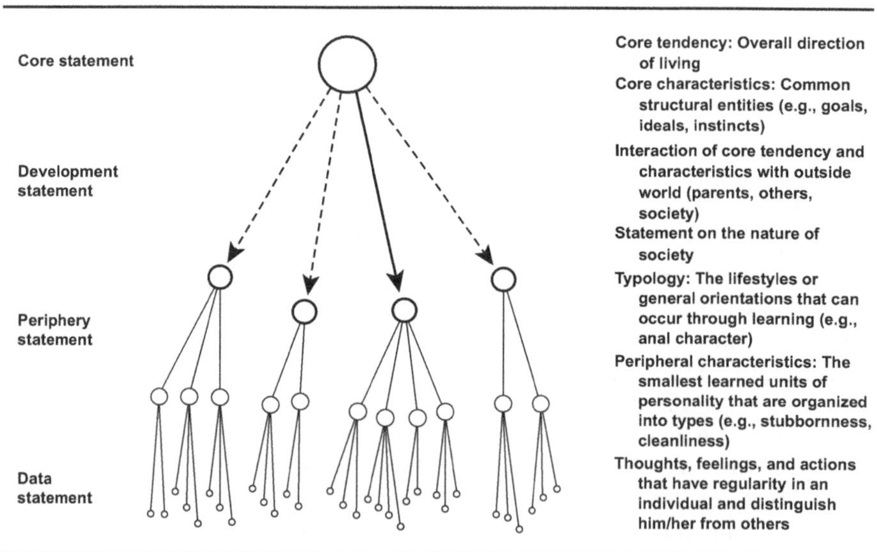

Figure 8.3 Schematic representation of the parts of a personality theory (Maddi, 1996: 16); reproduced by permission of Waveland Press Inc.

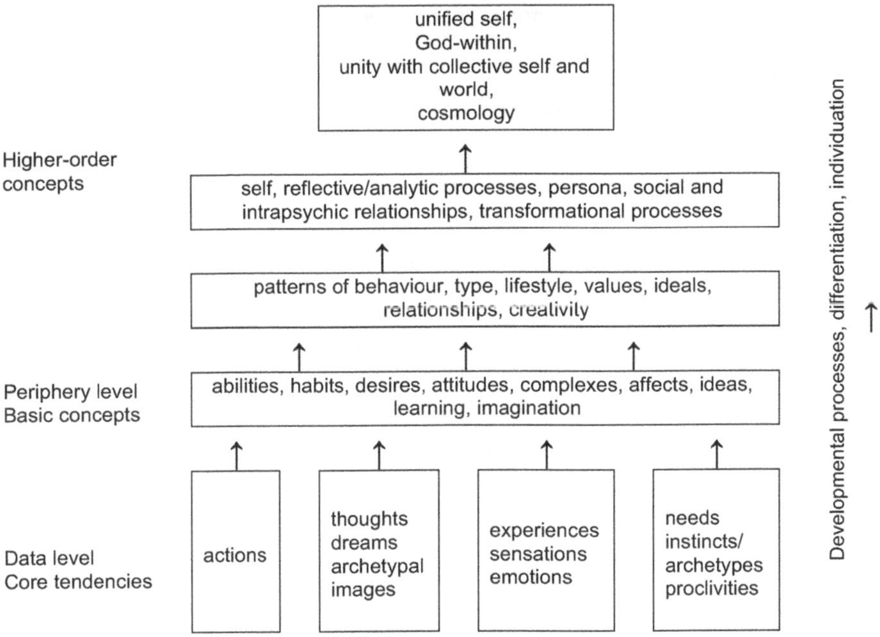

Figure 8.4 Schematic representation of the structure of Jung's personality theory

statements. Weakness of logical coherence limits a theory's potential to generate clear hypotheses and reduces its heuristic and generative value (Millon, 1969: 40).

Although Jung's theory has been criticised on the grounds of alleged vagueness (Ryckman, 1993; Hjelle & Ziegler, 1992) and alleged diffuseness (Levy, 1970), his theory has a clear structure, which I summarise schematically (Figure 8.4). There are data statements, peripheral characteristics, statements of general orientation, and intervening variables. Millon describes intervening variables as processes that have to be assumed but which are anchored in empirical fact. Jung's theoretical structure includes intervening variables (such as attitudes, ideals, and transformational processes shown in levels two, three, and four). There is also a clear developmental theory. There are core characteristics in the form of goals and ideals, and a prominent developmental role is given to instincts. This is implied in the function of archetypes as developmental drivers. The unifying concept of self is set at the highest level, with all its connotations, human and divine.

Is the structure that of a scientific theory?

For the following reasons, I consider that it is also possible to conceptualise the elements of Jung's theory to show correspondences with a schematic model of the structure of a science such as Millon proposed; see Figure 8.5 (Millon, 1969: 41).

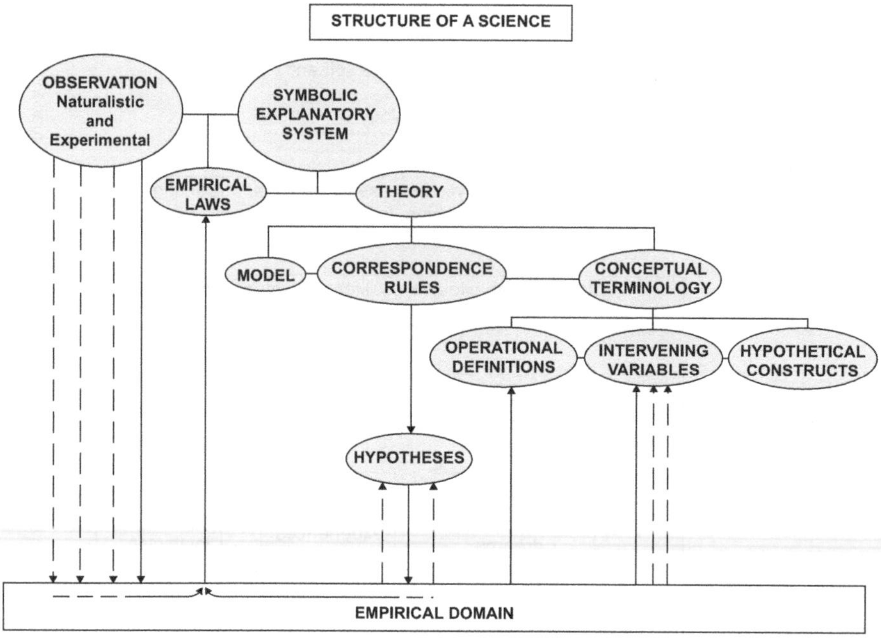

Figure 8.5 Structure of a science. Relationships among the elements of science are signified by connecting lines and arrows. Dotted lines denote a less formal or more imprecise relationship; unbroken lines indicate greater precision or formality (Millon, 1969: 41, Figure 2-1).

The empirical domain would comprise Jung's basic-level data. We know that Jung respected the value of empirical data, his observations. That he did so is exemplified by his diligence in collecting instances and examples of symbolism from different eras and from many parts of the world. It is true that Jung's theory includes data that some theorists would argue are not empirical, but Jung was not alone amongst his contemporaries in including mental phenomena as empirically valid. One might mention Wilhelm Wundt, whose early laboratory experiments were based on introspection, and William James, who made a study of the verbal reports of religious experience.

At the next level in the diagram are hypotheses. Jung's hypotheses may be considered unconventional, but they are explicit. Consider, for example, the hypothesis that new attitudes, ideas, and positions emerge initially as archetypal images. Another example is Jung's hypothesis that men and women carry some vestige of the opposite gender within their natures and his hypothesis that the collective unconscious is represented in mythology.

The next level in the diagram includes 'correspondence rules'. Millon defines these as the logical relationships that form the links between the theory's constructs. Such links are present in Jung's theory. For example, there are statements describing the relationship between the ego and the unconscious as one of interdependence and balance, such as 'The conscious self is merely the marionette dancing upon the stage to a hidden automatic impulse' (*CW*2 1904–7/1910 §246), and 'The more one-sided and cramped the conscious standpoint is, the more painful and dangerous will be the unconscious reaction' (*CW*14 1955–56 §184), as well as statements about the function of opposites in human psychology and their underlying connectedness, such as 'Paradox is the natural way for expressing transconscious facts' (*CW*14 1955–56 §90). In addition to the correspondence rules, at the next level in Millon's structure of a science, there are empirical laws. Jung's theoretical constructs are underpinned by a number of universal empirical laws such as biological and psychological developmental processes, the constraints and limits set by biology, and the inevitability of death, all of which have significant functions in Jung's explanatory system.

An important component in Millon's structure of a science is the hypothetical construct. Jung's archetypes, the concept of the collective unconscious, and the concept of individuation are all hypothetical constructs. An important issue for evaluating the structural coherence of Jung's theory is to examine the function and value of its hypothetical constructs. In this connection, it is useful to return to Millon's remark that the use of hypothetical constructs in theories is often questioned since they are 'speculative concepts which are formulated without explicit reference to observable phenomena'. He warned against the inappropriate application of unrealistic standards of empirical anchorage in the early stages of theorising, as this 'may discourage the kind of imaginative speculation necessary to decipher elusive and obscure phenomena', and concluded that vagueness and surplus meaning can be both weaknesses and also strengths of hypothetical constructs (Millon, 1969: 40). Millon saw vagueness and surplus (not tightly defined) meaning as necessary tools in the development of a productive theory. This latter point has particular significance in relation to the validity of Jung's constructs of the archetype and the collective unconscious, since Jung explicitly favoured and used ambiguous language in order to preserve the complexity and paradoxicality that is inherent in these concepts (*CW*8 1931b §680).

Whilst a 'tree diagram' makes the scientific structure of Jung's personality theory visible, alternative schematic models can be used to reveal other aspects. Circle diagrams capture a different kind of relationship between parts, with opposites in balance, facing one another, opposing and at the same time relating, with the possibility of affecting one another. Circles also suggest the possibility of distinctive types of motion, for example, from inner to outer or vice versa, and rotation, in which opposition and relatedness vary with the rotation. Jung's theory can be equally aptly illustrated in a circular form, as all its contents, structures, and processes revolve around the concept of self as the centre, itself a microcosmic reflection of God. This is why Jung painted mandalas. They are a kind of idiographic representation of personality structure in relation to both the outer and inner world and therefore a graphic expression of his theory.

I conclude that Jung's theory has a demonstrable scientific and dynamic structure which can be revealed through comparisons with schematic representations of personality structure (the clinical picture), personality theory, and the hypothesised structure of a science. I now turn to consideration of a further aspect of theoretical coherence, the clarity of a theory's terms.

Clarity of terms

According to Millon, drawing from the philosophy of science, the logical coherence of a theory depends to a significant extent on the clarity of its terms, its operational definitions (Millon, 1969: 40 and Figure 8.5). Millon acknowledges that the more philosophical the concept (the further from empirical anchorage), the more difficult it becomes to be specific. As we have seen, Jung did provide operational definitions for most of the terms and concepts in his theory, albeit that many of his terms are highly abstract. Jung's definition of *abstraction* itself exemplifies his approach to the problem of defining abstract terms. The definition is precise and shows clearly how abstractions are derived from their empirical sources:

> ABSTRACTION, as the word itself indicates, is the drawing out of a content (a meaning, a general characteristic, etc.) from a context made up of other elements whose combination into a whole is something unique or individual and therefore cannot be compared with anything else . . .
>
> Abstraction . . . is a form of mental activity that frees this content from its association with the irrelevant elements by distinguishing it from them or, in other words, *differentiating* it (v. *Differentiation*). . . .
>
> The more abstract a concept is, the more it is irrepresentable. I subscribe to Kant's view that a concept gets more abstract 'the more differences of things are left out of it', in the sense that abstraction at its highest level detaches itself absolutely from the object, thereby attaining the extreme limit of irrepresentability. It is this pure 'abstract' which I term an *idea* (q.v.). Conversely, an abstract (sic) that still possesses some degree of representability or plasticity is a *concrete* concept (v. *Concretism*).
>
> (*CW*6 1921 §676–680)

Jung's definition gives a clear sense of the process of abstracting, then takes the definition to its highest level, as a pure 'idea', and finally, illustrates the concept by saying what the opposite would be. Inasmuch as it uses other precise terms with known meanings for its description, it is not tautological, and, where a term in the definition has a specific meaning within Jung's work (e.g. 'idea'), a cross-reference is given to its definition.

Jung, no less than Millon, was aware of the dangers of abstract conceptualisation getting further and further away from its empirical ground. Indeed, in 1939 he remarked that Western culture's habit of analysing and theorising made it like 'a madhouse of abstractions' (*CW*10 1939b §988).[2] When Jung defined the significant terms of his theory, he was acknowledging the established conventions of the field of personality theory and writing as a psychiatrist/psychologist within that field. This practice suggests that Jung thought of himself as a scientific personality theorist not only in 1921 when the definitions were first published but also in 1960 when he revised them. It is inevitable, given the complexity of his ideas, that the meanings he gives for significant terms are rich in extended connotations. They are elaborate rather than reductive, but they are at the same time precise in specifying their range of meanings: in fact, Jung's definitions followed a pattern comprising an initial definitive statement, some derivational references, a statement about what is not meant, and finally a more detailed description of his own usage. The following definition of *affect* is typical of the style and format of Jung's definitions:

> AFFECT. By the term *affect* I mean a state of feeling characterized by marked physical innervations on the one hand and a peculiar disturbance of the ideational process on the other. I use *emotion* as synonymous with affect. I distinguish – in contrast to Bleuler (v. *Affectivity*) – *feeling* (q.v.) from *affect*, in spite of the fact that the dividing line is fluid, since every feeling, after attaining a certain strength, releases physical innervations, thus becoming an affect. For practical reasons, however, it is advisable to distinguish affect from feeling, since feeling can be a voluntarily disposable function, whereas affect is usually not. . . . Affect, becomes cumulative through the sensation of the physical innervations released by it. This observation gave rise to the James-Lange theory of affect, which derives affect causally from physical innervations. As against this extreme view, I regard affect on the one hand as a psychic feeling-state and on the other as a physiological innervations state, each of which has a reciprocal effect on the other.
>
> (*CW*6 1921 §681)

Clarity can be characterised by whether definitions are precise enough for their purpose. This must largely be a matter of opinion. Some readers of Jung's work, especially those who sample his work piecemeal, will find it difficult to follow his thinking if they have not built up an understanding of his terms both from his definitions and also from immersion in his work so as to become familiar with his usage of them. Furthermore, it is important to balance clarity of definition with creative and innovative thinking, which must necessarily seek to extend the accepted meaning of technical and common language terms (Millon, 1969). Clarity of terms is partially dependent on the consistency of their use. Before concluding this section on the structural coherence of Jung's theory, I will briefly discuss the issues involved in evaluating Jung's consistency or otherwise in his use of the key terms of his theory.

Consistency

The criticism has been levelled at Jung that he used his terms inconsistently. If true, this would be a serious flaw; however, one must consider the context of the use of terms in a theory that develops over many decades. In the early stages of a theory's development, terms are tentatively put forward; their meaning develops over time. There are perhaps two different questions that are raised in the criticism: clarity of terms and researchability. Lack of clarity has a negative impact on researchability. Furthermore, the less precise the terms are, the more variation there will be in their use across different contexts. I think that some of the difficulty Jung had was that, in writing scientifically, he was in a sense, translating. Whilst he was influenced by outside sources, the real source of his ideas was his imagination. He then transformed his material into a publicly acceptable form. It is not surprising that, as his ideas were nourished from a different source than the world of science, his terms sometimes alternate between a philosophical and a psychological usage, and between technical meanings and the connotations of 'common language' forms. This must be particularly so with a common language term like 'self', which had different meanings for Jung depending on the semantic world he was temporarily inhabiting, as it must do for everyone. Jung's *Collected Works* include a wide range of texts, some well-prepared books, essays, and papers, and other less formal contributions which include letters, talks, and seminars in which Jung, in talking to his followers, engaged in 'ad hoc' theorising and expressed opinions in one-off remarks. Like any theorist talking to groups of people who shared his views, Jung made 'guru-like' statements that were speculative, not rooted in a framework or structure. Such statements may or may not be useful. For the most part, I have based my descriptions of Jung's personality theory on his more formal writing, where one can best see the ideas that he consistently develops.

Summary

This section considered how the criterion of structural coherence can be applied to Jung's theory and argues that, far from lacking structural coherence, his theory has a clear and evident structure that corresponds with schematic representations of a scientific personality theory. The two related questions of clarity and consistency of terms were also discussed. It can be seen that Jung took pains to provide clear definitions for his terms, being an early pioneer in this respect. I suggest that the variation in Jung's use of his terms should be understood in the light of their similarity with everyday-language words[3] and in the context of the range of audiences he was addressing in formal and informal contexts.

Criterion 2: Validity

In recent years, there have been a number of popular reviews by neuroscience research specialists (notably Damasio[4] and Schore[5]) which psychoanalysts have examined for evidence that supports psychoanalytical ideas. There are problems with this approach. One is the tendency to seek confirmation rather than disconfirmation. Another is that the research is selected by the author. Damasio's and Schore's are not academic review papers with a specific and transparent methodology. Although written by eminent figures, they are interpretive overviews which include speculation. What is needed rather is a comprehensive review of evidence in the neurosciences undertaken scientifically by collaborating experts in both the neurosciences and analytical psychology. Such a review is outside the scope of this thesis, but it may be useful to point out some examples of recent experimental research that enrich Jung's work in particular ways. In doing so, I have drawn on material from both primary and secondary sources and include some speculative material. My purpose is not to offer a substitute for a much more comprehensive review but rather to draw attention to areas of research that have yielded promising and interesting results in order to suggest fruitful areas for continued evaluation.

I have selected two contrasting examples from Jung's key concepts. The first is Jung's conceptualisation of the relationship between consciousness and the unconscious. Accumulated experimental results from the study of consciousness indirectly validate Jung's conceptualisation of the unconscious, and experimental evidence that might have falsified Jung's concept of the unconscious in fact supports it. I should emphasise that, by consciousness, I do not mean a state of neurological alertness but a state of awareness of self and environment that is simultaneously capable of reflecting on its own processes.

My second example is Jung's concept of the archetypes, since, if archetypes were found to have been invalidated, then individuation itself, a pivotal concept of Jung's personality theory, would be placed on shaky ground. The evidence that could validate or falsify the concept of archetypes is more difficult to identify, but recently reviewed evidence from neuroscience, palaeontology, and evolutionary biology appears to point to a conclusion that Jung's concept of archetypes is largely harmonious with 'a biology that was poorly understood [in Jung's time] and consistent with biological facts that are better understood now' (Haule, 2011: 126).

Example A. Experimental research on consciousness and the unconscious

1. Consciousness

Over the last twenty years, research on mental processing has consistently demonstrated that in perception, memory, language, and thought, most mental processes are completed prior to any conscious awareness. For example, saccadic eye movements (jumps) take place completely outside of awareness, so much so that these movements were only discovered in the last decades of the twentieth century despite being the most frequently occurring behavioural acts of human beings (Bridgeman, 1992: 76). Aphasia research has shown that, in language puzzle tasks, people with aphasia fixated the correct solutions longer even though they failed to solve the puzzles, suggesting that there was some unconscious recognition of the correct solutions but that this was dissociated from both performance and consciousness (Bridgeman, 1992: 77). Bridgeman concluded that 'most of the business of the brain concerns functions that remain unconscious . . . hidden from view and . . . only dimly understood' (1992: 85–86). In the light of such research findings, the relationship of consciousness to the unconscious and the difference in their modes of operation in the sequences of cognitive processing are beginning to emerge. Dynamic and potent unconscious functions are revealed, with consciousness in a secondary, dependent position.

Reviews of cognitive science research have been undertaken by Power and Brewin (1991) in relation to Freud's concept of the unconscious and by Velmans (1989, 1990, 1993, 2009) in relation to the functions and limits of consciousness. The ultimate focus of Jung's work and the goal of his therapy was the development of a particular kind of consciousness through individuation; as Meier stressed, Jung's 'main concern was to indicate the process of *becoming* conscious' (Meier, 1989: 7). I briefly discuss the potential for future Jungian research of Power and Brewin's comparative approach before outlining examples from Velmans's work that I believe have a bearing on the validity of Jung's concepts. Finally, I discuss research (Weiskrantz, 1988; Milner & Dijkerman, 2001; Morris & Dolan, 2001) which has direct bearing on the powers of the unconscious mind and Steele and Morawski's (2002) reappraisal of work on unconscious cognition and implicit memory in relation to social factors.

Power and Brewin (1991) compared cognitive science's approach to the unconscious with that of Freud, taking into consideration the prevailing computer models and other clinical and experimental data such as Marcel's (1983) experiments in information processing and word recognition and Markus's work (1977; Markus & Nutrius, 1986) on self-schemata. They concluded that both cognitive psychology and Freudian theory include provision for innate prewired programmes to organise incoming stimuli, that the control of behaviour involves both autonomous and semi-autonomous structures, and that both allow for unconscious thought processes that defy time and logic. They found less evidence from cognitive science and hence less agreement about the repression of inadmissible ideas and experiences to the unconscious (Power & Brewin, 1991:301–302). They propose an evidence-based synthesis model which would include innate emotional reactions that prepare for action, innate programmes that enable humans to acquire basic competencies such as self- and child-care, the ability to compete and to cooperate socially, well-learned information and skills that have become automatic, and representations based on the accumulation of repeated experiences, such as the self-schema, as well as the coexistence of relatively autonomous self-states and 'personalities' (Power & Brewin, 1991: 302–305, 307). Power and Brewin's approach could be used as a model for a similar comparative review of cognitive science research data and Jung's concept of the unconscious, which, according to Power and Brewin's conclusions, more closely corresponds with the cognitive research data than Freud's does.

Velmans also systematically analysed key experiments on the processes of cognition and, in some cases, critically reinterpreted the results. For example, in the area of focal attention, he noted that in Cherry's (1953) studies imitating the 'cocktail party effect', while foreground speech signals were delivered to one ear, background speech signals delivered to the other ear must have been unconsciously analysed to a degree, since the physical characteristics of the background message were able to be reported (Velmans, 1989: 2–3). The cocktail-party phenomenon is named after the observation that people suddenly become aware of the previously unattended conversations in another part of the room in which their own name is mentioned. He also reviewed Treisman's (1964) experiments in dichotic listening[6] (one message is played to one ear while a different message is played to the other ear through earphones) in which just under half of the listeners who had been directed to concentrate on the message delivered to one ear recognised that the text spoken in the nonattended ear was a French translation of the message they were hearing in the attended ear, though the degree of recognition was related to the level of skill the person had in the language concerned. Velmans argued that, to have recognised this, the listeners must have unconsciously processed the meaning of the nonattended text (Velmans, 1989: 11).

Experimental results in language processing (reviewed by Marslen-Wilson, 1984) also demonstrate that syntactic analysis is largely carried out unconsciously. For example, the way a word is pronounced when reading aloud may be determined by the whole of the sentence occurring before *and after* the word concerned. This is not under voluntary control. On the basis of this and other evidence on the speed of verbal processing, Velmans concludes that stimuli are constantly being analysed to a high level without entering consciousness. It is only subsequently that preconsciously 'chosen' items receive conscious attention. The choice of which items will and will not be attended to has therefore been made unconsciously, and consciousness follows that choice (Velmans, 1989: 14; 2009: 2248). These results shift many of the functions we habitually associate with consciousness and relocate them in the unconscious (Velmans, 1989: 27). This picture of consciousness as secondary to the unconscious corresponds with Jung's view that the conscious ego is, to a large extent, the servant of the unconscious, not its ruler.

In *Understanding Consciousness* (2009), Velmans asks what is left for consciousness to do if analysis of meaning and significance takes place unconsciously. Consciousness is shown to be surrounded and supported by unconscious contents and processes. The interaction between the two forms 'a reflexive interaction of perceptual processing with entities, events and processes in the surrounding world, body and mind/brain itself' (Velmans, 2009: 296).

Consciousness, Velmans concludes, brings a private, subjective, and unique awareness. Individual conscious presentations of the world are the result of 'an exact mix of perceptual, cognitive, affective, social, cultural and historical influences which enter into the "construction" of a given experience'. Taken together, these provide a *view* of the wider universe but are not the *thing-itself*. Velmans proposes a concept of 'reflexive monism' to describe humans' participation in a reflexive process whereby the universe experiences itself: reflexive monism expresses the idea that human consciousness is the conscious element of a conscious universe. 'There is *one* universe (the thing-itself), with relatively differentiated parts in the form of conscious beings like ourselves, each with a uniquely conscious view of the larger universe of which it is a part' (Velmans, 2009: 298). There is a striking correspondence between this vision of the human mind/brain as the part of the universe that experiences itself and Jung's perception of the conscious world, the *unus mundus* (see *CW*10 1958c §780).

To illustrate his assertion that phenomenal representation, the experience of living, is the main function of consciousness, Velmans proposed a thought experiment in which we are invited to imagine that consciousness is stripped away whilst all other human functions are left intact.[7] The effect, he suggests, is that 'the lights go out'. Although we would continue to live in the world, we could not experience ourselves living in it. Having no thoughts, emotions, or dreams, we could not have any awareness of ourselves. Whilst the world would still function, it could not be subjectively real, as this is lost when consciousness is lost. This imaginal exercise, taken together with the strong evidence for a multitude of pre- or unconscious processes, convinced Velmans that the sole function of consciousness is that it enables us to 'real-ise' the world (2009: 322–323). His concluding speculations relate so closely to Jung's view of the function and purpose of consciousness that Velmans chose to cite in full Jung's account of his personal experience while travelling in Nairobi, a moment in which he felt as if he had been present at 'the eternal beginning of the world as it had always been', and as if he had created it:

> Now I know what it was, and know even more: that man is indispensable for the completion of creation; that, in fact, he himself is the second creator of the world. . . . Human consciousness created objective existence and meaning . . .
>
> (Jung & Jaffé, 1983: 284, cited in Velmans, 2009: 350)

Support for Jung's suggestion that ideas arrive 'whole' from the unconscious and are instantly available and accessible to consciousness in the form of images can be found in the work of Penrose (1989) and Greenfield (2000). Penrose suggests that conscious processes could not all be algorithmic in a computational sense (passing through a logical sequence of operations). Instead, he speculated that, in the case of selecting, judging, and comprehending, that is, 'seeing' that something is right or wrong, a more global 'quantum' process is likely to be involved in which ideas arrive whole and not in a conventionally time-ordered framework (Penrose, 1989: 515–581). More recently, Greenfield has suggested that the neurotransmitter acetylcholine may provide the underlying chemical basis for enabling the necessary 'quantum coherence' for assemblies of neurons acting in concert (Greenfield, 2000: 188–193).

2. *The unconscious*

1. Jung and unconscious processing

Jung described the unconscious as containing all that has been seen and experienced, whether within or outside awareness (*CW*8 1947/1954 §382). Turning to research with direct bearing on the powers of the unconscious mind, de Gelder, de Haan, and Heywood reviewed the experimental evidence for a variety of implicit unconscious processes (de Gelder et al., 2001: chapter 2). Their volume acknowledges the contribution of Weiskrantz's work on the phenomenon of 'blindsight'. Weiskrantz investigated the phenomenon that people with neurological blindness showed greater than chance accuracy in pointing by guesswork in the direction of visual stimuli that they reported they were unable to see and concluded that unconscious modes of visual processing retained residual capacity after damage to the visual cortex (Weiskrantz, 1986, 1988). Research by Weiskrantz and others raised the question whether blindness is actually a loss of vision or the loss of the *conscious experience* of vision. This research revealed the extent to which sensory perception is processed unconsciously.

Jung's word-association tests had shown that unconscious emotions affect verbal responses to word lists. Emotional memory, an aspect of unconscious processing thought to involve the amygdala, was investigated by Milner and Dijkerman (2001). They found that facial expressions that people could not see and were not aware of could influence processing in another sensory modality such as responses to spoken sentences. There appeared to have been some unconscious processing of emotional stimuli, perhaps through a different automatic visual pathway that works in parallel to the rest of the visual system. This parallel pathway, it was thought, might not result in a conscious visual experience but in an enduring mental representation affecting subsequent tasks, just as Jung had shown (Milner & Dijkerman, 2001: 241–265; see also Milner & Goodale, 2008).

Support for Jung's view that unconscious emotional factors such as archetypes exist and are innate and instinctual is found in experiments carried out by Morris and Dolan (2001). The amygdala is believed to be the site of both learned and innate fear. Morris and Dolan reviewed neuroimaging studies which showed that fear processing in the amygdala could occur with no conscious awareness of the fear-inducing stimuli (Morris & Dolan, 2001: 185–190). In the experiments reviewed by Morris and Dolan, picture stimuli were coupled with electric shocks in 'conditioning experiments' in order to induce learned fear of the pictured images. When presented for too short a time to be consciously processed, happy faces and other not normally fear-inducing stimuli did not elicit enhanced autonomic responses, but faces with expressions of fear did do so. They concluded that this finding supports Seligman's (1971) theory that fears that occur frequently of snakes, spiders, and angry or fearful faces are the result of an innate 'preparedness' to fear things that would have been threatening or alarming to human ancestors. Not only could such fear-related stimuli be processed by the amygdala without being consciously perceived, but a lack of cognitive awareness could sometimes lead to stronger fear responses (Morris & Dolan, 2001: 188–189). Morris and Dolan's results provide some support for Jung's view that unconscious emotional factors exist that are innate and instinctual.

Experiments using neuroimaging techniques provided Morris and Dolan with evidence for the existence of parallel autonomous visual systems in the human brain associated with different levels of conscious awareness. They suggest that parallel subcortical and cortical pathways exist, one of which is rapid and secondary, and the other, a primary pathway, serves visual analysis and object recognition (Morris & Dolan, 2001: 195). The data indicate that in some circumstances, these parallel systems exhibit a degree of autonomy (2001: 199–200). Jung's idea that old ancestral patterns of learning and behaviour (archetypal patterns) are stored deep in the unconscious and can function autonomously begins to make biological sense in the light of these findings. It is interesting that, like the concept of the archetypes, Seligman's innate 'preparedness' poses questions about how a facility initially learned by experience can be passed on, if not through 'Lamarckian inheritance'. Haule suggests a process by which such learning could indeed be passed down through the generations that is compatible with Darwinian evolution. He points out that the hereditable genetic component is in the emergent properties of the developing human brain that forms structures and (hormonal) processes capable of supporting basic human action patterns for functions like language but which are essentially 'empty forms' of instincts to be shaped by experience and culture. The individual brain is made by its experiences, formed from its own 'memories' which fill the 'empty structures' in just the same way that Jung said that experience 'fills' the empty structures of instinct with the individual image and expression of the instinct in each person (Haule, 2011: 11–28).

Not only do the above findings support the existence of a general concept of the unconscious that contains and processes information of which the conscious mind is unaware, but these data support a specifically Jungian conceptualisation of the unconscious as the matrix that surrounds and gives rise to consciousness, as that which directs, guides, and influences what consciousness will attend to, as the source of ideas that come into consciousness, and as the source of innate instinctual and autonomous predispositions that lead to patterns of behaviour.

A further area of research lends support to yet another aspect of Jung's theory: his developmental notion of the child's unconscious participation in the parental milieu.

2. *Jung and unconscious social processing*

Jung claimed that early development takes place within a parental milieu unconsciously absorbed by the child who participates in it (*CW*17 1928a §107). Steele and Morawski (2002) reappraised empirical work on unconscious cognition and implicit memory in cognitive psychology. Citing Reber (1993), who proposed that people's unconscious model of the power, gender, and other social factors that make up their surrounding social world is formed of unconscious structures and projected unconscious contents, which, in turn, affect and shape the social world, they found evidence that the norms of culture are learnt implicitly during childhood. An unconsciously acquired social order is formed which may have negative power so long as it remains hidden from conscious awareness (Steele & Morawski, 2002: 38). The idea that complex social learning is unconscious but can be made conscious by turning attention towards it is similar to Jung's hypothesis that a child's' view of the world is acquired unconsciously through unconscious participation in the parental milieu. The link I am making here is tentative but promising and points to an area for further investigation and research.

Concluding remarks on Jung and contemporary research on conscious and unconscious processes

Data from other areas of psychology which demonstrate correspondences with Jung's conclusions suggest a project for a comprehensive overview of existing research would be fruitful. The findings discussed in the preceding section, which reveal insights into the fundamental nature, phenomenology, and neural biology of conscious and unconscious processes, were not available to Jung. From different points of departure, a number of researchers are in significant agreement with Jung in concluding that consciousness does not lead the unconscious, that unconscious processes precede and influence conscious processes, and that most mental functions proceed independently of conscious awareness. Most importantly, all of these experiments were open to falsification and could have demonstrated the contrary.

Example B. Validity and the concept of archetype

Although the concept of the archetypes has been in human culture in some form since Plato, it is only recently that scholars have begun to gather and evaluate experimental work across disciplines that would support or falsify Jung's concept of the archetype.

Samuels questions a literal interpretation of the archetype as something in the person (Samuels, 1989: 24–27), and Shamdasani concluded that Jung's ethological idea of archetypes as instincts was weakened by the fact that attempts to reformulate the concept in line with modern biology had failed (Shamdasani,

2003: 259–267). Ethology moved away from the idea of 'inborn images' guiding instinctual behaviour. By contrast, Stevens (2002: 23–33, 53–55) concluded that adequate scientific evidence exists for the evolutionary biological concept of instinct and that the same evidence can be used as scientific validation for Jung's archetype-as-instinct. Stevens's argument is based on a view that links archetypes closely with instincts. From the perspective of personality theory, however, it is the link between archetypes and individuation that has a value for the psychology of personality. In Chapter 5, we saw the various ways in which Jung defined archetypes. His emphasis on the archetype as the principle of formation, by which 'primordial' thoughts shape personality and influence personal choices, is crucial in evaluating Jung's contribution to personality theory.

I want to suggest a possible link with the psychological concept of cognitive schemata, frameworks that organise information such as the self-schema, which, like assumptions and presuppositions, are available to conscious awareness, but the origins of which are not always conscious.[8] It is believed that they colour and influence conscious thinking and emotional responses, and they are the subject of cognitive psychotherapy. Jung's archetypes are similarly dynamic influencers of thought processes and of psychic development itself. It is difficult to devise experimental procedures that would isolate the epistemological process that Jung was convinced exists or to demonstrate that no other process could have caused the experimental outcome. A project to review potentially relevant cognitive studies directly and comprehensively would be fruitful for seeing what light existing research on cognitive processes and structures might throw on Jung's archetypes.[9] A similar review is needed of neuroscience research. For example, Haule (2011) looked closely at the suggestive results from neuroscience on slow and fast fear-learning pathways in the amygdala. This research tells us that a fast pathway exists that alerts the person to the presence of danger, while a slower pathway *such as the archetype* stores more lasting information. These may be the brain pathways in which Jung's postulated thought-forming process and images as well as complexes might be carried (Haule, 2011: 125–137).

Support for Jung's archetypes as primordial forms of ideas was found by Mattoon (1981). Mattoon categorised two types of evidence for archetypes, inferential and empirical. As inferential support, she includes Jung's analogical parallel with the botanical system, based on discerned structures or forms that do not exist as entities but are reflected in the morphological and functional similarities that can be observed in nature (Jung cited in Mattoon, 1981: 43). Jung understood the botanical system as a set of 'norms' which drive, influence, shape, and limit the variety of botanical forms and functions that can exist and be observed in nature. Whilst the 'norms' are not themselves observable, they are discernible by the effects they produce. Jung deduced that similar 'norms' exist in psychological life and that they are ultimately biological in origin. His logic seems to be that if something takes a certain form, develops in a certain way along certain lines, one must assume the existence of something like 'rules' that guide development along those lines, just as the axial system in a crystal shapes the crystalline structure that the crystal will take. For humans, archetypes are a species-specific system reflecting the putative 'arrangers' of psychological contents into specifically human forms.[10] Jung's point is 'Why not?' (Mattoon, 1981: 47). The answer may need to take into consideration the critique that the assumption that evolved forms must have a creator or a guiding purpose is false, as Dawkins (1986: 1–18) has argued.

Mattoon cites a range of possible evidence for archetypes, for example: Penfield's discoveries from experimental brain stimulation in which stimulation of a particular area produced experiences of bright lighted object shapes such as stars, squares, or streaks (although this could be interpreted more simply as evidence for specificity of function in groups of brain cells); Lorenz's studies of imprinting in birds and animals; anthropological evidence that similar artefacts are found in cultures that had no contact with one another as noted by Hawkes (1963, cited in Mattoon, 1981, although it is not clear whether this phenomenon might have other causes such as environmental conditions and opportunities); and Ross's experiments (1976, cited in Mattoon, 1981) in which people judged squares to be more perfectly square than they were, a phenomenon Ross explained by hypothesising that the participants imposed a kind of ideal squareness similar to one of Plato's ideal forms (Mattoon, 1981: 46–47). Mattoon also cites Jung's comparative research on archetypal images and Spiegelman's 1955 finding that Thematic Apperception Test responses could be explained as archetypal images projected onto the test stimuli (Mattoon, 1981: 48).

Nevertheless, Jung's concept of the archetypes remains controversial. We are left with the question of whether the concept should be best understood as an empirical observation about a natural entity or as a metaphysical/quasi-philosophical concept. I agree with Brooke (1991: 14) that Jung sought both to understand phenomena *and* to bring them into the realm of empiricism, which at times may seem to extend *empirical* beyond its usual meaning. Jung's comparative method for dreams and fantasies is clearly empiricist. He was not alone in regarding his comparative results *per se* as an adequate empirical basis for the existence of archetypes (Maduro & Wheelwright, 1977). Brooke refers to a [1960] letter from Jung to Bennet in which he situates psychology in a European tradition, in which 'historical and comparative methods are scientific' (Jung, cited in Brooke, 1991: 74). On the other hand, comparative mythology is the subject of a nature/nurture debate because of the difficulty of specifying what is inherent in a species-specific mode of transmission and what is socially and culturally transmitted. A programme of future research could look for ways of exploring the limits of social transmission to establish what aspects of human personality are socially constructed and what is left unaccounted for. Brooke makes two useful and subtle distinctions: that validation is not verification but is a logic of uncertainty and probability rather than certainty (Ricoeur, 1973, cited in Brooke, 1991: 74–75) and, secondly, that Jung's work emphasises process more than structures (Brooke, 1991: 78–80), the connecting link between psychological functions and the world being archetypal fantasy (Brooke, 1991: 80–81).

One area of potential empirical evidence is the practice of Jungian psychotherapy, which seeks to facilitate the function of the archetypes in individuation. However, without a systematic programme of investigation including comparison with alternative explanations, Jung's concept of the archetypes remains vulnerable to the critique that endless positive instances constitute consensus, not proof.

Demonstrating the empirical validity of archetypes is crucial since, if archetypes were found to be unsupportable (a dead end), this would negate Jung's account of personality and his concept of the Self. When talking about mandala symbols, Jung asserted that mandala-like images reflected in the symbols that people drew, painted, and recounted from dreams have empirical reality as the symbolic expressions of the emergent process of self-formation, which can be empirically tracked via these images. Much Jungian psychotherapy and art psychotherapies are based on this assumption. It is entirely possible that a future theorist could offer a superior account of archetypes and archetypal processes, in which case Jung's interpretation would shift to being of historical importance. Indeed, such an outcome might be expected if Jung's ideas generated a programme of further research. There would be amendments and developments of his theory that would take account of new data. In fact, this would increase rather than decrease the heuristic and generative value of the concept of the archetypes and would develop the idea beyond Jung's original intuition.

Emergence theory and archetype

The recent development of emergence theory has combined several preexisting strands of research which correspond quite closely with some aspects of Jung's theory of archetypes. Emergence theory describes the capacity of simple structures to spontaneously generate complex structures in a self-organised 'bottom-up' way. Separate strands of thinking were brought together that enabled the emergence of self-organised behaviour to be studied in a unified way. Johnson (2001) summarised key studies such as Keller's work on the behaviour of slime moulds,[11] the work of the Santa Fe Institute (founded 1984) on chaos theory (the study of orderly patterns emerging from lower-level randomness), Jacob's observations of the organised systems that emerge in cities, and Minsky's work on self-organised phenomena in the human mind, as well as studies from the 1960s onwards of ant colonies by Gordon, Hamilton, and Wilson and Holldobler (all cited by Johnson, 2001: 236–238 and 274). Johnson notes that, in 1952, when Turing extended his pattern-detection approach to biology, he posed such questions as 'How does a seed know how to become a flower?' (Johnson, 2001: 42) and that Weaver, the author of the field's 1948 founding text, saw that organised complexity was present everywhere in nature, in genes, in plant behaviour, and in how the genetic constitution of a living organism expresses itself in the development of the adult (Johnson, 2001: 48). It is this latter point that has direct relevance for Jung's conception of the role of archetypes in the development of personality.

Computer models were developed to see *how* these phenomena could work. The Jefferson and Taylor computer programme 'Tracker' imitated the process of evolution through inheritance of genetic variation in generations of computer 'ants' and provided a means of testing the theory's hypotheses about what the simple rules are that enable patterns to form. The link between Jung's concept of the archetypes and the emergence of complex patterns in biology is still at the level of analogy in which the detail of the correspondences has not been fully worked out. Are archetypes like DNA, master components that command, trigger, and suppress the activity of other components? Do they emerge from the brain, or are they preexisting properties present everywhere in the body, inherently active? Is the brain itself an emergent process? Haule notes that Jung thought that the brain was a process rather than an entity (Jung 1924, cited in Haule, 2011: 81–82). But how similar is the question 'How does an egg "know" how to become a chicken?' to 'How does a person "know" how to become what they may be?'? Emergence theory suggests that there is no awareness, no seeing of the whole pattern that is emerging, and no guiding image. Emergence phenomena occur by mechanisms that enable cells to 'look' to their neighbouring cells for cues about how to behave, as in neural networks, where a cell at a higher level will 'fire' only if the cells in the lower levels reach a certain level of activity (Johnson, 2001: 86). At the cell level, emergence is automatic. No one cell 'knows' what it is doing. By contrast, at the level of the human person, each individual does, to a degree, know what they are doing. So the analogy has limits. Humans, ants, and cells *are* different from one another. But Johnson (2001: 98) makes the interesting observation that the phenomenon of human self-consciousness exists only in the relatively short term, whereas in the very long term, humans are not aware of consequences when considered over cycles of thousands of years, the time scales that concerned and interested Jung.

At the level of the brain, Johnson finds plausible similarities between the organisation that emerges in ant colonies and how the brain organises itself, the 'colony brain' being the sum of thousands of decisions taken by individual cells which, like individual ants, do not themselves have a 'personality'. The resulting organisation depends on feedback loops between the cells (Johnson, 2001: 113). The self (i.e. self-awareness) is understood as an emergent property of the brain's neural networks, but the brain/mind in aggregate arrives at a state of self-awareness by predicting the behaviour of its neighbours (that is, neurons residing in other brains), in the same way that individual cells respond to feedback from neighbouring cells (Johnson, 2001: 203). This analogy, if correct, would suggest that an intimate (therefore 'collective') human brain structure exists capable of supporting the development of universal archetype-like phenomena, but that, as Jung himself suggests, archetypal images develop through (are 'clothed by') individual experience. I conclude that emergence theory offers an interesting but partial analogy with the 'image' aspect of Jung's archetypes, leaving the epistemological aspects as yet unconfirmed; it is an area of great promise for future, more detailed, comparison with Jung's ideas.

Concluding remarks on the validity of archetypes

In my view, Jung's concept of the archetypes provides a new angle on the process of thinking as an emergent process, a concept that was not developed or well understood until a decade after Jung's death. All that can be concluded, as things stand at present, is that the theory of archetypes and their involvement in a putative process of individuation has neither been refuted nor completely demonstrated, although Haule (2011) has gone further than any other author to date in gathering comparative evidence from other fields of enquiry. Although its validity is still obscured by lack of direct research, Jung's concept of the archetypes has demonstrable heuristic value in studies of mythology and considerable aesthetic value in terms of its contribution to understanding the psychological aspects of symbolism in the arts, as well as demonstrable and widespread therapeutic value as a guiding metaphor for psychotherapists and counsellors (see p. 179). It also has the value of simplicity as an explanatory concept, since it 'captures' a wide range of phenomena (emergent thought processes, imagery, and personality development) in one hypothesis. When validation issues have been resolved, Jung's concept of the archetypes could emerge as the most parsimonious of Jung's concepts.

I have discussed the criteria of structural coherence and validity in greater detail as programmatic examples of the use of empirical 'hard scientific' evidence from other areas of research to evaluate Jung's key concepts. In the following paragraphs, I consider the potential of five further criteria: complexity and scope, heuristic value, morality, originality, and therapeutic value. These may be described as 'soft science' criteria, since they concern philosophical and applied values, but they are equally important as evaluation criteria. Indeed, morality may be considered primary and a fundamental value against which other criteria must be matched. The following discussion illustrates the potential contribution of more appropriate 'soft science' criteria to revealing Jung's originality.

Criterion 3: Complexity and scope

There is always a trade-off between simplicity and complexity. High value does not necessarily accrue to complex or wide-ranging theories, but a wide scope can bring added value in terms of the meaningfulness and wide applicability of the theory, especially when explained as simply as possible without sacrificing meaningfulness (see Chapter 7 on Inference to the Best Explanation). Complexity and scope can be evaluated by comparison with other similar personality theories. Allport and Murray, the 'personologists' mentioned in Chapters 1 and 6, were interested in the person as developed over a whole life. Theirs was not a snapshot focus on aspects of particular behaviour at one moment. Rather, these personality theorists tried to describe the person as an individual functioning across many situations, contexts, and times. Their scope is wide and long. Jung's scope is at least as broad as theirs and his theory as complex. In fact, Jung's theory does not really have a comparator in terms of scope. No other personality theory ventures as far beyond the boundaries of birth and death in defining a human life, and there is no competing theory of the collective unconscious that is fully worked out and accounts for the same data. The alternative could only be the null hypothesis, according to which there is no need for a *collective unconscious.*

Jung's scope included the social in several ways. The goal of individuation is to foster a type of personal development that can balance individual needs with a response to outer social demands and pressures (see also the section which follows on the morality criterion and Jung's moral purpose). On the one hand, the individuated person must rescue his or her self from being smothered by the collective and resist 'going with the crowd'.[12] On the other hand, the individuated personality must recognise the need to follow social norms for the good of society as a whole. Jung tried to show that collective psychic contents are social, holding that human beings share with one another a common humanity in nature that yokes them together at root level, like a rhizome (*CW*5 1911–12/1952 p. xxiv). I agree with Progoff's conclusion (1953) that Jung made important but unrecognised contributions to the development of a social vector for psychoanalytical personality theories. For example, since Jung held that complexes in the personal psyche are autonomous, the psyche itself is a social entity, a group. The individual is a social entity in dialogue with itself. Jung also applied the concept of psychic energy to society. Whereas Freud constituted the human as in *conflict* with society, for Jung, the individuated person gains an outflow of energy which can be transformed to serve a broader sociality (Progoff, 1953: 226–227).

In his work on typology, Jung had much to say about social interaction, about what happens when different types of personalities come together. On the wider cultural scale, Jung gave prominence in his theory to archetypal symbols, both in the individual psyche and within a culture. He believed that Western society needed new symbols. He considered such symbols to be dynamic within society and in the shaping of history as well as within individuals (see Progoff, 1953: 233–286). Progoff believed this insight opened up a totally new area of the study of historical symbols; Jung's perception of the individual's interaction with the environment offered an anthropological perspective on the cultural functions of unconscious symbols.[13] Progoff suggests that Jung brought an attitude that is focussed as much towards the social as towards the biological and psychological into psychoanalytical approaches to the study of personality and that this facet of Jung's work is not widely recognised. However, he noted that the all-inclusiveness of Jung's theory led to difficulties for laying out a programme of further study and that some of his concepts will have to be reformulated and redefined in relation to the specific problems of social study (Progoff, 1953: 286–287).

Criterion 4: Heuristic value

Theories are judged partly by the quantity of empirical studies that quickly follow their reception. With the exception of the concepts of introversion and extraversion, Jung's theory did not generate that kind of response. Furthermore, the apparently solid research base of introversion and extraversion may itself be misleading, since few of the empirical studies of introversion/extraversion are based on a version of these concepts that accurately reflects Jung's. Eysenck's concepts, for instance, diverged from Jung's over the years. Eventually, they differed so markedly from Jung's that Eysenck ceased to acknowledge Jung's influence (Eysenck, 1965: 58). Yet Eysenck's work is still cited in support of Jung's typology. Only research that is directly based on Jung's own concepts, and perhaps studies that use the Myers Briggs Type Indicator, can reliably be cited as support for Jung's typological concepts.

In evaluating the heuristic potential of Jung's theory, as opposed to the quality of existing research, the most important question is whether the theory is 'waiting in the wings' and will eventually attract a productive research programme or whether it has now been irretrievably marginalised. I believe that psychology has not yet emerged sufficiently from the influence of behaviourism and cognitive behaviourism to develop a research programme with techniques that could do justice to Jung's more philosophical approach to psychology. One reason psychologists have shown little interest in Jung's work is psychology's historic need to regard itself as a science. Stenner argues that Jung became a casualty of psychology's weakness in this respect and was rejected as a function of psychology's self-making as a science, a rejection that Jung himself was able to predict (Stenner, 2008, pers. comm.). Doubt about the scientificity of Jung's theory has made it unattractive to research-oriented psychologists. The question of whether Jung's theory and indeed whether psychological theories in general are or are not scientific is a matter of ongoing discussion. I have offered some brief thoughts on this issue in relation to Jung's theory (see pp. 126–132).

We must accept that academic neglect of Jung's ideas has delayed the development of a systematic programme that might establish the predictions and testable hypotheses that can be derived from the theory. Several textbook authors (Maddi, 1972; Maduro & Wheelwright, 1977; Smith & Vetter, 1982) concluded that systematic testing of hypotheses is feasible with respect to the typology. Others (such as Ryckman, 1993) concluded that Jung's metaphysical concepts such as the archetypes are not amenable to testing (see Chapter 6, pp. 111 and 113). The disinclination of many Jung scholars, who have not been scientifically oriented, to work with quantitative data in experimental paradigms also hindered the development of a fully articulated programme for Jungian research. In addition, the exploitation of Jung's ideas by nonscientific groups has served to further marginalise Jung's work from academia.

Undoubtedly, the historical and philosophical context in which the theory sits must have contributed to the failure to develop a programme of Jungian research. The ineffable nature of some of the phenomena under study makes it difficult to see how to measure inferred concepts and processes objectively. But this is generally the case in subject areas like sociology and psychology compared with physics, where there are many concrete phenomena to research that are different in kind from the observer. The unavoidable reflexivity of the self looking at the self is inherent to psychology and is its dilemma. One aspect of Jung's value is that he never fell into the illusion of objectivity but clearly stated that 'psychology . . . lacks the Archimedean point outside and hence the possibility of objective measurement' (*CW*17 1926/1946 §163). His comparative method was his incomplete solution.

A theory is considered poor if it fails to guide a coherent research programme that leads to the discovery of at least some novel phenomena (Lakatos, 1974, cited in Chalmers, 1986: 84). Jung's work on personality did generate a 'research programme', but its trajectory was limited. One could argue that although its indications for future research were well understood by some of his immediate colleagues and collaborators such as Marie-Louise von Franz, who carried on Jung's alchemical research, there has been little further development of their research after their deaths. There have, however, been very significant onward developments of Jung's ideas on personality that are close to being personality theories in themselves, such as the work of Michael Fordham, Erich Neumann, and James Hillman. Michael Fordham (1905–1995) pioneered the Jungian analysis of children and theorised the childhood development of self. Erich Neumann (1905–1960) developed theories of feminine development and of creativity and made major contributions to the Jungian study of myths and tales. James Hillman (1926–2011) founded a movement that reinstated and developed archetypal approaches to psychology and a therapy based on this. Hillman's phenomenological approach placed soul-making in the centre of personality development. In addition, very significant new therapeutic approaches, such as art psychotherapy and adult sand-play therapies, have been developed based on Jung's concept of individuation. Jung's notion of the archetypes was taken up by Hillman and developed into a widely known literature and therapy which promotes the concept of individuation (see Hillman, 1996, 1999). Furthermore, Jung's work on personality has itself inspired other personality theories, for example, that of Carl Rogers, which in turn inspired the growth of counselling over the last forty years. Jung's ideas are also acknowledged by other theorists, for example, Maslow (1954: 35) and Laing (1990: 165).

In addition, there is heuristic value in the unanswered questions that are Jung's legacy to personality theory. For example, *is* there a process of individuation? If so, is it universal or culturally specific? Is it a conscious process, or do some people go through this process in a totally unconscious way? *Is* there a period of readjustment that occurs in midlife? Whilst research has been limited, people continue to ask the questions Jung proposed, questions like: What is it that draws people toward religion in a modern and relatively secular world? Do primordial ideas or archetypes exist, and do they have a dynamic influence within the personality? If so, how does this happen? For Jung, the biggest question of all was the problem of *opposites*. This had enormous implications for his personality theory with respect to his arrangement of personality types on opposite dimensions, as the motivation for the development of the transcendent function as a unifier, and in thinking about the problems of evil and how to influence morality on a worldwide scale. Moreover, raising questions about the meaning of symbols and mythology for individual and human development extended the scope of personality theory by emphasising the positive functions of nonrational thinking and the role of imagination in creativity. Academic psychologists and the psychological professionals of the future, less constrained by academic psychology's preference for quantitative research, will be able to benefit from pursuing the questions that concerned Jung.

Many nonpsychologists are interested in the questions that fascinated Jung, such as the function of religions as systems of personal development, the creative value of irrational modes of thinking, and the limits of free will. Unique to Jung's legacy are questions about the existence, nature, and function of archetypes, the phenomenology of individuation, the nature of nonrational logic, and the role of creative imagination in personality development. For almost a century, Jung's ideas have remained highly visible on the margins of psychology, functioning as a reminder, keeping these questions in view, if only at the edge of psychology's visual field. It can take many decades and even centuries after a theorist's death for an integrated and coherent research programme to develop from his or her work. The theory then is pulled in from the shadows, reexamined, and seen in a different light (Chalmers, 1986: 75).[14]

If a research programme were to be developed today based on Jung's ideas, it is unlikely to develop canonically. An International Association for Jungian Studies (IAJS) now exists which consists of scholars and academics from many disciplines who are interested in addressing 'Jungian' questions. They represent the disciplines of literature, media studies, religious studies, anthropology, philosophy, and psychology. Few are in a position to offer courses in Jungian studies in their universities, but they bring Jung's vision to their areas of academic interest, including the field of education itself. The diversity of IAJS members mirrors the wide interests and cross-disciplinary contacts that Jung himself had. This organisation and the Philemon Foundation, a non-profit-making foundation dedicated to the preparation and bringing to publication the complete works of C.G. Jung, have promoted much new Jungian scholarship and brought academic standards and multidisciplinary breadth of vision into the Jungian field.

In conclusion, although Jung's theory did not initially give rise to the development of a programme of research, it has been developed onwards in significant ways by subsequent theorists who were interested in personality, and it has influenced the development of other major personality theories and therapies, including the development of counselling. There is a great deal of valuable Jungian scholarship which is not research oriented. In addition, Jung's theory continues to raise important questions and has kept alive some of the most important unanswered questions in psychology. A research programme is now developing, although there remains a need for methodological creative ingenuity.

Criterion 5: Morality/ethical value

As we saw in Chapter 5, Jung believed he had discovered how to save humanity, through psychologically informed self-awareness, from the consequences of humans' dissociation from themselves. Obviously, Jung did not expect to fully succeed in his wider aims. People are still distressed and the world is still at war. But personal 'growth' ideas, based on knowledge of the less agreeable sides of oneself, have spread. Evaluating the ethical impact of Jung's theory of personality would require establishing that people who have taken Jung's message seriously are less inclined to project evil onto others and to act aggressively as a result. But there has been no systematic collection of data on this difficult question. However, this is an important area for research in the future since Jungians give great importance to the potential moral value of Jung's project, as Jung himself did.

Jung's theory is morally appealing for a number of reasons – firstly, because his concept of individuation is highly creative, nonprescriptive, nondogmatic, and nonfundamentalist, in that Jung is not showing '*the* way' but theorises an internal mechanism by which individuals can generate their own way through finding a new attitude or position. At its best, therapy based on Jung's concept of personality fosters diversity through the creation of individual solutions and promotes responsible freedom. Jung's concept of balance has moral value too inasmuch as his approach to individual personality development involves a two-way adaptation both to one's own and to society's needs.

Secondly, the theory offers creative solutions to conflict through seeking a new attitude or a 'third term' that finds commonality in conflicting spheres. Its value lies in its focus on the future, on possibility, and on resolution. The concept of the transcendent function (see Chapter 1, p. 13) embodies an ideal of creative compromise whilst also suggesting how individuals might achieve this in practice. Finding a new position on the individual level opens the possibility of advancing social and political pluralism.[15]

Thirdly, the theory is morally valuable because of its optimism. Jung's position that good and evil should be understood as two related aspects of life, as a duality that exists in everyone, also has therapeutic value. Acknowledging the evil in human nature can lead to pessimism, but the concept of individuation brings a transcendent purpose to confronting evil within the self. Jung offered a way of balancing hope and despair within the personality and potentially in the world. In this way, Jung's theory adds moral value to personality theory by bringing a transcendent aspect into the psychology of personality.

A fourth facet of its moral and ethical value lies in its therapeutic applications. For example, Jung's view that the purpose of life is to 'become as fully as possible what one is' can be helpful to older people as a counter to the prevailing ideals of 'usefulness', bodily youth, health, and activity. It offers a positive philosophical position in a post-religious world. A further aspect is his understanding of psychosis as meaningful and amenable to transformational processes. People are not marginalised for being in a different state of being. Jung's understanding of psychosis as a response to extreme conflict within the self and his position on the meaningfulness of symbols point to the reparative use of fantasies and images. After his clinic years, Jung was no longer active as a practising pioneer of ways of understanding psychotic states, but his theory continues to offer ways of understanding psychosis and, in its time, influenced a move away from a sexual interpretation and towards a broader conceptualisation of the meaning and function of psychoses (see 'therapeutic value', pp. 178–180).

I have suggested reasons Jung's theory is morally appealing and optimistic in its emphasis on the human transformative potential. All theories can be used for immoral and unethical purposes. Behaviourism, for example, can be used in immoral as well as moral ways, since it offers techniques for controlling others that can be applied without their consent. The theory that there is an unconscious mind that can influence behaviour has been exploited by advertisers, who have used subliminal effects to influence people's purchasing habits. Whilst no one can prevent the misuse of a theory, its moral value rests, to some degree, on the theorist's responsible consideration of its potential consequences. Jung's personality theory, emphasising as it does creativity and transcendence and transformation, has been taken up in extreme New Age ideas. There may be moral value in this. Such ideas may not be an accurate reflection of Jung's own, but they do not in themselves increase the level of division and violence in the world and may contribute positively a softening influence on a potentially disastrous competitive and economically dominated zeitgeist.

Criterion 6: Originality

Originality can be assessed by identifying what is new in a theory, though, for Jung, originality does not seem simply to mean having different ideas from other people. On the contrary, he seems quite delighted and enthuses when he discovers that someone else is thinking along the same lines (such as when he discovered Wilhelm's translation of *The Secret of the Golden Flower* and in his discovery of similarities between his own and Paracelsus's ideas). On the other hand, Jung disapproved of 'imitation', since copying others is not a way of expressing one's *self*. Jung, for the most part, aligned himself with the ideas of other thinkers *after* his ideas had emerged within himself. At the same time, he acknowledged that thoughts arise partly because of ideas absorbed from other influences. Hence, he does not claim originality, merely that he has produced 'new vines from old roots'.

Whilst Jung isn't overtly claiming originality, Ira Progoff sees Jung along with Adler and Rank as having contributed something very original to the psychology of personality: 'It was in fact, the realization that the unconscious depths of man contained much more than Freud's first formulations had described that began the process which has resulted in the transformation of psychology' (Progoff, 1956: 259). I consider that Jung's way of placing the person within an individual cosmology and bringing this into the psychology of personality is highly original. Jung's scheme not only situates individuals within a family, a social sphere, and the human species, but links them to the cosmos, however far that reaches. This implies that psychology's scope in thinking about personality must stretch well beyond the perceptual world and beyond the span of a lifetime. Jung's originality is his vision – the breadth of his conception of what it is to be human. No other theory of personality conceives individuality in such cosmological terms. Whether or not one is in tune with it, Jung was unique in amplifying his psychological thinking with alchemical parallels and bringing the alchemical vision of a microcosm reflecting a vast macrocosm into psychology.

Jung's originality also lies in the prominence he gave to creative imagination as a fundamental and defining characteristic of all individuals. More than any other personality theorist, Jung gave value to the imaginal processes in therapy. Descriptions from people who were in therapy with Jung reveal how he acted on hunches and impulses. Analysands realised that when he appeared to have been musing, Jung seemed to have expressed something that was in *their* unconscious. Their experience was that Jung had intuitively 'tuned in' and had faith that a thought that might seem irrelevant or even inappropriate might in fact be in tune with the other's process in a way that was not yet evident in the conscious material (Haule, 1999: 255–272). Jung had long practice in training his openness to the products of his own unconscious. His letting his *imagination* have free play within the therapy session, productively and in the service of the other, opens up interesting possibilities for therapists' ways of working, bringing the therapist's *unconscious* into the field as the therapist becomes 'midwife' to the emerging individuating unconscious developments within the analysand. That some other psychodynamic psychotherapies also do this may be the result of Jung's influence. This, together with his innovative practice of working with the archetypes themselves, resulted in a therapy of the whole personality very different in its focus from today's cognitive psychotherapy, for example, with its emphasis on conscious thoughts and beliefs. Jung is working further up the line, where thoughts are not yet fully formed or integrated and where information is transmitted unconsciously from person to person. The value of the alchemical metaphor as a way of understanding the moment-by-moment changes in the therapeutic encounter, as well as providing a theory of the stages of personal change and transformation of personality, illuminates both synchronic (moment-by-moment 'snapshots') and diachronic (longer-term changes over time) processes for both therapist and analysand (see Samuels, 1989: 175–193). Given the huge readership that Jung's work has had and the availability of his work in many countries, and its indirect influence through the work of Rogers in counselling, it is likely that his ideas have either explicitly or implicitly influenced the development of most of today's psychodynamic approaches.

I have suggested that, in evaluating Jung's originality, one would have to look beyond his attempts to emphasise the historical lineages of his ideas and concepts, as this conceals his originality behind a too-rational mask. Rather, it is his imaginative vision for human beings and his use of imagination in therapy as well as in his theorising that merits prominence in any reappraisal as something that is unique to Jung's conceptualisation both of personality and of its psychotherapy.

Criterion 7: Therapeutic value

I have mentioned in the previous section the therapeutic potential of Jung's theory of personality in relation to older people and for psychosis. However, Jungian psychotherapy shares with all psychotherapies a dearth of outcome data which urgently needs to be rectified,[16] even though outcomes are not the only indicators of the therapeutic value of a theory. Therapeutic value and moral value are linked especially with respect to how the human person is constituted. The theory's descriptive value, its scope, the openness of its boundaries, and its social value are also related to therapeutic value.

Jung made a number of advances in theorising the practice of therapy: firstly, his practice was to work in a face-to-face position. This reflects his relational approach to theorising the connection between analyst and analysand. Insights derived from alchemical notions, understood as a metaphor for the therapeutic process and expressed in Jung's emphasis on the mutual creative connection between the unconscious of the analyst and the unconscious of the patient, were also a theoretical and therapeutic advance.

Secondly, Jung's understanding of transference as a two-way transformative process and his emphasis on the positive aspects of countertransference add moral as well as therapeutic value, as it fosters a relationship that is based on equality and in which both analyst and analysand learn and grow.

Thirdly, Jung theorised the goal of analytical psychotherapy as transformation and emphasised becoming rather than cure. Hillman (1996, 1999) took up and developed Jung's position on the teleological purpose of all life in his use of the metaphor of the acorn, whose purpose is to become as fully as possible the specific oak tree that its potential is to become (see Hillman, 1996: 3–40). Jung's theory and Jungian psychotherapy rest on the assumption that deep in the personality is a sense of the person's future direction that can be made conscious and activated through a process of therapy. Hence the Jungian approach allows for individual and diverse outcomes.

Fourthly, whilst Jung's theory does not ignore environmental influences, his enduring contribution is in the importance he gave to inherited aspects of personality, including the archetypes in their accessible forms (see Appendix 1 for examples of significant archetypal figures and their psychic functions), the therapeutic benefit of bringing these to conscious awareness, and his drawing attention to the dangers of being too much guided by social influences.

Fifthly, there may be a particular value in some therapy situations in Jung's recognition that there is a way that the dead can have an influence on the psyche that restricts people's psychological range of freedom if not brought into conscious awareness. Jung held that the residue of 'unlived life' that has not been realised by ancestors can be unconsciously lived out in subsequent generations, creating difficulty for living out one's own nature. When unconscious 'knowledge' of this kind is made conscious, the result is an increase in the degree of freedom. Jung's recognition of the psychological grip of ancestral inheritance as possibly overwhelming makes otherwise puzzling phenomena seem understandable and therapeutically accessible. Jung's acknowledgement of the possibility that unacknowledged and even unknown factors *may* have a transgenerational effect if not (and sometimes even if) brought into conscious awareness was a pioneering contribution.[17]

A Jungian approach to therapy makes available a set of values that differ from those in the prevailing culture. The idea that life is a challenge to become more fully oneself is radically different from viewing life's challenges solely in relation to one's economic status, youthfulness, or social usefulness. In this respect, a therapy based on the application of Jung's ideas on personality frees older people and people facing personal or economic failure in mid- or late life from the oppression of negative social values.

A further aspect of Jung's understanding of personality that has therapeutic value is his idea that, as human people, we are all connected to one another and to nature at the level of the collective unconscious. This idea has particular therapeutic value for older people since death may be viewed as joining that of which one was always a part. This is a counterinfluence to the current ideas about death's approach as exclusively signifying loss of self and loss of the world, replacing these with the idea of a special state of consciousness, of readiness to return to the collective.

Jung did not attempt to set out categories of personality disorder beyond the interpersonal difficulties he outlines in his typology; thus he is not a theorist of personality disorder, but therapy derived from his theory has potential application within the field of personality disorder. One Jungian psychotherapist, R. Ledermann, developed specifically Jungian approaches to working with a specific personality disorder (narcissistic personality), and Dougherty and West (2007) offer an archetypal and developmental approach to each of the personality disorders categorised in the American Psychiatric Association's *Diagnostic and Statistical Manual* (DSM II, III, and IV). Like many other psychotherapists, I have direct experience of the benefits of bringing Jungian ideas into integrated therapy for people described and diagnosed as having personality disorders, but there has been little documentation of its effectiveness beyond single case reports.

Jungian therapy is nonprescriptive, but it is also challenging. Like all good therapy which leads to lasting change, Jungian therapy does not end. Rather, it leads to a way of life. Jung's theory fosters the examination of a kind of psychological conscience over a lifetime, a constant striving which only ends at the moment of death. Of course Jung was not alone in this. All good therapy, based on useful theories of what it is to be human, should have the effects of raising consciousness on the individual and collective levels.[18]

If Jung's theory had not been a personality theory, which is to say if it had been restricted to the treatment of illness alone, it would have much less therapeutic potential. Jung was interested in the person in their lived life, in relation to their culture, history, their ancestral line, and ultimately, their place in the universe. This wide approach to defining a person is therapeutically valuable because of the potential of Jung's vision to open people's eyes to the infinite, to the hugeness of their own potential, to be worked out within the limits of their situations, capacities, and possibilities.

Conclusions

Jung left many things unfinished. His theory sets out as many questions as it gives answers, and he hinted at rather than defined a research programme which is only now beginning. In the preceding chapters, I have shown why we should not expect to evaluate Jung's ideas on personality in terms of their having established truths or general laws. The question should rather be whether his ideas, viewed as a personality theory, offer advances to understanding or not. Personality theorists of the twenty-first century advocate the need for a synthesis of psychological work and research from other disciplines. This was always Jung's position, not only at the beginning of his career when psychology was not established as a separate discipline but also at the end of his life when anthropological, mythological, and parapsychological studies continued to engage his interest.

As well as setting out to test those of his hypotheses that are amenable to experimental research, it may be fruitful to follow the directions he opened up and develop further theories about these: to dream the dream onward. The practical value of Jung's method as a tool for thinking and its implications as an empirical demonstration of Jung's own ideas has yet to be explored.[19] Jung was on a journey of *discovery*. His life-work was an attempt to present to the scientific community the fruits of his *imagination*, which, in his epistemology, is the origin of all ideas. Because Jung was against imitation, the real test of his legacy for personality theory is whether people can be inspired by his openness to having an attitude of enquiry towards far-reaching questions about the nature of personhood.

Future generations of scholars will be better able to see the impact of the 2009 publication of Jung's *Red Book* and to consider its value as an insight into the process of thinking itself, into the role and functions of imagination within this emergent process, and into the psychosocial processes by which emerged ideas come to be expressed scientifically and are subsequently embedded in academic culture.

I might have been led to the conclusion that Jung's theory is not a personality theory, or that it is a personality theory with limited value. On the contrary, Jung shows how far it is possible for a personality theory to go. Its value is its vision. If Jung had not been part of psychology's history and a part of the early history of personality theory, there would have been a loss of a visionary conceptualisation of psychology itself. That Jung failed to leave an adequate legacy of empirical or other alternative research methods that would further his own ideas may not be negative, as it does not constrain the freedom to use modern research methods for those with a sympathetic understanding of his theory. What Jung did leave was his own method of active imagination, which may be why he offered no other methods, since he saw that as having almost infinite potential. This *was* his method of thinking and from it most of his theory emerged. Perhaps it should be ours.

Notes

1 Becher's seventeenth-century theory of combustion postulated a substance called 'phlogiston' that was later found not to exist, having been replaced by the discovery of oxygen.
2 This was not a specific comment on theorising as such. Here Jung was making a more general point, contrasting the earthy life of India with the cerebral life of the West, in 'The Dreamlike World of India' (1939b).
3 This is a problem for all personality theorists which is sometimes solved by inventing distinctive terms. Allport, for example, invented the term *proprium* for his concept of the self.
4 See *Descartes' Error, Emotion, Reason and the Human Brain* (Damasio, 1994); *The Feeling of What Happens: Body and Emotion in the Making of Consciousness* (Damasio, 1999); and *Self Comes to Mind: Constructing the Conscious Brain* (Damasio, 2010).
5 See *Affect Regulation and the Origin of the Self: The Neurobiology of Emotional Development* (Schore, 1994).
6 Treisman's studies were based on Cherry's earlier work.
7 A similar idea to the 1970s thought experiment of the philosophers' zombies. 'Zombies in philosophy are imaginary creatures used to illuminate problems about consciousness and its relation to the physical world. Unlike those in films or witchcraft, they are exactly like us in all physical respects but without conscious experience' (*Stamford Encyclopedia of Philosophy* http://plato.stanford.edu, accessed November 29, 2011).
8 Cognitive schemata originated with Piaget (1896–1980), who proposed that children learn by gradually developing cognitive frameworks, the totality of which form the cognitive structure which guides and influences the way the child deals with the

world. Initially formed from genetically inherent reflexes, these become consciously available and used to structure thinking (Hergenhahn, 1986: 541). Cognitive schemata were taken up by Beck in developing his cognitive therapy. Beck sees schemata as prototypes or templates of specific life experiences that include emotional and affective responses and which orient the direction of attention and provide meaning for incoming information (Millon, 2004: 401).

9 Power and Brewin's (1991) comparison of Freud's theory of the unconscious and that of cognitive science is a good model, though less comprehensive than I am suggesting.

10 Jung was influenced, *inter alia*, by Kant's categories, which were forms of judgement, pure concepts of understanding, which themselves have been the subject of debate. See Nagy (1991: 59–74; 229–236).

11 Slime moulds are phenomena that occur in forests. The moulds spend most of their lives as single cells but can be observed moving together to form large masses when the right conditions occur.

12 See Shamdasani (2003: 283–386) on Jung's interest in crowd psychology and the work of Le Bon.

13 See Progoff (1953: 266) on Jung's interest lying in the principles of society that derive from the spiritual, psychological, and experiential aspects of human beings rather than specific social phenomena, and thus have a different frame of reference from the one that is more common in the social sciences.

14 Chalmers cites the case of the development of the electrical field. The initial vague concept was only able to be clearly defined and precisely measured when another theory was developed that provided the means to do so (Chalmers, 1986: 79).

15 See Samuels (1989) for a fuller exploration of the social and political potential of Jung's ideas.

16 But see Shedler (2010) for a review of meta-analyses of the long- and short-term effectiveness of psychodynamic psychotherapy. In addition, outcome data have been systematically gathered as part of the Increasing Access to Psychological Therapies (IAPT) project in the UK, but there is as yet no comparison of outcomes between therapeutic approaches, between therapists, or between different services or providers. There are no outcome figures for the thousands of private psychotherapies that are undertaken, or for therapies provided in a public setting which is privately funded (non-NHS). Although this situation is changing rapidly at the moment, there is still much to be done in this respect.

17 For Jung, this was a spiritualist belief that the actual dead can influence the living. However, he also acknowledged the huge unconscious pressures that exist within the immediate living family (see *CW*4 1909/1949).

18 There is evidence from studies of cognitive therapy outcomes that lasting change is only achieved when there has been a shift in understanding towards developing the capacity to doubt previously unexamined and unquestioned assumptions, a kind of wise self-scepticism.

19 A beginning has been made by Romanyshyn (2007) in developing his alchemical method of research.

Afterword

Having been inspired to undertake this investigation by my colleagues' challenges, questions, and puzzlement over the years, I hope that this work will help to bring Jung's value to the attention of the psychological professions. Practitioner psychologists, particularly in the UK, do themselves and their clients a disservice by keeping themselves in ignorance of Jung's work and its therapeutic potential. I wanted, in writing this thesis, to find an effective way of speaking simultaneously from my professional psychologist self and my Jungian self.

In my description and detailed exposition of the religious and alchemical aspects of the theory, I have provided a picture that is broader than is usual in surveys of Jung's personality theory. I have shown how Jung brings into the centre of personality theory the *unity* of personality as well as *individuality*. His theory balances these two aspects within one theory. I have shown that his theory incorporates a very early notion of synthesis and crosses disciplinary boundaries, anticipating almost a century ago a trend that has only recently been acknowledged as a need by personality theorists.

I have taken into consideration the major and significant critiques of Jung's theory and have embedded within the text alternative views and arguments. I wished to place my own evaluation on a sound basis of *appreciation* of Jung's ideas – something that is missing from many of the textbooks – but this is a critically evaluative and not a naive appreciation. Whilst I have not taken an adversarial approach, in my review of the treatment of Jung in textbooks of personality psychology, I have shown that some criticisms are ill founded. Others will no doubt continue to be debated.

I have shown why the work of evaluation of a personality theory requires cross-disciplinary collaboration, and I have indicated the future directions of this work. I introduce and propose a systematic programme of research and evaluation which embraces Jungian scholars and the psychological professions, thereby suggesting a way of unifying the field and healing the divisions between Jung's theory and the academic world.

By reviewing the theoretical aspects of theory evaluation and the theory of explanatory value, offered by Inference to the Best Explanation, I have given theoretical reasons a full re-evaluation is not immediately feasible. However, I believe I have offered a sound basis and given models and suggestions for the programme of evaluation that is needed.

Appendix 1

Examples of significant archetypal figures and their psychic functions for personality

Animus and anima

The two concepts, *animus* and *anima*, have an important place in Jung's typology, where they are used to explain gender differences in so far as personality types and modes of experience are expressed differently in men and women. Jung introduced the concepts in the commentary on *The Secret of the Golden Flower* (*CW*13 1929d) comparing anima and animus to the Chinese concepts of *yin* and *yang*, remarking that, in the Chinese tradition, these principles go in opposite directions after death, the animus (*shen* or *yang*) reaching upwards as a higher breath-soul, while the anima, being the earth-bound and bodily soul, reaches down towards the earth (*CW*13 1929d §57). He noted that in Chinese literature, whilst these two principles are united in human nature, they are distinct in terms of their creative function. Since affects have an autonomous nature, Jung spoke of anima as moods which hold people under their power. Jung's Logos, however, is impersonal in nature, rational, and not expressed in moods. Jung remarked that *yin* and *yang* were aspects of the masculine psyche (*CW*13 1929d §58–59). He continued by saying that, in the text *The Secret of the Golden Flower*, consciousness appeared to come from the anima, which would assign the utmost importance for both individual and human development to the anima (*CW*13 1929d §60).

Jung explained that he used the term 'anima' so as not to confuse his concept with the Christian idea of 'soul' or with any previous philosophical conceptions of it. He also distinguished his concept from *p'o* or *kuei* in Classical Chinese philosophy, which he understood as the feminine or Chthonic part of the soul. He regarded his concept of anima as empirical even though the form in which it appears could only be described in phenomenological terms (*CW*9.1 1936/1954 §119). Jung maintained that anima is empirical because it can be seen in projected forms, such as in the Divine Syzygies (male/female pairs of deities) and the Chinese pair concept of *yin* and *yang* (*CW*9.1 1936/1954, §120). Jung added that the notion of a pair of lovers, the parental pair, and the incest fantasy are also contained in these ideas, as well as the feminine aspect which corresponds to the anima (*CW*9.1 1936/1954 §130). Because the anima seemed to have definite characteristics when projected, Jung warned that it should not be assumed that the archetype has these characteristics in itself. Rather, the archetype has no exactly demonstrable form in its quiescent, unprotected state but is, as Jung repeatedly asserted, an indefinite structure (an archetypal idea) which can only assume definite form in projection (*CW*9.1 1936/1954 §142).

Archetype of the 'great mother'

Jung argued that experience in its widest sense cannot originate exclusively in the outside world, since the psyche is itself part of what is experienced (*CW*9.1 1938/1954b §150). He assigned structure and form to the psyche, which he considered to be like every other organism, whose structures are 'given' (*CW*9.1 1938/1954b §152). Jung thought that this inherent structure within the psyche was experienced psychologically as the *mother*, the matrix, the form into which all experience is poured. He distinguished this from the imago of the *father*, which he felt represented the dynamism and energy of the archetype itself, archetype being both form and energy (*CW*9.1 1938/1954b §187). The origin of the mother archetype was the actual mother, who was the carrier of the archetype (the form) in the first instance. Jung assumed that children initially live in complete participation with their mother or mother-figures such that the mother or mother-figure is the psychic precondition of the child. Later in their development, children differentiate their own character from the mother in her personal aspect. The archetypal aspects of the mother imago then fall into the image of the grand-mother or become part of the mythology of the 'great mother's' paradoxical qualities and powers, as Queen of Heaven, wisdom, witch, and Earth Mother (*CW*9.1 1938/1954b §188).

Archetype of the father

In 'A Psychological Approach to the Trinity' (1942/1948), Jung describes the father imago as, by definition, the creator, the *auctor rerum*, who can only be one, adding that 'The other follows from the One by splitting off from it'. Such splitting did not detract from the unity of the Father. Instead, 'a feeling of oneness, far removed from critical judgment and moral conflict, leaves the father's authority unimpaired' (*CW*11 1942/1948 §199). Speaking of the clothing of the idea in projected form, Jung described the father idea in the following terms: 'The world of the Father typifies an age which is characterised by a pristine oneness with the whole of Nature' (*CW*11 1942/1948 §201). However, he added that there are problems for this oneness as soon as the question of the origin of evil arises, since the logical conclusion would be that the Creator had not created properly, and thus, as a consequence, the Father must be criticised; or it has to be acknowledged that the goodness of the Father cannot be the only principle of the cosmos, since the One has to be supplemented by the Other (*CW*11 1942/1948 §201).

Jung was giving expression to the inherent tension of opposites that occupied his thoughts since his earliest years: that is the paradox of unity versus diversity, which was also the concern of the alchemists. Jung believed this oppositeness was expressed psychologically in the tension between conscious and unconscious and was ultimately resolved by the formation of a unified Self. This sense of a primal unity, from which form emerges, broods over Jung's work, especially in his work on archetypes, and is most powerfully seen in his concept of the father archetype.

The archetype of the child and child-souls

Jung believed that a child's psyche was born populated with the forms of ideas. This was evident in the dreams of three- and four-year-old children which could be shown to be strikingly like those of adults. Children's dreams revealed vestiges of a collective psyche – an infinite soul which was 'limitless and ageless'. He believed this was behind the primitive belief that the child's soul was an ancestral spirit. Since, in Jung's view, the forms of ideas were inherited, he thought that the child's psyche contained archetypes of the collective human psyche, such as the primordial image of the father, and the magical figure of the Magna Mater (the Great Mother).[1] He concluded that the child projected these preconscious dominants onto the natural parents so that, internalised, the images of the parents (the parental imagos) began to act like divine agencies in the psyche (*CW*17 1927/1931a §93–97).

When the child appears in adult dreams or as a myth motif, Jung insisted that the image is not a copy of a real child but is a symbol, recognisable as such by its being a wonder-child, a divine child, who, in the dream, is born and brought up in extraordinary circumstances (*CW*9.1 1940 §273 and footnote). An essential element of the child image when it was expressing an archetypal idea was its futurity. The child, when it appeared in dreams, paved the way for a future change in personality, as if it anticipated the symbol of wholeness, the self (*CW*9.1 1940 §278). However, when many children appear in dreams or in myths, Jung understood the image to represent the dissolution of the synthesis of the self and to be an indication that the ego of the dreamer or mythological character may be still in a stage of the kind of unconscious identification with the plurality of the group (*CW*9.1 1940 §279). Jung, following Malinowski and Lévy-Bruhl, took group identification to be a universal stage of human development that preceded individual differentiation and assumed that the principle that ontogeny recapitulates phylogeny could be applied to the development of each human being (*CW*17 1943a §250).

Jung maintained through comparison with myths and stories that an important aspect of the appearance of the child image in active imagination, dreams, and visions was as a bringer of light, one who overcomes darkness or an earlier unconscious state. For Jung, the child image is of something that is developing and evolving towards differentiation, independence, and hence towards aloneness, since the development of higher consciousness brings in essence a psychological state of being alone in the world. Thus, for Jung, the child is both a beginning and an end – the goal, the self, oneness (*CW*9.1 1940 §288 & 298–300).

Christ as archetype

The figure of Christ can sometimes appear as the Divine child or the child of alchemy who is the product of the *hieros gamos*. Jung stated that the life of Christ was understood by the Church as both a historical life and an eternal mystery. Whilst Christ lived a personal life, the Biblical story of his life, Jung noted, had archetypal features such as the way he is narrated as a hero with the changes of fortune that are characteristic of mythological heroes. Jung emphasised that the biographical details of the life of Christ had numerous connections with world-wide myth motifs and that the gospel authors constituted their meaning by weaving factual reports, legends, and myths into a whole. Ordinary human folk, Jung asserted, also live archetypal forms, and their dreams reveal archetypal patterns. Psychic events, deeply grounded in archetypal ideas, are interwoven with the human psyche. Hence, each person's life reveals its hidden unconscious grounding and, in consequence, is continuously historical. For Jung, the archetype of Christ represents both Christ and every human person, since what happened in the life of Christ happens always and everywhere (*CW*11 1938/1940 §146).

The archetype of the tree

Jung's comparative studies led him to the conclusion that throughout its history, the tree symbol generally represented a process of growth. He listed and illustrated a diversity of representations of the tree image in myths, dreams, and visions in a paper published in 1945 (*CW*13 1945/1954) and pointed out that this archetypal idea had developed over centuries. Although the outward form of the tree image had changed over time, he discerned a number of basic features. From his knowledge of comparative mythological material, Jung formed the view that all archetypal symbols need to be understood through the entirety of the rich connotations that they have come to carry over hundreds of years. The full meaning of the tree symbol he said is expressed over time in its changes and varieties of meaning:

> The commonest associations to its meaning are growth, life, infolding of a form in a physical and spiritual sense, growth from below upwards and from above downwards, the maternal aspect (protections, shade, shelter, nourishing fruits, source of life, solidity, permanence, firm-rootedness, but

> also being 'rooted to the spot'), old age, personality, and finally death and rebirth.
>
> (*CW*13 1945/1954 §350)

Here it may seem that Jung is talking about an archetype, not as an 'empty idea' but in its fully clothed form as an archetypal image. Such passages have been the source of some confusion and irritation to those who have criticised Jung for his inconsistency in his use of terms. Jung acknowledged that he had sometimes slipped into talking about archetype and image interchangeably, but the quoted passage shows that he differentiated the two as he considered these various representations and images of the tree to be manifestations of an underlying form that is dynamic and has to do with growth, whether this be in the religious, personal, physical, or psychological spheres.

Anima mundi

Medieval thinking allowed for the existence of different kinds of souls. Jung believed that primitive and medieval thinking lived on in a deeply unconscious layer of the twentieth-century Western psychic experience. One specific archetypal image Jung referred to in 1929 was the '*anima mundi*', the 'primordial image of creative matter' on which Paracelsus's ideas were based and which Jung traced to Plato through Ficino. Jung linked the *anima mundi* with Plato's *eide*, the archetype or germinal idea of an intangible spiritual principle that proceeds from matter and in which everything is contained. (Medieval alchemists believed the macrocosm was contained within the microcosm and vice versa.) Humankind and the world are conceived as being contained in and part of animate matter (*CW*15 1929c §12). Jung suggested that the foundation of alchemical philosophy was the archetype of creative matter and appears when conditions are favourable, such as when a spiritual view of the world is fading. In its place, an image of creative animate matter sometimes emerges (*CW*15 1929c §11).

Creation myth as a projection of the archetype of division, and of consciousness and unconsciousness

In 1938, Jung said that the unconscious was mythology's place of origin and asked:

> How else would it have occurred to man to divide the cosmos, on the analogy of day and night, summer and winter, into a bright day-world and a dark night-world peopled with fabulous monsters, unless he had the prototype of such a division in himself in the polarity between the conscious and the invisible and unknowable unconscious.
>
> (*CW*9.1 1938/1954b §187)

He invokes ancient and modern traditions of descriptions of creation that are imbued with the observable light/dark contrasts in the world, claiming that these reflect the internal divisions inherent in the human psyche which have been projected onto the world. It is a convoluted idea based on correspondences and is not logical reasoning; hence, Jung's work has attracted the criticism of loose thinking. However, Jung was not trying to reason with conventional logic but was attempting to penetrate with his understanding the layers of rich symbolism that have come to us from earlier eras when reasoning took a different form. The creation myth was never far from his thinking. Even his concept of personality is imbued with the notion that the unconscious harbours autonomous self-forming archetypes which have creative, generative power and which drive the process of differentiation and individuation as naturally as, in the early creation myths, night and day, land and sea.

The archetype of four, the quaternity, in the typology and as God

In the 'Visions of Zosimos' (1938/1954a), Jung wrote of his realisation that he had unconsciously used, in his fourfold typology of personality types, the idea of dividing the chaos of the elements into four, as a way of creating the beginnings of order and bringing the rule of harmony into his typology based on the four functions of consciousness (*CW*13 1938/1954a §111). In 'Psychology and Religion', a Terry Lecture given in the same year, Jung wrote that quaternity is a representation of the God who is manifest in creation (*CW*11 1938/1940 §101 and §105). Essentially, Jung thought that modern dream symbols involving four pointed to a meaning similar to the Self or 'the God within', even when the dreamer would be unlikely to recognise it as such (*CW*11 1938/1940 §101–102).

The mandala

Like the archetypal idea of the quaternity, the mandala was a form of archetypal image that Jung believed represented the self. When activated, it assisted and influenced the development of the self as the centre of personality by being, as he explained, a central point around which every other aspect of the personality is arranged, ordered, and contained. For Jung, the circular mandala was the quintessential archetype by which the psyche could both see and become itself. As well as representing a central point to which everything is related and a concentric arrangement of contradictory and irreconcilable elements, the mandala was the psyche's instinctual attempt at self-healing and was an aspect of instinct itself: '[W]hat psychology designates as an archetype is really a particular, frequently occurring, formal aspect of instinct, and is just as much an *a priori* factor as the latter' (*CW*9.1 1955 §714). In 1944, he stated that the mandala archetype, which he acknowledged was expressed in distinct form in only a few cases, nevertheless functioned for everyone as a concealed pole around which everything ultimately revolves (*CW*12 1944a §330). The relevance of this for his ideas on personality is revealed in the continuation of this statement: 'every life is the realisation of a whole, a self, an individuation – an individual destiny and destination, the realisation of which makes sense of life' (*CW*12 1944a §330). The mandala symbol could express all of this in a composite symbol, the exact form of its image differing in each case and at different times, since Jung held that the mandala archetype is the carrier of an emergent self which is being realised in each person in its own way (ibid.). In Jung's way of conceptualising it, the mandala represents life and functions as a kind of value, a direction which has to be realised (made real) through being made conscious and through being clothed in personal meaning through the lived life of each and every person.

The archetype of the self

Jung's definition of *self* (*CW*6 1921 §789) describes it as 'only *potentially* empirical' because it encompasses experience and 'not yet experienced' factors. One can see immediately that Jung is thinking about the self in the same way as archetypes, as a form of an idea that only gradually emerges and becomes 'clothed' in the individual's experience. As with all archetypes, Jung states that the self appears initially in images in dreams and in myths and fairy tales. Image forms of the self are the abstract forms of circle (mandalas) and square (the quaternity), human images of the king, hero, prophet, and saviour, and symbols of united duality such as the Chinese *yin/yang* symbol (*CW*6 1921 §790–791). The self, Jung said, is 'the point of reference for the unconscious psyche'; hence, Jung's mythological research suggested that this archetype was expressed in the form of a superordinate personality, the God-image or the Anthropos (*CW*18 1948 §1158). It was also seen by Jung as biologically the archetype of order and, dynamically, the source of life (*CW*18 1956/1957 §1638), which is to say that it can be understood as the archetypal image of archetype itself.

Jung always linked the archetype of the self with religions. One reason was that he viewed the self as an organiser as well as a unifier: 'The archetype of the self has, functionally, the significance of a ruler of the inner world' (*CW*5 1911–12/1952 §576) and is projected into the symbols of Christ as God-man. Jung has the interesting idea that the precise reason for the success of some of the world's great religions, such as Christianity, Buddhism, and Islam, is that they were founded by historical personages and conjoin a unique human personality to an indeterminable divine nature, thus combining uniqueness with eternity and the individual with universality (*CW*12 1944a §22). Jung also linked the archetype of the self with the Indian idea of the self as *brahman* and *atman*; 'the hearing of the ear, the thinking of the mind . . . that which speech cannot express, by which speech is expressed, . . . which the mind cannot think, by which the mind thinks' (Kena Upanishad cited in *CW*9.2 1951a §348). At the same time, Jung reminds us that his postulate of the self represents a kind of unity that is not 'complacent bliss but preserves a painful sense of its innate duality and discord, expressed in Christ's life which ended on the cross' (*CW*16 1946 §400).

Note

1 The cult of the Great Mother is thought to be the oldest religion, as 6,000-year-old 'Mother Goddess' sculptures have been found. Her cult was known in Rome, and a temple of Magna Mater was excavated in the nineteenth century, from the Hadrianic period. The Roman cult involved a bull sacrifice that led to a symbolic rebirth. http://faculty.cua.edu/pennington/churchhistory220/lectureone/MagnaMater.htm; www.ostia-antica.org/regio4/1/1.htm accessed 28/08/2011.

Appendix 2

Textbooks reviewed in Chapter 6

1 US textbooks

Allport, G. W. (1937) *Personality: A Psychological Interpretation,* London: Constable, 1949 (originally published in USA).

Allport, G. W. (1961) *Pattern and Growth in Personality,* New York: Holt, Rinehart & Winston.

Arndt, W. J. Jr, (1974) *Theories of Personality,* New York: Macmillan.

Bischof, L. J. (1964) *Interpreting Personality Theories,* New York: Harper & Row, 1970.

Blum, G. S. (1953) *Psychoanalytic Theories of Personality,* New York: McGraw Hill.

Borgatta, E. F. & Lambert, W. W. E. (eds) (1968) *Handbook of Personality Theory and Research,* Chicago: Rand McNally.

Byrne, D. (1966) *An Introduction to Personality: A Research Approach,* Englewood Cliffs: Prentice-Hall.

Carver, C. S. & Scheier, M. F. (2000) *Perspectives in Personality,* Boston: Allyn & Bacon.

Cattell, R. B. (1950) *Personality: A Systematic Theoretical and Factual Study,* New York: McGraw-Hill.

Cloninger, S. C. (1996) *Theories of Personality: Understanding Persons,* Upper Saddle River: Prentice-Hall.

Corsini, R. (ed.) (1977) *Current Personality Theories,* Itasca, IL: Peacock.

Ewen, R. B. (1980) *An Introduction to Theories of Personality,* New York: Academic Press.

Feist, J. (1985) *Theories of Personality,* New York: Holt, Rinehart & Winston.

Guilford, J. P. (1959) *Personality,* New York: McGraw-Hill.

Hall, C. & Lindzey, G. (1978) *Theories of Personality,* New York: Wiley. [First published 1957.]

Hampson, S. (1988) *The Construction of Personality: An Introduction,* 2nd edn, London: Routledge & Kegan Paul. [First edition 1982.]

Hergenhahn, B. R. (1994/1999) *An Introduction to Theories of Personality,* Upper Saddle River/Englewood Cliffs: Prentice-Hall. [First published 1980.]

Hjelle, L. A. & Ziegler, D. J. (1992) *Personality Theories: Basic Assumptions, Research and Applications,* 3rd edn, New York: McGraw-Hill. [First published 1976.]

Hogan, R. Johnson, J. & Briggs, S. (eds) (1997) *Handbook of Personality Psychology,* San Diego: Academic Press.

Khunrath H. *Von hylealischen Chaos,* Pp54f. *Magdeburg, 1597.*

Levy, L. H. (1970) *Conceptions of Personality: Theories and Research,* New York: Random House.

Lindzey, G., Hall, C. S. & Manosewitz, M. (1973) *Theories of Personality: Primary Sources and Research,* New York: John Wiley & Sons. [First published in 1965.]
Maddi, S. (1972) *Personality Theories: A Comparative Analysis,* Homewood: Dorsey
Maddi, S. (1996) *Personality Theories: A Comparative Analysis,* Prospect Heights: Waveland.
Magnavita, J. (2002) *Theories of Personality: Contemporary Approaches to the Science of Personality,* New York: John Wiley & Sons.
Massey, R. F. (1981) *Personality Theories: Comparisons and Synthesis,* New York: Van Nostrand.
McCary, J. L. (ed) (1956) *Psychology and Personality: Six Modern Approaches,* New York: Logos.
Mehrabian, A. (1968) *An Analysis of Personality Theories,* Englewood Cliffs: Prentice-Hall.
Mischel, W. (1971/1981/1999) *Introduction to Personality,* New York: Holt, Rinehart & Winston, 1971; New York: CBS College Publishing, 1981; New York: Harcourt Brace, 1999.
Monte, C. F. (1977/1980/1987/1995) *Beneath the Mask: An Introduction to Theories of Personality,* New York: Praeger 1977; New York: Holt, Rinehart & Winston, 1980, 1987; Fort Worth: Harcourt Brace, 1995.
Murphy, G. (1947) *Personality: A Biosocial Approach to Origins and Structure,* New York: Harper & Row.
Norbeck, E., Price-Williams, D. & McCord, W. (eds) (1968) *The Study of Personality: An Interdisciplinary Appraisal,* New York: Holt, Rinehart & Winston.
Pervin, L. A. & John, D. P. (2001) *Personality Theory and Research,* 8th edn, New York: John Wiley & Sons.
Progoff, I. (1956) *The Death and Rebirth of Psychology,* New York: The Julian Press.
Ryckman, R. (1993) *Theories of Personality,* Pacific Grove: Brooks/Cole.
Sahakian, W. S. (ed) (1965) *Psychology of Personality: Readings in Theory,* Chicago: Rand McNally.
Schultz, D. (1976) *Theories of Personality,* Monterey: Brooks Cole.
Schultz, D. (2001) *Theories of Personality,* 7th edn, Belmont: Wadsworth Thomson.
Smith, B. D. & Vetter, H. J. (1982) *Theoretical Approaches to Personality,* Englewood Cliffs, NJ: Prentice-Hall.
Stolorow, R. D. & Atwood, G. E. (1979) *Faces in a Cloud: Subjectivity in Personality Theory,* New York: Jason Aronson.
Sullivan, H. S. (1953–1964) *Collected Works of Harry Stack Sullivan,* 2 vols, New York: Norton.
Thorpe, L. P. (1938) *Psychological Foundations of Personality,* New York: McGraw-Hill.
Wepman, J. M. & Heine, R. W. (eds) (1963) *Concepts of Personality,* 6th edn, Chicago: Aldine, 1970.

2 UK textbooks

Cook, M. (1993) *Levels of Personality,* London: Cassell.
Ewen, R. B. (1984) *An Introduction to Theories of Personality,* 2nd edn, London: Academic Press. [UK edition of Ewen (1980)].
Eysenck, H. J. (1947) *Dimensions of Personality,* London: Kegan Paul.
Eysenck, H. J. (1953) *Uses and Abuses of Psychology,* Harmondsworth: Penguin.

Eysenck, H. J. (1957) *Sense and Nonsense in Psychology,* Harmondsworth: Penguin.
Eysenck, H. J. (1965) *Fact and Fiction in Psychology,* Harmondsworth: Penguin.
Foulds, G. A., Caine, T. M., Adams, A. & Owen, A. (1965) *Personality and Personal Illness,* London: Tavistock.
Hampson, S. (1988) *The Construction of Personality: An Introduction,* 2nd edn, London: Routledge & Kegan Paul. [First edition 1982].
Lazarus, R. S. & Opton, E. M. (eds) (1977) *Personality,* Harmondsworth: Penguin.
Notcutt, B. (1953) *The Psychology of Personality,* London: Methuen.
Peck, D. & Whitlow, D. (1975) *Approaches to Personality,* London: Methuen.

Appendix 3

Primary sources (Jung's works) cited by textbook authors: by number of citations

Title	*No. of citations*
Psychological types	34
McGuire: The Freud-Jung letters	12
Two essays on analytical psychology	11
Archetypes and the collective unconscious	10
Psychology of dementia praecox, The	10
Relations between the ego and the unconscious	10
Theory of psychoanalysis, The	10
On psychic energy	9
Symbols of transformation	9
Psychology of the unconscious	9
Aion	8
Stages of life	8
Structure of the psyche, The	8
Structure and dynamics of the psyche	8
Instinct and the unconscious	7
Modern man in search of a soul	7
Psychology and religion	7
Answer to Job	6
Concept of the collective unconscious, The	6
Concerning the archetypes with special ref. to the anima concept	6
Psychological aspects of the mother archetype	6
Psychology and alchemy	6
Analytical psychology, its theory and practice	5
Collected papers on analytical psychology	5
Contributions to analytical psychology	5
General aspects of dream psychology	5
Man and his symbols	5
Secret of the golden flower, The	5
Synchronicity	5

(*Continued*)

Title	*No. of citations*
Transcendent function, The	5
Undiscovered self, The	5
Conscious, unconscious and individuation	4
Flying saucers	4
Jung & Kerenyi: Essays on a science of mythology	4
Mandalas	4
Marriage as a psychological relationship	4
Mysterium coniunctionis	4
On the nature of the psyche	4
Psychology of the child archetype, The	4
Studies in word association	4
Alchemical studies	3
Analytical psychology and education	3
Association method, The	3
Child development and education	3
Concerning rebirth	3
Experimental researches	3
On the doctrine of complexes	3
On the nature of dreams	3
On the psychology of the unconscious	3
On the relation of analytical psychology to poetry	3
Practical use of dream analysis, The	3
Psychological diagnosis of evidence, The	3
Psychology of the transference, The	3
Review of the complex theory	3
Shadow, The	3
Significance of constitution and heredity in psychology, The	3
Structure of the unconscious, The	3
Study in the process of individuation, A	3
Aims of psychotherapy	2
Analytical psychology	2
Concerning mandala symbolism	2
Development of personality, The	2
Fight with the shadow, The	2
Gifted child, The	2
Integration of the personality	2
Letters 1906–1950	2
Letters 1951–1961	2
On the psychology and pathology of so-called occult phenomena	2
Philosophical tree, The	2

Problems of modern psychology	2
Psyche and symbol	2
Psychological theory of types	2
Psychology of the conscious, The	2
Psychology of the trickster figure, The	2
Psychotherapy today	2
Synchronicity, On	2
Animus and anima	1
Archaic man	1
Association experiments	1
Basic writings of C G Jung	1
Civilization in transition	1
Content of the neuroses, The	1
Die Beziehungen zwischen dem Ich und dem Unbewissten 1928	1
Ego, The	1
Eros Theory, The	1
Foreword to Suzuki's Introduction to Zen Buddhism	1
Foreword to the I Ching	1
Four archetypes; Mother, rebirth, spirit, trickster	1
Freud and Jung contrasts	1
Freud and psychoanalysis	1
General aspects of psychoanalysis	1
Individual dream symbolism in relation to alchemy	1
Interpretation of a dream, An	1
Jung & Pauli: The integration of nature and the psyche	1
Jung & Riklin: The associations of normal subjects	1
McGuire: C G Jung speaking	1
Nach der Katastrophe	1
New paths in psychology	1
On psychological understanding	1
On the psychogenesis of schizophrenia	1
Persona as a segment of the collective psyche, The	1
Phenomenology of the spirit in fairy tales	1
Practice of psychotherapy	1
Principles of practical psychotherapy	1
Problem of the attitude type, The	1
Psychic conflicts in a child	1
Psychoanalysis and association experiments	1
Psychogenesis of mental disease	1
Psychological commentary on the Tibetan Book of the Dead	1
Psychological factors determining human behaviour	1

(Continued)

Title	*No. of citations*
Psychological reflections, an anthology	1
Psychology and literature	1
Psychology of eastern meditation	1
Psychotherapy or the clergy	1
Significance of the unconscious in individual education, The	1
Some aspects of modern psychology	1
Soul and death, The	1
Special phenomenology of the child archetype	1
Spirit and life	1
State of psychotherapy today, The	1
Symbol formation	1
Synchronicity, an acausal connecting principle	1
Tavistock lectures, The	1
What is psychotherapy?	1
Wotan	1
Zur gegenwartigen Lage der Psychotherapie	1
	428

Appendix 4

Secondary sources on Jung cited by textbook authors

Work	*No. of citations*
Jung, C. G. & Jaffé, A., *Memories, dreams, reflections.* 1963	18
Fordham, F., *An introduction to Jung's psychology.* 1953	11
Progoff, I., *Jung's psychology and its social meaning.* 1953	8
Stern, P. J., *Jung the haunted prophet.* 1976	8
Ellenberger, H. F., *The discovery of the unconscious.* 1970	6
Jacobi, J., *The psychology of C. G. Jung.* 1962	6
Dry, A. M., *The psychology of Jung.* 1961	5
Hannah, B., *Jung: His life and work.* 1976	5
van der Post, L., *Jung and the story of our time.* 1975	5
Brome, V., *Jung, man and myth.* 1978	4
Glover, E., *Freud or Jung.* 1950	4
Jacobi, J., *Complex, archetype, symbol. On the psychology of C. G. Jung.* 1959	4
Wehr, G., *Portrait of Jung: An illustrated biography.* 1971	4
Hall, C. S. & Nordby, V. J., *A primer of Jungian psychology.* 1973	3
Jaffé, A., *From the life and work of C. G. Jung.* 1971	3
Progoff, I., *The death and rebirth of psychology.* 1956	3
Progoff, I., *Jung, synchronicity and human destiny.* 1973	3
Storr, A., *Jung.* 1973	3
von Franz, M. L., *Jung: His myth in our times.* 1975	3
Campbell, J., *The hero with a thousand faces.* 1971	2
Campbell, J., *The portable Jung.* 1971	2
Cohen, E. D., *C. G. Jung and the scientific attitude.* 1975	2
Evans, R. I., *Conversations with Carl Jung* 1964	2
Goldbrunner, J., *Individuation: A study of the depth psychology of Carl Jung.* 1956	2
Jaffé, A., *The myth of meaning: Jung and the expansion of consciousness.* 1971	2
Jaffé, A., *Word and image.* 1979	2

(Continued)

Work	*No. of citations*
Mattoon, M. A., *Jungian psychology in perspective*. 1981	2
Serrano, M., *C. G. Jung and Herman Hesse*. 1966	2
Singer, J., *Boundaries of the soul*. 1973	2
Bennett, E. A., *C. G. Jung*. 1961	1
Campbell, J., *Myths to live by*. 1972	1
Clark, R. A., *Six talks on Jung's psychology*. 1953	1
Ellenberger, H. F., 'Carl Gustav Jung: His historical setting', in H. Reise (ed), *Historical explorations in the history of psychiatry*. 1978	1
Evans, R. I., *Jung on elementary psychology: A discussion*. 1976	1
Franz, M. L. von, 'Science and the unconscious' [conclusion in *Man and his symbols*]. 1964	1
Frey-Rohn, L., *From Freud to Jung: A comparative study of the unconscious*. 1974	1
Hostie, R., *Religion and the psychology of Jung*. 1957	1
Jahoda, G., Chapter 7, in *The psychology of superstition*. 1969	1
Marcowitz, E., *Jung's three secrets*. 1982	1
Mattoon, M. A., *Applied dream analysis: A Jungian approach*. 1978	1
McGowan, D., *What is wrong with Jung*. 1994	1
Noll, R., *The Aryan Christ*. 1997	1
Noll, R., *The Jung cult*. 1994	1
Odajnyk, V. W., *Jung and politics: The political and social ideas of C. G. Jung*. 1976	1
Progoff, I., 'At a journal workshop'. 1975	1
Stevens, A., *On Jung*. 1990	
Time Magazine, 'Biographical sketch of Carl Gustav Jung'. 1952	1
Time Magazine, 'The old wise man'. 1956	1
Toynbee, A., *The value of C. G. Jung's work for historians*. 1956	1
Wehr, D. S., *Jung and feminism*. 1987	1
Whitmont, E., *The symbolic quest*. 1979	1

Bibliography

References in the text to Jung's papers cite paragraph numbers rather than page numbers, as the pagination of the European and American editions of the *Collected Works* (*CW*) is different. For the same reason, the pagination of the papers is not included here.

Adler, G. (1948) *Studies in Analytical Psychology,* New York: Norton.

Allport, G. W. (1937) *Personality: A Psychological Interpretation,* London: Constable, 1949 (originally published in USA).

Allport, G. W. (1955) *Becoming: Basic Considerations for a Psychology of Personality,* New Haven, CT: Yale University Press.

Allport, G. W. (1961) *Pattern and Growth in Personality,* New York: Holt, Rinehart & Winston.

Arndt, W. J., Jr (1974) *Theories of Personality,* New York: Macmillan.

Ball, P. (2006) *The Devil's Doctor: Paracelsus and the World of Renaissance Magic and Science,* London: Heinemann.

Bargh, J. A. & Chartrand, T. L. (1999) 'The unbearable automaticity of being', *American Psychologist,* 54.7: 462–479.

Barker, R. & Wright H. (1955) *The Midwest and its Children. The Psychological Ecology of an American Town,* New York: Row, Peterson and Co.

Bennet, E. (1985) *Meetings with Jung: Conversations Recorded During the Years 1946–1961,* Zurich: Daimon.

Berlin, I. (2001) 'The state of psychology in 1936', *History and Philosophy of Psychology,* 3.1: 76–83.

Bischof, L. J. (1964) *Interpreting Personality Theories,* New York: Harper & Row, 1970.

Blackney, R. B. (1941) *Meister Eckhart: A Modern Translation,* New York: Harper & Row.

Blum, G. S. (1953) *Psychoanalytic Theories of Personality,* New York: McGraw Hill.

Borgatta, E. F. & Lambert, W. W. E. (eds) (1968) *Handbook of Personality Theory and Research,* Chicago: Rand McNally.

Boring, E. G. (1950) *A History of Experimental Psychology,* New York: Appleton Century Crofts.

Boring, E. G. (1961) *Psychologist at Large,* New York: Basic Books.

Bridgeman, B. (1992) 'Conscious versus unconscious processes: The case of vision', *Theory & Psychology,* 2.1: 73–88.

Brody, N. (1972) *Personality Research and Theory,* London: Academic Press Inc.

Bromley, D. B. (1977) *Personality Description in Ordinary Language,* Chichester: John Wiley & Sons.

Brooke, R. (1991) *Jung and Phenomenology,* Pittsburgh: Trivium, 2009.

Brown, R. P. (2011) 'The origins and development of Carl Jung's relationship with Wolfgang Pauli', *Spring,* 86: 193–222.

Burckhardt, T. (1997) *Alchemy: Science of the Cosmos, Science of the Soul,* Louisville, KY: Fons Vitae.

Buys, C. J. (1976) 'Freud in introductory psychology texts', *Teaching of Psychology,* 3.4: 160–167.

Byrne, D. (1966) *An Introduction to Personality: A Research Approach,* Englewood Cliffs: Prentice-Hall.

Capaldi, E. J. & Proctor, R. W. (2008) 'Are theories to be evaluated in isolation or relative to alternatives? An abductive view', *American Journal of Psychology,* 121.4: 617–641.

Carlson, R. (1971) 'Where is the person in personality research?' *Psychological Bulletin,* 75: 203–219.

Carver, C. S. & Scheier, M. F. (2000) *Perspectives in Personality,* Boston: Allyn & Bacon.

Cattell, R. B. (1950) *Personality: A Systematic Theoretical and Factual Study,* New York: McGraw-Hill.

Chalmers, A. F. (1986) *What Is This Thing Called Science?* 2nd edn, Milton Keynes: Open University Press.

Cheetham, T. (2003) *The World Turned Inside Out: Henry Corbin and Islamic Mysticism,* New Orleans: Spring Journal Books.

Cherry, E. C. (1953) 'Some experiments on the recognition of speech, with one and with two ears', *Journal of the Acoustical Society of America,* 25.5: 975–979.

Cloninger, S. C. (1996) *Theories of Personality: Understanding Persons,* Upper Saddle River: Prentice-Hall.

Cohen, E. D. (1975) *C.G. Jung and the Scientific Attitude,* New York: Philosophical Library.

Cook, M. (1984) *Levels of Personality,* New York: Holt, Rinehart & Winston.

Cook, M. (1993) *Levels of Personality,* London: Cassell.

Corsini, R. (ed) (1977) *Current Personality Theories,* Itasca, IL: Peacock.

Cox, D. (1964) *How Your Mind Works: An Introduction to the Psychology of C.G. Jung,* London: Hodder & Stoughton, 1980.

Craib, I. (1992) *Modern Sociological Theory: From Parsons to Habermas,* 2nd edn, London: Harvester Wheatsheaf.

Crellin, C. (1987) 'Cognitive titles in the *Psychological Index* and the *Psychological Abstracts* 1897–1941', paper presented at Cheiron: European Society for the History of the Behavioural and Social Sciences VIth Cheiron-Europe Conference, Brighton, September 1987.

Crellin, C. (2003) 'Does Jung have a bad press? The undergraduate textbook as an introduction to the personality theory of C.G. Jung', paper presented at the British Psychological Society History and Philosophy of Psychology Section Annual Conference, April 2003.

Damasio, A. R. (1994) *Descartes' Error: Emotion, Reason, and the Human Brain,* New York: Putnam; revised edition, 2005, New York: Penguin.

Damasio, A. R. (1999) *The Feeling of What Happens: Body and Emotion in the Making of Consciousness,* New York: Harcourt Brace.

Damasio, A. R. (2010) *Self Comes to Mind: Constructing the Conscious Brain,* New York: Pantheon.

Danziger, K. (1997) *Naming the Mind: How Psychology Found its Language,* London: Sage.

Darwin, C. (1859) *The Origin of Species,* Harmondsworth: Penguin, 1986.
Dawkins, R. (1986) *The Blind Watchmaker,* Harlow: Longman.
Dougherty, N. J. & West, J. J. (2007) *The Matrix and Meaning of Character: An Archetypal and Developmental Approach,* London: Routledge.
Dry, A. M. (1961) *The Psychology of Jung: A Critical Interpretation,* London: Methuen.
Ebbinghaus, H. (1905–1913) *Grundzüge der Psychologie,* 2 vols, 2nd edn, Leipzig: Veit.
Eliade, M. (1978) *The Forge and the Crucible: The Origins and Structures of Alchemy,* trans. S. Corrin, 2nd edn, Chicago: University of Chicago Press.
Ellenberger, H. F. (1970) *The Discovery of the Unconscious,* New York: Basic Books.
Erwin, E. (1997) *Philosophy and Psychotherapy: Razing the Troubles of the Brain,* London: Sage.
Ewen, R. B. (1980) *An Introduction to Theories of Personality,* New York: Academic Press.
Ewen, R. B. (1984) *An Introduction to Theories of Personality,* 2nd edn, London: Academic Press. [UK edition of Ewen (1980)].
Eysenck, H. J. (1947) *Dimensions of Personality,* London: Kegan Paul.
Eysenck, H. J. (1953) *Uses and Abuses of Psychology,* Harmondsworth: Penguin.
Eysenck, H. J. (1957) *Sense and Nonsense in Psychology,* Harmondsworth: Penguin.
Eysenck, H. J. (1965) *Fact and Fiction in Psychology,* Harmondsworth: Penguin.
Feist, J. (1985) *Theories of Personality,* New York: Holt, Rinehart & Winston.
Flournoy, T. (1994) *From India to the Planet Mars: A Case of Multiple Personality with Imaginary Languages,* ed. S. Shamdasani, Princeton: Princeton University Press.
Fordham, F. (1953) *An Introduction to Jung's Psychology,* Harmondsworth: Penguin, 1983.
Foulds, G. A., Caine, T. M., Adams, A. & Owen, A. (1965) *Personality and Personal Illness,* London: Tavistock.
Franz, M. L. von (1975) *Jung: His Myth in our Times,* New York: Putnam.
Franz, M. L. von (1977) *Alchemical Active Imagination,* Boston: Shambhala, 1979.
Franz, M. L. von (1988) *The Way of the Dream: Conversations on Dream Interpretation with Marie-Louise von Franz,* Boston: Shambhala, 1994.
Franz, M. L. von (1997) *Archetypal Patterns in Fairy Tales,* Toronto: Inner City Books.
Gelder, B. de, de Haan, E. H. F. & Heywood, C. (eds) (2001) *Out of Mind: Varieties of Unconscious Processes,* Oxford: Oxford University Press.
Giere, R. N. (1985) 'Philosophy of science naturalized', *Philosophy of Science,* 52: 331–356.
Goethe, J. W. (1808) *Faust. Part One,* trans. D. Luke, Oxford: Oxford University Press, 1987.
Goethe, J. W. (1808) *Faust. Part Two,* trans. D. Luke, Oxford: Oxford University Press, 1994.
Goldbrunner, J. (1956) *Individuation. A Study of the Depth Psychology of Carl Gustav Jung,* New York: Pantheon.
Glover, E. (1950) *Freud or Jung,* London: George Allen & Unwin.
Greenfield, S. (2000) *The Private Life of the Brain,* London: Allen Lane.
Guilford, J. P. (1959) *Personality,* New York: McGraw-Hill.
Haig, B. D. (2009a) 'Inference to the best explanation: A neglected approach to theory appraisal in psychology', *American Journal of Psychology,* 122.4: 219–234.
Haig, B. D. (2009b) 'Evaluating explanatory theories', *The Psychologist,* 22.11: 948–950.
Hall, C. & Lindzey, G. (1978) *Theories of Personality,* New York: Wiley. [First published 1957].
Hampson, S. (1988) *The Construction of Personality: An Introduction,* 2nd edn, London: Routledge & Kegan Paul. [First edition 1982].

Hannah, B. (1976) *Jung: His Life and Work,* New York: Putnam.

Happold, F. C. (1964) *Mysticism: A Study and an Anthology,* Harmondsworth: Penguin.

Haule, J. (1999) 'Analyzing from the self: an empirical phenomenology of the "third" in analysis', in R. Brooke (ed) *Pathways into the Jungian World,* pp. 255–272, London: Routledge.

Haule, J. R. (2011) *Jung in the 21st Century. Volume One: Evolution and Archetype,* London: Routledge.

Heidegger, M. (1968) *What Is Called Thinking?* trans. J. Glenn Gray, New York: Harper & Row.

Heisig, J. W. (1979) *Imago Dei: A Study of C.G. Jung's Psychology of Religion,* London: Associated University Press.

Hergenhahn, B. R. (1986) *An Introduction to the History of Psychology,* 2nd edn, Belmont: Wadsworth Publishing Co.

Hergenhahn, B. R. (1994/1999) *An Introduction to Theories of Personality,* Upper Saddle River/Englewood Cliffs: Prentice-Hall. [First published 1980.]

Hillman, J. (1985) *Anima: An Anatomy of a Personified Notion,* Dallas: Spring.

Hillman, J. (1990) *The Essential James Hillman: A Blue Fire,* ed. T. Moore, London: Routledge.

Hillman, J. (1996) *The Soul's Code: In Search of Character and Calling,* New York: Grand Central Publishing.

Hillman, J. (1999) *The Force of Character and the Lasting Life,* New York: Ballantine.

Hjelle, L. A. & Ziegler, D. J. (1992) *Personality Theories: Basic Assumptions, Research and Applications,* 3rd edn, New York: McGraw-Hill. [First published 1976.]

Hobbs, S. & Chiesa, M. (2003) 'Errors of omission and commission: the analysis of misrepresentation in secondary sources', *History & Philosophy of Psychology,* 5.1: 46–56.

Hogan, R., Johnson, J. & Briggs, S. (eds) (1997) *Handbook of Personality Psychology,* San Diego: Academic Press.

Holmyard, E. J. (1957) *Alchemy,* Harmondsworth: Penguin.

Hostie, R. (1957) *Religion and the Psychology of Jung,* trans. G. R. Lamb, New York: Sheed & Ward.

Hubel, D. H. & Wiesel, T. N. (1959) 'Receptive fields of single neurones in the cat's striate cortex', *Journal of Physiology,* 148: 574–591.

Hubel, D. H. & Wiesel, T. N. (1962) 'Receptive fields, binocular interaction and functional architecture in the cat's visual cortex', *Journal of Physiology,* 160: 106–154.

Hyde, M. & McGuinness, M. (1992) *Introducing Jung,* Cambridge: Icon Books, 2001.

Ireneus, Saint. *Adversus* [or *Contra*] *haereses libri quinque.* See Migne, P.G., vol. 7, cols. 433–1224. For translation, see: *The Writings of Ireneus.* Translated by Alexander Roberts and W. H. Rambaut. (Ante-Nicene Christian Library, 5, 9.) Edinburgh, 1868. 2 vols.

Jacobi, J. (1962) *The Psychology of C.G. Jung,* London: Routledge & Kegan Paul.

Jaffé, A. (1971) *From the Life and Work of C.G. Jung,* New York: Harper & Row.

Jensen, R. & Burgess, H. (1997) 'Mythmaking: how introductory psychology texts present B.F. Skinner's analysis of cognition', *The Psychological Record,* 47.2: 221–232.

Jeromson, B. (2006) 'Systema Munditotius and Seven Sermons: symbolic collaborators in Jung's confrontation with the dead', *Jung History,* 1.2: 6–10.

John, O. P., Pals, J. L., & Westenberg, P. M. (1998) 'Personality prototypes and ego development: conceptual similarities and relations in adult women', *Journal of Personality and Social Psychology,* 74: 1093–1108.

Johnson, S. (2001) *Emergence: The Connected Lives of Ants, Brains, Cities and Software,* London: Allen Lane.
Jung, C. G. (1904–7/1910) *Studies in Word Association* (*Collected Works, Vol. 2*), London: Routledge & Kegan Paul, 1969.
Jung, C. G. (1906) 'Reviews of psychiatric literature', in *Collected Works, Vol. 18. The Symbolic Life,* London: Routledge, 1977.
Jung, C. G. (1907/1936) 'The psychology of Dementia Praecox', in *Collected Works, Vol. 3. The Psychogenesis of Mental Disease,* London: Routledge & Kegan Paul, 1960.
Jung, C. G. (1908/1914) 'The content of the psychoses', in *Collected Works, Vol. 3. The Psychogenesis of Mental Disease,* London: Routledge & Kegan Paul, 1960.
Jung, C. G. (1909/1949) 'The significance of the father in the destiny of the individual', in *Collected Works, Vol. 4. Freud and Psychoanalysis,* London: Routledge & Kegan Paul, 1961.
Jung, C. G. (1910/1946) 'Psychic conflicts in a child', in *Collected Works, Vol. 17. The Development of Personality,* 2nd edn, London: Routledge & Kegan Paul, 1964.
Jung, C. G. (1911) 'Morton Prince, "The Mechanism and Interpretation of Dreams": a Critical Review', in *Collected Works, Vol. 4. Freud and Psychoanalysis,* London: Routledge & Kegan Paul, 1961.
Jung, C. G. (1911–12/1952) *Collected Works, Vol. 5. Symbols of Transformation,* London: Routledge & Kegan Paul, 1956.
Jung, C. G. (1912) 'New paths in psychology', in *Collected Works, Vol. 7. Two Essays on Analytical Psychology,* London: Routledge & Kegan Paul, 1953.
Jung, C. G. (1913) 'The theory of psychoanalysis', in *Collected Works, Vol. 4. Freud and Psychoanalysis,* London: Routledge & Kegan Paul, 1961.
Jung, C. G. (1914a) 'On psychological understanding', in *Collected Works, Vol. 3. The Psychogenesis of Mental Disease,* London: Routledge & Kegan Paul, 1960.
Jung, C. G. (1914b) 'Crucial points in psychoanalysis (Jung and Loÿ)', in *Collected Works, Vol. 4. Freud and Psychoanalysis,* London: Routledge & Kegan Paul, 1961.
Jung, C. G. (1916/1920) 'Psychoanalysis and neurosis', in *Collected Works, Vol. 4. Freud and Psychoanalysis,* London: Routledge & Kegan Paul, 1961.
Jung, C. G. (1916/1957) 'The transcendent function', in *Collected Works, Vol. 8. The Structure and Dynamics of the Psyche,* London: Routledge & Kegan Paul, 1960.
Jung, C. G. (1916/1970) 'Adaptation, individuality, collectivity', in *Collected Works, Vol. 18. The Symbolic Life,* London: Routledge, 1977.
Jung, C. G. (1916a) 'The structure of the unconscious', in *Collected Works, Vol. 7. Two Essays on Analytical Psychology,* London: Routledge & Kegan Paul, 1953.
Jung, C. G. (1916b) 'Adaptation, individuation, collectivity', in *Collected Works, Vol. 18. The Symbolic Life,* London: Routledge, 1977.
Jung, C. G. (1917/1926/1943) 'The psychology of the unconscious', in *Collected Works, Vol. 7. Two Essays on Analytical Psychology,* London: Routledge & Kegan Paul, 1953.
Jung, C. G. (1919) 'Instinct and the unconscious', in *Collected Works, Vol. 8. The Structure and Dynamics of the Psyche,* London: Routledge & Kegan Paul, 1960.
Jung, C. G. (1921) *Psychological Types* (*Collected Works, Vol. 6*) London: Routledge & Kegan Paul, 1971.
Jung, C. G. (1926) 'Spirit and life', in *Collected Works, Vol. 8. The Structure and Dynamics of the Psyche,* London: Routledge & Kegan Paul, 1960.
Jung, C. G. (1926/1946) 'Analytical psychology and education', in *Collected Works, Vol. 17. The Development of Personality,* 2nd edn, London: Routledge & Kegan Paul, 1964.

Jung, C. G. (1927/1931a) 'Introduction to Wickes's *Analyse der Kinderseele*', in *Collected Works, Vol. 17. The Development of Personality,* 2nd edn, London: Routledge & Kegan Paul, 1964.

Jung, C. G. (1927/1931b) 'The structure of the psyche', in *Collected Works, Vol. 8. The Structure and Dynamics of the Psyche,* London: Routledge & Kegan Paul, 1960.

Jung, C. G. (1928/1931) 'The spiritual problem of modern man', in *Collected Works, Vol. 10. Civilization in Transition,* London: Routledge & Kegan Paul, 1964.

Jung, C. G. (1928a) 'Child development and education', in *Collected Works, Vol. 17. The Development of Personality,* 2nd edn, London: Routledge & Kegan Paul, 1964.

Jung, C. G. (1928b) 'The relations between the ego and the unconscious', in *Collected Works, Vol. 7. Two Essays on Analytical Psychology,* London: Routledge & Kegan Paul, 1953.

Jung, C. G. (1928c) 'On psychic energy', in *Collected Works, Vol. 8. The Structure and Dynamics of the Psyche,* London: Routledge & Kegan Paul, 1960.

Jung, C. G. (1929a) 'Problems of modern psychotherapy', in *Collected Works, Vol. 16. The Practice of Psychotherapy,* London: Routledge & Kegan Paul, 1954.

Jung, C. G. (1929b) 'Freud and Jung: contrasts', in *Collected Works, Vol. 4. Freud and Psychoanalysis,* London: Routledge & Kegan Paul, 1961.

Jung, C. G. (1929c) 'Paracelsus', in *Collected Works, Vol. 15. The Spirit in Man, Art and Literature,* London: Routledge & Kegan Paul, 1966.

Jung, C. G. (1929d) 'Commentary on *The Secret of the Golden Flower*', in *Collected Works, Vol. 13. Alchemical Studies,* London: Routledge & Kegan Paul.

Jung, C. G. (1931) 'Basic postulates of analytical psychology', in *Collected Works, Vol. 8. The Structure and Dynamics of the Psyche,* London: Routledge & Kegan Paul, 1960.

Jung, C. G. (1932) 'Psychotherapists or the clergy', in *Collected Works, Vol. 11. Psychology and Religion: West and East,* London: Routledge & Kegan Paul, 1958.

Jung, C. G. (1933) *Modern Man in Search of a Soul,* trans. W. S. Dell & C. F. Baynes, London: Routledge & Kegan Paul, 1981.

Jung, C. G. (1934/1950) 'A study in the process of individuation', in *Collected Works, Vol. 9 Part 1. The Archetypes and the Collective Unconscious,* London: Routledge & Kegan Paul, 1959.

Jung, C. G. (1934/1954) 'Archetypes of the collective unconscious', in *Collected Works, Vol. 9 Part 1. The Archetypes and the Collective Unconscious,* London: Routledge & Kegan Paul, 1959.

Jung, C. G. (1934a) 'The development of personality', in *Collected Works, Vol. 17. The Development of Personality,* 2nd edn, London: Routledge & Kegan Paul, 1964.

Jung, C. G. (1934b) 'The state of psychotherapy today', in *Collected Works, Vol. 10. Civilization in Transition,* London: Routledge & Kegan Paul, 1964.

Jung, C. G. (1934c) 'Foreword to Schleich: *Die Wunder der Seele*', in *Collected Works, Vol. 18. The Symbolic Life,* London: Routledge, 1977.

Jung, C. G. (1934d) 'The practical use of dream analysis', in *Collected Works, Vol. 16. The Practice of Psychotherapy,* London: Routledge & Kegan Paul, 1954.

Jung, C. G. (1934e) 'A review of the complex theory', in *Collected Works, Vol. 8. The Structure and Dynamics of the Psyche,* London: Routledge & Kegan Paul, 1960.

Jung, C. G. (1935) 'The Tavistock Lectures', in *Collected Works, Vol. 18. The Symbolic Life,* London: Routledge, 1977.

Jung, C. G. (1936/1954) 'Concerning the archetypes, with special reference to the anima concept', in *Collected Works, Vol. 9 Part 1. The Archetypes and the Collective Unconscious,* London: Routledge & Kegan Paul, 1959.

Jung, C. G. (1936a) 'Yoga and the West', in *Collected Works, Vol. 11. Psychology and Religion: West and East,* London: Routledge & Kegan Paul, 1958.
Jung, C. G. (1936b) 'The concept of the collective unconscious', in *Collected Works, Vol. 9 Part 1. The Archetypes and the Collective Unconscious,* London: Routledge & Kegan Paul, 1959.
Jung, C. G. (1938) 'Foreword to Jung: "Phénomènes Occultes",' in *Collected Works, Vol. 18. The Symbolic Life,* London: Routledge, 1977.
Jung, C. G. (1938/1940) 'Psychology and religion', in *Collected Works, Vol. 11. Psychology and Religion: West and East,* London: Routledge & Kegan Paul, 1958.
Jung, C. G. (1938/1954a) 'The visions of Zosimos', in *Collected Works, Vol. 13. Alchemical Studies,* London: Routledge & Kegan Paul.
Jung, C. G. (1938/1954b) 'Psychological aspects of the mother archetype', in *Collected Works, Vol. 9 Part 1. The Archetypes and the Collective Unconscious,* London: Routledge & Kegan Paul, 1959.
Jung, C. G. (1939/1947) 'Foreword to Jacobi: *The Psychology of C.G. Jung*', in *Collected Works, Vol. 18. The Symbolic Life,* London: Routledge, 1977.
Jung, C. G. (1939/1954) 'Psychological commentary on *The Tibetan Book of the Dead*', in *Collected Works, Vol. 11. Psychology and Religion: West and East,* London: Routledge & Kegan Paul, 1958.
Jung, C. G. (1939a) 'On the psychogenesis of schizophrenia', in *Collected Works, Vol. 3. The Psychogenesis of Mental Disease,* London: Routledge & Kegan Paul, 1960.
Jung, C. G. (1939b) 'The dreamlike world of India', in *Collected Works, Vol. 10. Civilization in Transition,* London: Routledge & Kegan Paul, 1964.
Jung, C. G. (1939c) 'Foreword to Suzuki's *Introduction to Zen Buddhism*', in *Collected Works, Vol. 11. Psychology and Religion: West and East,* London: Routledge & Kegan Paul, 1958.
Jung, C. G. (1940) 'The psychology of the child archetype', in *Collected Works, Vol. 9 Part 1. The Archetypes and the Collective Unconscious,* London: Routledge & Kegan Paul, 1959.
Jung, C. G. (1940/1950) 'Concerning rebirth', in *Collected Works, Vol. 9 Part 1. The Archetypes and the Collective Unconscious,* London: Routledge & Kegan Paul, 1959.
Jung, C. G. (1942) 'Paracelsus as a spiritual phenomenon', in *Collected Works, Vol. 13. Alchemical Studies,* London: Routledge & Kegan Paul.
Jung, C. G. (1942/1948) 'A psychological approach to the dogma of the Trinity', in *Collected Works, Vol. 11. Psychology and Religion: West and East,* London: Routledge & Kegan Paul, 1958.
Jung, C. G. (1942/1954) 'Transformation symbolism in the Mass', in *Collected Works, Vol. 11. Psychology and Religion: West and East,* London: Routledge & Kegan Paul, 1958.
Jung, C. G. (1943/1948) 'The spirit Mercurius', in *Collected Works, Vol. 13. Alchemical Studies,* London: Routledge & Kegan Paul.
Jung, C. G. (1943/1969) 'Depth psychology and self-knowledge', in *Collected Works, Vol. 18. The Symbolic Life,* London: Routledge, 1977.
Jung, C. G. (1943a) 'The gifted child', in *Collected Works, Vol. 17. The Development of Personality,* 2nd edn, London: Routledge & Kegan Paul, 1964.
Jung, C. G. (1943b) 'The psychology of eastern meditation', in *Collected Works, Vol. 11. Psychology and Religion: West and East,* London: Routledge & Kegan Paul, 1958.
Jung, C. G. (1944a) *Psychology and Alchemy* (*Collected Works, Vol. 12*) 2nd edn, Bollingen Series, Princeton: Princeton University Press.

Jung, C. G. (1944b) 'The holy men of India', in *Collected Works, Vol. 11. Psychology and Religion: West and East,* London: Routledge & Kegan Paul, 1958.

Jung, C. G. (1945) 'Marginalia on contemporary events', in *Collected Works, Vol. 18. The Symbolic Life,* London: Routledge, 1977.

Jung, C. G. (1945/1948) 'The phenomenology of the spirit in fairy tales', in *Collected Works, Vol. 9 Part 1. The Archetypes and the Collective Unconscious,* London: Routledge & Kegan Paul, 1959.

Jung, C. G. (1945/1954) 'The philosophical tree', in *Collected Works, Vol. 13. Alchemical Studies,* London: Routledge & Kegan Paul.

Jung, C. G. (1946) 'The psychology of the transference', in *Collected Works, Vol. 16. The Practice of Psychotherapy,* London: Routledge & Kegan Paul, 1954.

Jung, C. G. (1946/1968) 'Foreword to a Catalogue on Alchemy', in *Collected Works, Vol. 18. The Symbolic Life,* London: Routledge, 1977.

Jung, C. G. (1947/1954) 'On the nature of the psyche', in *Collected Works, Vol. 8. The Structure and Dynamics of the Psyche,* London: Routledge & Kegan Paul, 1960.

Jung, C. G. (1948) 'Depth psychology', in *Collected Works, Vol. 18. The Symbolic Life,* London: Routledge, 1977.

Jung, C. G. (1949/1954) 'Foreword to Neumann: *The Origins and History of the Unconscious*', in *Collected Works, Vol. 18. The Symbolic Life,* London: Routledge, 1977.

Jung, C. G. (1950) 'Concerning mandala symbolism', in *Collected Works, Vol. 9 Part 1. The Archetypes and the Collective Unconscious,* London: Routledge & Kegan Paul, 1959.

Jung, C. G. (1951a) *Aion: Researches into the Phenomenology of the Self (Collected Works, Vol. 9, Part 2)*, London: Routledge & Kegan Paul, 1959.

Jung, C. G. (1951b) 'Fundamental questions of psychotherapy', in *Collected Works, Vol. 16. The Practice of Psychotherapy,* London: Routledge & Kegan Paul, 1954.

Jung, C. G. (1952/1973) 'Religion and psychology: a reply to Martin Buber', in *Collected Works, Vol. 18. The Symbolic Life,* London: Routledge, 1977.

Jung, C. G. (1952a) 'Synchronicity: an acausal connecting principle', in *Collected Works, Vol. 8. The Structure and Dynamics of the Psyche,* London: Routledge & Kegan Paul, 1960.

Jung, C. G. (1952b) 'Answer to Job', in *Collected Works, Vol. 11. Psychology and Religion: West and East,* London: Routledge & Kegan Paul, 1958.

Jung, C. G. (1953) 'Foreword to Frieda Fordham: *Introduction to Jung's Psychology*', in *Collected Works, Vol. 18. The Symbolic Life,* London: Routledge, 1977.

Jung, C. G. (1954) 'Letter to Père Lachat', in *Collected Works, Vol. 18. The Symbolic Life,* London: Routledge, 1977.

Jung, C. G. (1955) 'Mandalas'. Appendix to 'Concerning Mandala Symbolism', in *Collected Works, Vol. 9 Part 1. The Archetypes and the Collective Unconscious,* London: Routledge & Kegan Paul, 1959.

Jung, C. G. (1955–56) *Mysterium Coniunctionis: An Inquiry into the Separation and Synthesis of Psychic Opposites in Alchemy (Collected Works, Vol. 14)* London: Routledge & Kegan Paul, 1963.

Jung, C. G. (1956/1957) 'Jung and religious belief', in *Collected Works, Vol. 18. The Symbolic Life,* London: Routledge, 1977.

Jung, C. G. (1957a) 'God and the Devil', *Atlantic Monthly,* 200, 5 Nov.

Jung, C. G. (1957b) 'The undiscovered self (present and future)', in *Collected Works, Vol. 10. Civilization in Transition,* London: Routledge & Kegan Paul, 1964.

Jung, C. G. (1958a) 'A psychological view of conscience', in *Collected Works, Vol. 10. Civilization in Transition,* London: Routledge & Kegan Paul, 1964.

Jung, C. G. (1958b) 'An astrological experiment', in *Collected Works, Vol. 18. The Symbolic Life,* London: Routledge, 1977.

Jung, C. G. (1958c) 'Flying saucers: a modern myth of things seen in the skies', in *Collected Works, Vol. 10. Civilization in Transition,* London: Routledge & Kegan Paul, 1964.

Jung, C. G. (1961) 'Symbols and the interpretation of dreams', in *Collected Works, Vol. 18. The Symbolic Life,* London: Routledge, 1977.

Jung, C. G. (1983) *The Zofingia Lectures,* supplementary Volume A in *Collected Works,* Bollingen Series, Princeton: Princeton University Press. [Delivered 1896–1899.]

Jung, C. G. (1995) *Dream Analysis Part 1: Notes of the Seminar Given in 1928–1930,* ed. W. McGuire, London: Routledge.

Jung, C. G. (2008) *Children's Dreams: Notes from the Seminar Given in 1936–1940,* ed. L. Jung & M. Meyer-Grass, Princeton: Princeton University Press.

Jung, C. G. (2009) *The Red Book. Liber Novus,* trans. and ed. S. Shamdasani, London: Norton.

Jung, C. G. & Jaffé, A. (1963) *Memories, Dreams, Reflections,* London: Fontana, 1977.

Khunrath, H. (1597) *Von hylealischen Chaos,* Magdeburg.

Kierkegaard, S. (1981) *The Concept of Anxiety,* Princeton: Princeton University Press.

Kirsch, T. B. (2000) *The Jungians: A Comparative and Historical Perspective,* London: Routledge.

Kluckhohn, C. & Murray, H. A. (eds) (1949) *Personality in Nature, Society, and Culture,* London: Jonathan Cape.

Kotsch, W. E. (2000) 'Jung's mediatory science as a psychology beyond objectivism', *Journal of Analytical Psychology,* 45: 217–244.

Laing, R. D. (1990) *The Divided Self,* London: Penguin.

Lammers, A. C. & Cunningham, A. (eds) (2007) *The Jung-White Letters,* Hove: Routledge.

Lazarus, R. S. & Opton, E. M. (eds) (1977) *Personality,* Harmondsworth: Penguin.

Levinas, E. (1930) 'Ethics as first philosophy', in S. Hand (ed) *The Levinas Reader,* pp. 76–77, Oxford: Blackwell, 1994.

Levy, L. H. (1970) *Conceptions of Personality: Theories and Research,* New York: Random House.

Lévy-Bruhl, L. (1966) *How Natives Think,* New York: Washington Square Press. [First published in French in 1910.]

Lindzey, G., Hall, C. S. & Manosewitz, M. (1973) *Theories of Personality: Primary Sources and Research,* New York: John Wiley & Sons. [First published in 1965.]

Lipton, P. (2004) *Inference to the Best Explanation,* 2nd edn, London: Routledge.

Lunt, P. (2004) 'Psychology, expertise and the consumer: an historical comparison', paper presented at the Annual Conference of the History and Philosophy Section of The British Psychological Society, York, 2004.

Maddi, S. (1972) *Personality Theories: A Comparative Analysis,* Homewood: Dorsey.

Maddi, S. (1996) *Personality Theories: A Comparative Analysis,* Prospect Heights: Waveland.

Maduro, R. J. & Wheelwright, J. B. (1977) 'Analytical psychology', in R. Corsini (ed) *Current Personality Theories,* pp. 83–123, Itasca, IL: Peacock.

Magnavita, J. (2002) *Theories of Personality: Contemporary Approaches to the Science of Personality,* New York: John Wiley & Sons.

Main, R. (2000) 'Religion, science and synchronicity', *Harvest: Journal for Jungian Studies,* 46.2: 89–107.

Main, R. (ed) (2003) 'Interview with Kathleen Raine', *Harvest: International Journal for Jungian Studies,* 49.1: 132–158.

Marcel, A. J. (1983) 'Conscious and unconscious perception: experiments on visual masking and word recognition', *Cognitive Psychology,* 15: 197–237.

Markus, H. (1977) 'Self-schemata and processing information about the self', *Journal of Personality and Social Psychology,* 35: 63–78.

Markus, H. & Nutrius, P. (1986) 'Possible selves', *American Psychologist,* 41: 954–969.

Marslen-Wilson, W. D. (1984) 'Function and process in spoken word recognition – a tutorial review', in H. Bouma and D. G. Bouwhuis (eds), *Attention and Performance X,* pp. 125–150, Hillsdale, NJ: Lawrence Erlbaum Associates.

Martin, S. (2005) 'President's welcome', *Jung History,* 1.1: 1.

Maslow, A. (1954) *Motivation and Personality,* 2nd edn, New York: Harper & Row.

Massey, R. F. (1981) *Personality Theories: Comparisons and Synthesis,* New York: Van Nostrand.

Mattoon, M. A. (1981) *Jungian Psychology in Perspective,* London: Collier Macmillan.

McCary, J. L. (ed) (1956) *Psychology and Personality: Six Modern Approaches,* New York: Logos.

McDougall, W. (1923) *An Outline of Psychology,* London: Methuen, 1949.

McDougall, W. (1933) *The Energies of Men. A Study of the Fundamentals of Dynamic Psychology,* New York: Charles Scribner's Sons.

McGuire, W. (ed) (1974) *The Freud/Jung Letters: The Correspondence Between Sigmund Freud and C.G. Jung,* trans. R. Manheim & R. F. C. Hull, Princeton: Princeton University Press.

Mehrabian, A. (1968) *An Analysis of Personality Theories,* Englewood Cliffs: Prentice-Hall.

Meier, C. A. (1977) *Personality: The Individuation Process in the Light of C.G. Jung's Typology,* trans. D. N. Roscoe, Einsiedeln: Daimon, 1995.

Meier, C. A. (1989) *Consciousness,* trans. D. N. Roscoe, Boston: Sigo.

Mendelssohn, G. A. (1993) 'It's time to put theories of personality in their place, or Allport and Stagner got it right, why can't we?', in K. H. Craik et al. (eds) *Fifty Years of Personality Psychology,* pp. 103–115, New York: Plenum Press.

Millon, T. (1969) *Modern Psychopathology,* Prospect Heights: Waveland Press.

Millon, T. (2004) *Masters of the Mind: Exploring the Story of Mental Illness from Ancient Times to the New Millennium,* Hoboken: John Wiley & Sons.

Milner, A. D. & Dijkerman, H. C. (2001) 'Direct and indirect visual routes to action', in B. de Gelder, E. H. F. de Haan & C. Heywood (eds) *Out of Mind: Varieties of Unconscious Processes,* pp. 241–265, Oxford: Oxford University Press.

Milner, A. D. & Goodale, M. A. (2008) 'Two visual systems reviewed', *Neuropsychologia,* 46: 774–785.

Mischel, W. (1971/1981/1999) *Introduction to Personality,* New York: Holt, Rinehart & Winston, 1971; New York: CBS College Publishing, 1981; New York: Harcourt Brace, 1999.

Monte, C. F. (1977/1980/1987/1995) *Beneath the Mask: An Introduction to Theories of Personality,* New York: Praeger, 1977; New York: Holt, Rinehart & Winston, 1980, 1987; Fort Worth: Harcourt Brace, 1995.

Morris, J. & Dolan, R. (2001) 'The amygdala and unconscious fear processing', in B. de Gelder, E. H. F. de Haan & C. Heywood (eds) *Out of Mind: Varieties of Unconscious Processes,* pp. 185–204, Oxford: Oxford University Press.

Murphy, G. (1947) *Personality: A Biosocial Approach to Origins and Structure,* New York: Harper & Row.
Murphy, G. (1958) *Human Potentialities,* New York: Basic Books.
Murray, H. & Kluckhohn, C. (1949) 'Outline of a conception of personality', in *Personality in Nature, Society, and Culture,* pp. 3–32, London: Jonathan Cape.
Myers, I. B. (1962) *The Myers-Briggs Type Indicator,* Princeton, NJ: Educational Testing Service.
Nagy, M. (1991) *Philosophical Issues in the Psychology of C.G. Jung,* Albany: State University of New York Press.
Noll, R. (1994) *The Jung Cult: The Origins of a Charismatic Movement,* Princeton: Princeton University Press.
Norbeck, E., Price-Williams, D. & McCord, W. (eds) (1968) *The Study of Personality: An Interdisciplinary Appraisal,* New York: Holt, Rinehart & Winston.
Notcutt, B. (1953) *The Psychology of Personality,* London: Methuen.
Origen (1936) *De Principiis,* trans. G. W. Butterworth, London: Society for the Promotion of Christian Knowledge.
Palmer, M. (1997) *Freud and Jung on Religion,* London: Routledge.
Papadopoulos, R. K. (ed) (2006a) *The Handbook of Jungian Psychology: Theory, Practice and Applications,* London: Routledge.
Papadopoulos, R. K. (2006b) 'Jung's epistemology and methodology', in R. K. Papadopoulos (ed) *The Handbook of Jungian Psychology: Theory, Practice and Applications,* pp. 7–53, London: Routledge.
Peck, D. & Whitlow, D. (1975) *Approaches to Personality,* London: Methuen.
Penrose, R. (1989) *The Emperor's New Mind: Concerning Computers, Minds, and the Laws of Physics,* London: Vintage.
Pervin, L. A. (1996) *The Science of Personality,* New York: Wiley.
Pervin, L. A. & John, D. P. (2001) *Personality Theory and Research,* 8th edn, New York: John Wiley & Sons.
Peters, R. S. (ed) (1953) *Brett's History of Psychology,* London: Allen & Unwin.
Philo Judaeus *De opificio mundi.* In: *Philo.* With an English translation by Francis Henry Colson and George Herbert Whitaker. (Loeb Classical Library) London and New York, 1929– . 12 vols. published. (Vol. 1).
Philp, H. L. (1958) *Jung and the Problem of Evil,* London: Rockliff.
Piattelli-Palmarini, M. (ed) (1980) *Language and Learning: The Debate between Jean Piaget and Noam Chomsky,* Cambridge: Harvard University Press.
Porter, R. (1997) *The Greatest Benefit to Mankind: A Medical History of Humanity from Antiquity to the Present,* London: Harper Collins.
Power, M. & Brewin, C. R. (1991) 'From Freud to cognitive science: a contemporary account of the unconscious', *British Journal of Clinical Psychology,* 30: 289–310.
Proctor, R. W. & Capaldi, E. J. (2006) *Why Science Matters: Understanding the Methods of Psychological Research,* Oxford: Blackwell.
Progoff, I. (1953) *Jung's Psychology and its Social Meaning,* New York: Grove Press.
Progoff, I. (1956) *The Death and Rebirth of Psychology,* New York: The Julian Press.
Progoff, I. (1973) *Jung, Synchronicity and Human Destiny,* New York: The Julian Press.
Psychological Index 1894–1935. Princeton, NJ: Psychological Review Company.
Rachman, S. (1971) *The Effects of Psychotherapy,* Oxford: Pergamon.
Read, H. E. (1945) *Education Through Art,* New York: Pantheon Books.

Reber, A. S. (1993) *Implicit Learning and Tacit Knowledge: An Essay on the Cognitive Unconscious,* New York: Oxford University Press.

Richards, G. (2004) 'The strange marginalisation of James Martineau (1805–1900) in late Victorian British psychology', paper presented at the Annual Conference of the History and Philosophy Section of The British Psychological Society, York, 2004.

Romanyshyn, R. D. (2007) *The Wounded Researcher: Research with Soul in Mind,* New Orleans: Spring Journal Books.

Roob, A. (2006) *The Hermetic Museum: Alchemy and Mysticism,* Köln: Taschen.

Rorty, R. (1989) *Contingency, Irony and Solidarity,* New York: Cambridge University Press.

Rosen, D. H., Smith, S. M., Huston, H. J. & Gonzalez, G. (1991) 'Empirical Study of Associations between symbols and their meanings: evidence of collective unconscious (archetypal) memory', *Journal of Analytical Psychology*, 36: 211–228.

Rowland, S. (2002) *Jung: A Feminist Revision,* Malden: Blackwell.

Rowland, S. (2005) *Jung as a Writer,* Hove: Routledge.

Rowland, S. (2010) *C.G. Jung in the Humanities. Taking the Soul's Path,* New Orleans: Spring.

Rowland, S. A. (2003) 'Jung, myth and biography', *Harvest: International Journal for Jungian Studies,* 49.1: 22–39.

Runyan, W. McK. (1981) 'Why did Van Gogh cut off his ear? The problem of alternative explanations in psychobiography', *Journal of Personality and Social Psychology,* 40.6: 1070–1077.

Runyan, W. McK. (1997) 'Studying lives: psychobiography and the conceptual structure of personality psychology', in R. Hogan, J. Johnson & S. Briggs (eds) *Handbook of Personality Psychology,* pp. 41–69, San Diego: Academic Press.

Rychlak, J. F. (1973) *A Philosophy of Science for Personality Theory,* 2nd edn, Malabar: Robert E. Krieger, 1981.

Rychlak, J. F. (2003) *The Human Image in Postmodern America,* Washington, DC: American Psychological Association.

Ryckman, R. (1993) *Theories of Personality,* Pacific Grove: Brooks Cole.

Sahakian, W. S. (ed) (1965) *Psychology of Personality: Readings in Theory,* Chicago: Rand McNally.

Salmon, P. (2003) 'How do we recognise good research?', *The Psychologist,* 16.1: 24–27.

Samuels, A. (1985) *Jung and the Post-Jungians,* London: Routledge & Kegan Paul.

Samuels, A. (1989) *The Plural Psyche: Personality, Morality and the Father,* London: Routledge.

Schaer, H. (1950) *Religion and the Cure of Souls in Jung's Psychology,* New York: Pantheon.

Schatzki, T. (2004) 'Sites, organizations and minds', paper presented at the Annual Conference of the History and Philosophy Section of The British Psychological Society, York, 2004.

Schore, A. N. (1994) *Affect Regulation and the Origin of the Self: The Neurobiology of Emotional Development,* Hillsdale: Lawrence Erlbaum.

Schultz, D. (1976) *Theories of Personality,* Monterey: Brooks Cole.

Schultz, D. (2001) *Theories of Personality,* 7th edn, Belmont: Wadsworth Thomson.

Segal, R. A. (1992) *The Gnostic Jung,* London: Routledge, 2008.

Segal, R. A. (2007) 'Jung and Lévy-Bruhl', *Journal of Analytical Psychology,* 52: 635–658.

Seligman, M. E. P. (1971) 'Phobias and preparedness', *Behavior Therapy* 2.3: 307–320.

Shamdasani, S. (1998) *Cult Fictions: C.G. Jung and the Founding of Analytical Psychology,* London: Routledge.

Shamdasani, S. (2003) *Jung and the Making of Modern Psychology: The Dream of a Science*, Cambridge: Cambridge University Press.

Shamdasani, S. (2005a) *Jung Stripped Bare by his Biographers, Even,* London: Karnac.

Shamdasani, S. (2005b) 'From the uncollected Jung: Jung in Oxford', *Jung History,* 1.2: 3–5.

Shedler, J. (2010) 'The efficacy of psychodynamic psychotherapy', *American Psychologist,* 65.2: 98–109.

Singer, J. (1973) *Boundaries of the Soul: The Practice of Jung's Psychology,* New York: Anchor Doubleday.

Smith, B. D. & Vetter, H. J. (1982) *Theoretical Approaches to Personality,* Englewood Cliffs: Prentice-Hall.

Smyth, M. M. (2001) 'Fact making in psychology: the voice of the introductory textbook', *Theory & Psychology,* 11.5: 609–636.

Steele, R. S. & Morawski, J. G. (2002) 'Implicit cognition and the social unconscious', *Theory & Psychology,* 12.1: 37–54.

Stenner, P. (2002) 'Social psychology and Babel', *History and Philosophy of Psychology,* 4.1: 45–57.

Stern, P. J. (1976) *Jung: The Haunted Prophet,* New York: Braziller.

Stevens, A. (2002) *Archetype Revisited: An Updated Natural History of the Self,* 2nd edn, London: Brunner-Routledge.

Stolorow, R. D. & Atwood, G. E. (1979) *Faces in a Cloud: Subjectivity in Personality Theory,* New York: Jason Aronson.

Storr, A. (1973) *Jung,* London: Fontana, 1986.

Sullivan, H. S. (1953–1964) *Collected Works of Harry Stack Sullivan.* 2 vols, New York: Norton.

Sullivan, H. S. (1962) *Schizophrenia as a Human Process,* included in *Collected Works of Harry Stack Sullivan. Vol. II,* New York: Norton, 1953–1964.

Sullivan, H. S. (1964) 'Beliefs versus a rational psychiatry', in *The Fusion of Psychiatry and Social Science,* included in *Collected Works of Harry Stack Sullivan. Vol. II,* New York: Norton, 1953–1964.

Tacey, D. (2001) *Jung and the New Age,* Hove and Philadelphia: Brunner-Routledge.

Tacey, D. (2006) *How to Read Jung,* London: Norton.

Taylor, E. (2009) *The Mystery of Personality: A History of Psychodynamic Theories,* New York: Springer.

Telesko, W. (2001) *The Wisdom of Nature: The Healing Powers and Symbolism of Plants and Animals in the Middle Ages,* Munich: Prestel.

Thagard, P. (1978) 'The best explanation: criteria for theory choice', *Journal of Philosophy,* 75: 76–92.

Thagard, P. (1992) *Conceptual Revolutions,* Oxford: Princeton University Press.

Thorpe, L. P. (1938) *Psychological Foundations of Personality,* New York: McGraw-Hill.

Thorpe, W. H. (1961) *Bird-Song,* Cambridge: Cambridge University Press.

Todd, J. T. & Morris, E. K. (1983) 'Misconception and miseducation: presentations of radical behaviorism in psychology textbooks', *The Behavior Analyst,* 6.2: 153–160.

Toulmin, S. (1948) 'The logical status of psycho-analysis', *Analysis,* 9: 23–29.

Treisman, A. M. (1964) 'Verbal cues, language, and meaning in selective attention', *The American Journal of Psychology,* 77.2: 206–219.

Velmans, M. (1989) 'The function of consciousness in human information processing', paper given at the Colloquium on The Function of Consciousness, 3rd Annual

Conference of the History and Philosophy of Psychology Section of the British Psychological Society, Lincoln, March 1989.

Velmans, M. (1990) 'Consciousness, brain and the physical world', *Philosophical Psychology,* 3.1: 77–99.

Velmans, M. (1993) 'A reflexive science of consciousness', *Experimental and Theoretical Studies of Consciousness (Ciba Foundation Symposium),* 174: 81–89.

Velmans, M. (2009) *Understanding Consciousness,* 2nd edn, London: Routledge.

Vieljeux, J. (2005) 'A new Jung bibliography', *Jung History,* 1.1: 16–18.

Waele, J. P. de & Harré, R. (1976) 'The personality of individuals', in R. Harré (ed) *Personality,* pp. 189–246, Oxford: Blackwell.

Weiskrantz, L. (1986) *Blindsight: A Case Study and Implications,* Oxford: Oxford University Press.

Weiskrantz, L. (1988) 'Some contributions of neuropsychology of vision and memory to the problem of consciousness', in E. Bisiach and E. Marcel (eds) *Consciousness in contemporary science,* pp. 183–199, Oxford: Oxford University Press.

Wepman, J. M. & Heine, R. W. (eds) (1963) *Concepts of Personality,* 6th edn, Chicago: Aldine, 1970.

Wickes, F. G. (1948) *The Inner World of Childhood,* New York: The New American Library.

Index

For Product Safety Concerns and Information please contact our
EU representative GPSR@taylorandfrancis.com Taylor & Francis
Verlag GmbH, Kaufingerstraße 24, 80331 München, Germany